RUANDA MISSION (CMS)
157 Waterloo Road, London SE1 8UU

For over 40 years the
Ruanda Mission (CMS)
has been associated
with the Revival in
East Africa.

The name 'Ruanda', with
its colonial spelling,
is no longer acceptable,
particularly in Africa.

The Mission has, therefore,
changed its name to
Mid-Africa Ministry (CMS)

Mid-
Africa
Ministry (CMS)
(Formerly Ruanda Mission)

FIRE IN THE HILLS

H. H. Osborn

HIGHLAND BOOKS

ISBN 0 946616 79 5

Cover design by Diane Drummond

Two names occur throughout this text which are
written in two different ways. The modern,
standard forms of the names are Rwanda and
Burundi. However, before Independence these
formed one territory: Ruanda-Urundi. The name
of the Ruanda Mission was retained after
Independence.

Printed in Great Britain for
HIGHLAND BOOKS
Broadway House, The Broadway,
Crowborough, East Sussex TN6 1HQ
by Clays Ltd, St Ives plc
Typeset by Rowland Phototypesetting Ltd,
Bury St Edmunds, Suffolk

Contents

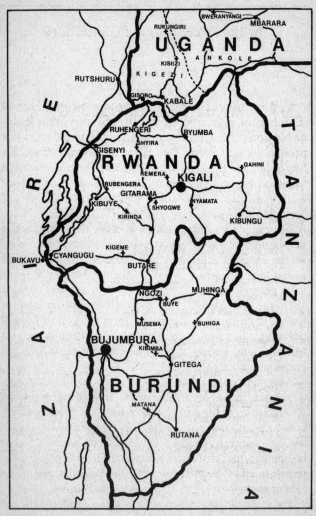

Map of South-West Uganda, Rwanda & Burundi

Foreword

by the Archbishop of Canterbury

All who are concerned with mission and with Africa will benefit, indeed be inspired, by this story of the Ruanda Mission (CMS). Its beginnings go back to the years just prior to the First World War, when two young doctors, Dr Len Sharp and Dr Algie Stanley Smith, became convinced that God was calling them to pioneer medical missionary work in Ruanda-Urundi, as it was then known, a part of German East Africa.

After military service as army doctors, they approached the Church Missionary Society. The Society was under severe financial difficulties and indicated its inability to accept the two doctors unless they could find their support from elsewhere. This they undertook to do. In February 1921, the two doctors, with their wives, started work at Kabale in the south-west corner of Uganda. From this small beginning, there grew the Ruanda General and Medical Mission, later known as the Ruanda Mission (CMS), an autonomous body within the CMS.

Although outwardly and numerically successful, the spiritual level of the developing work, nevertheless, proved disappointing to the early missionaries. They pleaded with God to break in to give the spiritual life of which they felt such a desperate need. In 1936, fifteen years after its beginnings, the African church and the mission began to be transformed as the fire of God's Holy Spirit burned in the hills of south-west Uganda, Rwanda and Burundi.

Those praying for revival today will note that with the great tidal wave of blessing there came the inevitable problems. Missionaries were divided in their understanding of some of the emotional expressions which sprang from powerful experiences of conviction of sin, joy of sins forgiven and liberation from Satanic forces. In his love for the Ruanda Mission the author has not attempted to conceal how an intolerance of compromise in any form led to a polarisation among both Africans and missionaries. And in it all, thousands came to a joyful experience of a living Christ.

Whatever our conclusions we can be grateful to Dr Osborn for sharing so frankly how the strongly lay leadership of the Mission came into conflict with the strong clerically based view of the Anglican Church structure current at that time. Potential harshness was mitigated, however, by one of the powerful evidences of revival – humility and brokenness. The widespread manifestations of revival subsided in the early 1950s, although there were further outbursts in the 1970s and later.

After World War II, missionary work expanded rapidly, aided by an influx of post-war missionaries and colonial government financial aid for medical and educational work. But by the late 1980s, the name of 'Ruanda', spelt in its pre-independence form, had become an increasing embarrassment when churches in Uganda and Burundi referred to 'The Ruanda Mission'.

This coincided with a review of the Mission's vision for the future and of its relationship with its parent body, the CMS. The outcome was the Mid-Africa Ministry (CMS), which came into being in 1990, still an autonomous body within the CMS but with a wider mandate for service further afield.

Thanks to Dr Osborn's splendid research the reader will sense when he concludes the book that from his armchair he has been privileged to witness a remarkable work of God including the revival which God brought to East Africa.

George Cantuar:

Introduction

To anyone who is not well informed about Christian missionary activity, the history of the way non-Christian countries have been evangelised appears to be the story of exceptional men and women who obeyed what they believed to be a call from God to undertake pioneering tasks in little-known, far away places. It is easy to gain the impression that everything depended on those missionaries, even to assume that the initiative lay with them.

Looking back with the benefit of our historical perspectives we can see that the numerous independent responses of individuals were, in fact, part of a Divine Master-plan. God was fulfilling, in His own sovereign way, the words spoken by Jesus Christ: "This gospel of the kingdom will be preached in the whole world" (Matthew 24:14). In His all-knowing wisdom He has woven a tapestry which has intertwined the lives of many different people, some of whom have never left their home countries, to bring a vast number of men and women throughout the world, into His kingdom.

The achievement of this has taken many different forms. One pattern has, however, been frequently repeated. A few have been convinced of a call from God to "Go and make disciples of all nations . . ." (Matthew 28:19). Then, for reasons which are usually humanly inexplicable, a further group of people has come to the equally strong conviction that they too were called of God to support them.

Such a group emerged in England soon after the end of the First World War. The few: Dr and Mrs Algernon C. Stanley Smith and Dr and Mrs Leonard E. S. Sharp, responded to the vision God gave them of taking the gospel to an area of central Africa which was unheard of to most people in the UK. The group, mainly relatives and friends of the two couples, expressed their certainty of God's leading in a commitment to support them by prayer and giving. From these beginnings grew the Ruanda General and Medical Mission, better known as the Ruanda Mission (CMS).

In February, 1921, the two doctors and their wives began the task of evangelising south-west Uganda with the intention of extending the work as soon as possible southwards into the countries of Rwanda and Burundi.

Less than eighteen months after work had begun, Dr Stanley Smith wrote home, in June 1922: "A safari round the village churches always sends one to one's knees in prayer for a revival of spiritual religion. But if our teachers are to be revived we who lead them must be abiding in the place of power."

Measured in numbers of converts to Christianity, early missionary outreach was very successful. The low spiritual level of the lives of many of those converts, however, disappointed the pioneers. Their zealous evangelistic efforts appeared to be so ineffective spiritually that some of them pleaded with God for many years to make real in power, what they sought faithfully to proclaim and teach from His Word. God answered those and many other such prayers as He showed missionaries, African evangelists, medical workers and teachers alike where the keys to His working in power lay.

The story, as it unfolded from the 1920's to the 1950's, was told in small booklets entitled *Ruanda's Redemption* and *Road to Revival*, written either by Dr Stanley Smith alone or jointly with Dr Sharp. There followed, in 1959, *A Grain of Mustard Seed* by Lindsay Guillebaud. Later still *Breath of Life*, by Patricia St John, extended the story to the end of the 1960's.

In 1991, the Episcopal Churches in Rwanda and Burundi celebrate their Silver Jubilee of Diocesan independence. Indications suggest that that year may prove to be a milestone in the relationships between the Ruanda Mission and the churches of Central Africa which it founded.

In addition, the Ruanda Mission (CMS), is changing its title. Many will regret the passing of a name which has many associations with the truths for which it stood and for the peculiarly warm and close fellowship which has grown among many missionaries and supporters. Fewer will be aware of the changing associations that the name conjures up in the minds of Church leaders in the Africa situation. The time for change has come.

Some day an expert may make a comprehensive assessment of the missionary enterprise of the Ruanda Mission. This is not such a work. This is a story, a story of ordinary men and women called to take the Good News of Jesus Christ to a particular part of Africa; only to find that their endeavours resulted in a largely formal and lifeless acceptance of the truths they proclaimed. Almost overwhelmed with a sense of impotence in the face of the forces of evil ranged against them, many were driven to their knees to pray that God would "breathe life" into them and into the biblical truths they taught. God answered in reviving power. The missionary task was completely transformed. This is the story of that transformation – its pains and disappointments and, above all, its testimony to the power of God to make living the cross of Christ in the lives of missionaries and Africans alike. A spiritual fire burst into flame in the hills of Africa which, like the bush fires of which it is a picture, spread far and wide. It left its mark in many lives and still bursts into flame in unexpected places.

The period of this story extends over seventy years. In that time the meanings and associations of words have changed. It is possible that, at a first reading, some of the terms used could be misunderstood. For instance, when the Germans first occupied the countries of Rwanda and Burundi (later to be succeeded by the Belgians) they referred to them as one territory, that of *Ruanda-Urundi*. The similarities of the two ethnic groups which inhabited them and of their two languages (actually two dialects of the same language) explain this confusion, despite the fact that the pronunciation of the names by the Africans did not change.

The terms *native* and *heathen* have acquired a pejorative sense. Instead of the former, reference is now made to *nationals* or simply *Africans*, *Ugandans*, *Rwandans* or *Burundians*. According to the dictionary, *heathen* means "an unconverted member of a people or nation that does not acknowledge the God of the Bible". It was in this sense that the word was used by the founders of the Mission. Where the terms *native* or *heathen* are quoted from the past there is no intention of implying anything of the depreciatory sense which the terms have acquired since then.

Similarly, reference is made to *lepers* and to *leper settlements*. It was realised many years ago that the term "leper" created a negative attitude in the minds of sufferers, especially as "leprosy" was used in the Bible as a picture of sin. In consequence, the term "leper" is never used today. *Leprosy patients*, *leprosy settlements* or *leprosaria* are modern terms which are used throughout, except for quotations and a few references related to the past.

Published documents and letters have provided much of the material of this story. However, many of the contemporary insights would have been impossible were it not for access to diaries and letters; hours of recorded memories of those early missionaries who are still alive today; as well as the memories of many of their successors. All this generous help and co-operation is gratefully acknowledged. While every effort has been made to respect the views of all who have contributed in these ways so generously, the sole responsibility for all the opinions expressed remains with the author.

Chapter 1

The smouldering
fire bursts into flame
1936

Darkness fell at about 6.30 pm on Gahini, a mission station built on the gentle slopes of a hill in north-east Rwanda. It was Sunday, 29 June 1936. The day had passed with nothing special to report. A morning service had been held in the whitewashed, mudbrick and corrugated iron roofed church. In the similarly built 30-bed hospital, Mildred Forder, a young nurse who had come to Gahini only six months previously, had attended the usual ward service. She was temporarily in charge as the Doctor, Joe Church, with Decie his wife, also a doctor, were in Mukono, Uganda where Joe was conducting some evangelistic meetings. Pupils from the boys' day school and students from the Evangelists' Training School had attended the morning service but nothing special had been arranged for them. In the boarding school of about one hundred girls, ranging from infants to late teenagers, Dora Skipper, a senior, very experienced missionary, assisted by Joy Gerson, a newcomer with only two months' experience in the country, had ended the day with the usual Sunday evening hymn singing and prayer.

"How did you get on?" enquired Mildred as Dora and Joy joined her in the house in which they lived together.

"Very dull!" Dora replied. "They are so solid and there's no life." It was a typical remark for Dora. She belonged to the "old school" of missionaries. She had worked for some years as a missionary of the Church Missionary Society in the foothills of Mount Elgon in Uganda. Her "senior missionary" had walked up from the coast! She was tough and needed to be. Now she was the senior missionary herself. She went on to enjoy an evening meal with her less experienced colleagues. Similarly occupied in another house further down the hill, were the only other two missionaries there at that time, the Rev. Cecil Verity and his wife, Nancy. It was nearing the close of a peaceful Sunday.

At about 9.30 pm, the silence of the night was suddenly broken. "We heard a noise in the school which, in the distance, sounded exactly like a Bank Holiday crowd on Hampstead Heath," wrote Joy Gerson. The three women rose hurriedly from the table and together set off in the direction of the girls' school from where the noise was coming. "As we got nearer," continued Joy, "we could hear that it was different. It was frightening!"

The gates to the school were locked at that hour and so Dora, Joy and Mildred clambered over a hedge to reach the inner compound. They saw some girls silently watching one of the school buildings. It was from there that the noise was coming. With difficulty Dora opened the door and they pushed their way in. Joy described the scene: "The girls seemed to have gone mad, some were on the floor, they were all throwing themselves about, they were absolutely uncontrolled, some were laughing, some weeping, most were shaking very much and they seemed to have supernatural strength. The powers of darkness seemed to be right on us. It felt like being in hell, as though Satan had loosed his armies." Some of the girls were foaming at the mouth and breaking up desks, chairs and windows. The noise was deafening and the atmosphere satanic.

Among the girls who showed such evidence of satanic power, a few appeared to be experiencing something totally different. "One or two girls had been very convicted of sin," remembered Mildred, "and they had a vision of the cross and were crying out, 'Can't you see Him! Can't you see Him dying there for us!'"

One by one Dora dragged the girls out of the building to question them. Looking on, not understanding the language, Joy could see that all of them looked very distraught. She learned later that "some were genuinely frightened, others were angry that they should be stopped in the middle of their experience of, as they believed, God. They were really and truly seeking Him and it was just then that Satan got in and nearly turned all their seeking to evil."

Hearing the noise, Cecil Verity came to the school to see what was happening and joined Dora in trying to restore order. Only Dora, however, appeared to be able to exercise any influence on the girls. Slowly they calmed down. Even as they did so, however, the sound of shouting and singing could be heard from different parts of the hill. And it went on all night!

At 3.30 am on Monday morning, the noise started again in the girls' school and Dora hurried there to investigate the cause. She found Geraldine Matama, a genial, round-faced teacher who had been recruited from the Toro area of Uganda, already there. Girls were shaking and crying uncontrollably and some were very frightened. "Geraldine impressed on them that God was only heard with a still, small voice," wrote Dora later. "And then they prayed and went on praying . . . All that day there was a fearful tense feeling and excitement everywhere and both Joy and I felt shaky for no reason. We came to the conclusion that it was a real fight going on between Christ and the devil."

What could have caused such a disturbance? The teachers in the school explained it simply. Four school-girls had been "in dead earnest about getting right with God". While they were praying quietly, some non-Christian girls came in. They too were seeking, but not for God; they were seeking contact with their ancestral spirits. The atmosphere changed. The sense of God's presence left the room and the spirit of *Nyabingi* – an evil spirit of sorcery – took over. "On the night of a wedding," Dora learned, "girls go with the bride and get into the same state (as these school-girls had been in) until the bride gets worked up in the same way and then she goes to her husband." The customary satanic ceremony had very strong sexual overtones. The Christian teachers were sure that the girls "had all got hopelessly tangled in their desperate longing to find God and be free from their sins." Of one thing there was no doubt: the pandemonium created was of the devil. It was certainly not of God.

The strange happenings were not limited to the girls' school. In the hospital, boys' school and Evangelists' Training School and among people visiting the hill, there were many emotional and spiritual outbursts but there was no more destruction of property nor was there anything further resembling the satanic atmosphere that had been experienced in the girls' school.

In the days that followed people in many different circumstances would suddenly begin to shiver, leading them at first to believe that they had a fever of some sort. Then a terrifying sense of their sin would overtake them and a fear of facing a holy God. The existence of unforgiven sin became unbearable. At that time the full meaning of the death of Christ for sin does not appear to have been generally grasped; but the separation from God and condemnation to hell that was the result of sin, was well understood. So was repentance and the assurance that sins were forgiven. This brought great relief, immeasurable joy and power to witness to the reality of Christ and to what He had done for them on the cross and was doing in them at that moment.

In the girls' school, Joy noted a new turn of events: some girls brought out blankets which, quite unsuspected by the missionaries, they had been given for sexual favours. The girls insisted that they be burnt. "The Lord has shown us", they explained, "that we have got to bring out everything that we have been given to do with sin." And they burnt the blankets!

"What a waste!" we said, but they insisted. "Anything associated with sin has to go." And that included things which had been stolen and objects used in totally unsuspected, sexual perversions. For those girls, it was not enough to repent of a sin unless that repentance was evidenced by a total rejection and removal of everything associated with that sin. The blazing light of God's holiness required nothing less. Then the joy and peace of forgiveness and liberation from the guilt and power of sin became almost overwhelming and expressed itself in wild singing and jubilation.

Joe Church and his team returned to Gahini from their evangelistic mission at Mukono to find the centre in a turmoil. "We cannot really explain or describe spiritual things. The medium of words is inadequate," Joe wrote of those events. "We cannot account for what happened in any other way. During that week men were gripped by uncontrollable forces, also spontaneously all over the district in the bush Churches and on some of the Stations. In some cases there were signs and dreams and outbursts of hymn singing, and prayer and remorse that often went on all night. In the Hospital, servants' quarters, Church, boys' school and in the houses and kraals of carpenters and headmen; even the government patients' Rest Camp was moved. The patients who were raw heathen and were lodging there behind the hospital were convicted."

The missionaries and African leaders at Gahini saw the need for immediate action and called in all the evangelists, teachers and church-attenders of the district on the Sunday following Joe's return from Uganda. A special weekend of teaching and guidance on how to deal with the happenings was arranged. That Sunday proved to be an unforgettable one for Joe. "About a thousand packed into and around the Gahini Church and we encouraged them, but at the same time dealt with the difficulties and the inevitable 'tares' which we knew would appear. At the end of the afternoon service many began praying aloud, and some cried out and fell on the floor weeping, while the others remained seated and we helped these out, and some prayed with them outside. We then closed the service and about one hundred and fifty remained behind and for three hours there were some of the most beautiful prayers I have ever heard offered up to God, interspersed with hymn singing, and apparently about fifteen or twenty were converted that afternoon."

Without any apparent connection, the same things were happening at Kabale and at Shyira, a new mission station in the north-west of Rwanda. Soon individuals and teams of men and women from these stations were visiting other centres and many outschools on the hills between them.

Two of the women whose testimony was used powerfully were Geraldine and Abisagi, two Toro teachers who had been asked to join the staff of the Gahini girls' school. "I found the presence of God very strong," remembered Geraldine years later. "Many people were repenting of their sins, and many of the children in the school were saved, and church teachers too . . . When I saw people confessing their sins, I was afraid and I thought it was a new religion. After a time God showed me the sins in my heart, but I feared to confess them and to repent of them, but the mercy of God showed me that Jesus loved me. How he loves the sinner! And I also repented in 1936. Jesus saved me and made me a new creature in the Spirit, the Lord be praised."

It is noteworthy that Dora Skipper, a missionary of long standing in Uganda as well as more recently in Rwanda, claimed that it was at this time that she was really saved. She had been a deeply committed, church-loving, zealous worker but she had not until then seen clearly what sin was in her life, nor repented of it so deeply, nor known such joyous assurance of sins forgiven. It is probably given to few people to pinpoint the exact moment of their conversion. Whatever may have been the true significance of this moment, for Dora it certainly represented the beginning of a new experience of a living Christ and effectiveness in His service.

On the 5th September, two months after the striking events at Gahini, Arthur Pitt-Pitts, Archdeacon of Kigezi and Ruanda-Urundi, wrote, "I have been to all the stations where this Revival is going on, and they all have the same story to tell, the fire was alight in all of them before the middle of June, but during that last week in June, it burst into a wild flame which, like the African grass fire before the wind, cannot be put out."

The flame grew even brighter and spread further afield. Missionaries were soon seriously divided in their assessment of what was happening and in their association with it. It was at times difficult to distinguish between behaviour which was the exuberant manifestation of the work of the Holy Spirit and that which was an

expression of satanic power. Although the need for
spiritual discernment continued, the evidence pointed
overwhelmingly to this being a notable intervention of a
holy God to authenticate His Word, point to His Son,
the crucified and risen Jesus Christ, and to His death on
the cross, as the only way to a saving relationship with
God the Father, and so achieve His purpose of calling
out a pure people from a corrupt world.

How did that smouldering fire start, which burst into
flame in the latter part of June 1936? What became of the
"wild flame" of revival? The answer is the story of the
Ruanda Mission and goes back to its beginnings over 20
years prior to these remarkable events.

Chapter 2

The beginnings
1908–1921

It was seeming chance that brought together two medical students, previously unknown to each other, as freshers to Trinity College, Cambridge, in October 1908. What followed from that convergence of two lives demands a deeper explanation.

Algernon Charles Stanley Smith was born in China, son of one of the famous "Cambridge seven" missionaries. His mother was Norwegian. She died while Algie was a baby. Leonard Ernest Stiegenberger Sharp was of Huguenot extraction. His father held a high position in the Civil Service in England and was decorated for his services and died at the age of 103. His mother was converted through D. L. Moody. Both students had received the best education that money could buy and Public Schools could offer; Algie at Winchester and Leonard at Harrow.

The two students differed in many ways. Len was tall, clean-shaven and with bushy eyebrows which were later to earn him as nickname the African equivalent to 'eyebrows'. Algie was of medium height and wore a moustache. But they shared common interests. Both enjoyed the games and sports facilities which the university provided and the study of medicine gave them a strong common concern. Stronger still was the bond formed by the discovery that they had both committed their lives to Jesus Christ.

The three years that the two students studied at Cambridge gave them ample opportunity to follow and imbibe the spirit of the two topics of debate which most engaged Evangelical Christians at that time: the defence of biblical truth and the challenge of world evangelisation.

The theological issue was focused in the relationship of two Christian student bodies: the Cambridge Inter-Collegiate Christian Union (CICCU) and the Student Christian Movement (SCM). Writing of the 'landslide away from biblical Christianity' between 1890 and 1909, Geraint Fielder wrote, in his *Story of sixty years of student witness*: "The Student Christian Movement (SCM) had tragically been in the vanguard of this. The evangelical Cambridge Inter-Collegiate Christian Union (CICCU), founded in 1887, had, by 1910, dissociated itself from the rest of SCM on the grounds that the latter was denying basic Bible truths. That process had continued, and by the end of the first world war there was, for example, hardly any theological college that had not downgraded its view of the Bible and Christ" (Geraint Fielder *Lord of the Years* IVP 1988 p 19). Len and Algie, as members of CICCU, shared in that dissociation of CICCU from the SCM in 1910 and a strong defence of biblical truth became a marked feature of the missionary task in which the two students were later engaged.

Those years at Cambridge University also allowed students in general, and Len and Algie in particular, ample opportunity of meeting missionary leaders and of catching something of the missionary fervour that stirred among Christian students at that time. They heard pioneers tell of the ways in which God was opening up the world to His gospel. The Edinburgh Missionary Conference of 1910 marked a milestone in world missionary outreach. Those were spiritually heady days as the students were presented with the challenge of "the evangelisation of the world in this generation".

Of particular significance was the Keswick Convention of 1910 which took place soon after the end of the Edinburgh Missionary Conference. Algie and Len joined others in a student camp associated with the Convention. Both young men faced and accepted the challenge of God to missionary service overseas. Len Sharp, in particular, looked back to that Convention as the time when God 'anointed him with the Holy Spirit' for further service.

"The Lord showed us," reflected Algie Stanley Smith many years later, "that we were not our own, but belonged to Him, and that we must listen to His voice and be ready to do what He commanded and go wherever He might send us. As we meditated on these things and sought to know what would please our Saviour most and make the best use of the one life He had given us, we began to pray daily that He would grant us the privilege of taking His Gospel to some heathen tribe which had never heard of our Saviour Jesus Christ, and prepare us for this task."

After their Cambridge years the two graduates moved to London for their clinical training; Algie Stanley Smith to St George's Hospital and Len Sharp to St Thomas's Hospital.

The first of many small but significant steps in which God guided the two young men towards their future sphere of service occurred while they were still students. In 1913, Algie and Len were invited to join a party of four men to visit the north-eastern corner of what was then the Belgian Congo, where missionaries of the

Africa Inland and the Heart of Africa Missions were working. To the east of them, like a great north-south gash in the vast continent of Africa, the western arm of the Great African Rift divided the seemingly never-ending, undulating tropical forest areas of the Belgian Congo from the mountainous highlands of western Uganda, Rwanda and Burundi; its course marked by a series of lakes and interconnecting rivers. Less than a degree south of the Equator, the Great Rift is cut by the Virunga mountains, a string of volcanoes of which only two are still active.

The two students learned that to the east of the Great Rift and south of the Virunga mountains there was a vast area of Africa which was little known and largely un-reached with the Gospel, although a few German Roman Catholic and even fewer Protestant missionaries were working there. The region was inhabited by two majority ethnic groups which remained distinct although there was intermarriage. The tall *Batutsi* or *Bahima* were considered to be of Nilotic origin and the shorter and more stocky *Bahutu* were probably derived from the *Bantu* tribes of southern Africa, but little more was known of them. The *Batwa* constituted a small but scattered minority of pygmies. Undeterred by the fact that the region was officially under German control, the two medical students returned to their studies with this vision of a wide-open door of opportunity before them.

A year later, both men became qualified doctors. Soon afterwards they were both invited by Dr Albert Cook, a missionary of the Church Missionary Society (CMS), to work for one year in Mengo Mission Hospital, Kampala, Uganda, where he was the doctor in charge. Missionary work had been carried on in that country for some years and they accepted the invitation with the double objective of acquiring experience in missionary methods and of investigating the un-evangelised countries to the south of Uganda.

However, political events overtook them and the visit was cancelled. In that same year, Great Britain was plunged into war. Algie, now Dr Stanley Smith, with the entire staff of St George's Hospital, London, was posted to the front line in France. He served as a Medical Officer to a battalion which suffered greatly in fighting around Ypres in the middle of 1915. During this period of front-line action he was mentioned twice in de-spatches and awarded the Military Cross.

Meanwhile, Mengo Hospital in Kampala, Uganda, had become a base hospital for the East African Cam-paign against the German forces in German East Africa. Dr Cook found it difficult to handle the extra heavy burden that this entailed and requested the release of two military doctors to help him in his responsibilities towards the armed forces in the area. At his request, Algie Stanley Smith was released from the war zone in France and drafted to Mengo Hospital. He sailed for Uganda under wartime maritime conditions in October 1915.

Len Sharp enlisted as a Medical Officer in the Native African Medical Corps and, from 1915 to 1917, served at a number of advance posts in Uganda before being posted to Mengo Hospital in Kampala. War service brought the young doctors together again at the very hospital to which they had been invited two years previously!

During the latter quarter of the nineteenth century, a large part of Africa was divided between European colonial powers in what appeared to be a somewhat arbitrary fashion. At the Berlin conference of 1884–85, called by the German Chancellor Otto Bismarck, agree-ment was reached between the great powers. In 1890, Ruanda-Urundi and Tanganyika became officially

German East Africa; Uganda became a British Protectorate; while Kenya and Congo became colonies of Britain and Belgium respectively.

The frontiers of these countries were not finally settled until 1912 when the border between Uganda and German East Africa was established along the crest of the Virunga mountains, and that between Uganda and Belgian Congo, along the Semliki River. This situation remained stable until the First World War. At the end of the conflict, Germany was forced to cede its East African territories of Tanganyika to Great Britain, and Ruanda-Urundi, treated as one country, to Belgium. Ruanda-Urundi became a Belgian mandated territory and Uganda remained a British Protectorate.

In 1916, the two doctors came across a book entitled "*In the Heart of Africa*". Published by Cassell in 1910, it was an English translation of a German account of an expedition across Central Africa in 1907–8, led by its author, the Duke of Mecklenburg. The route followed started in German East Africa and ended, according to the author "by crossing the Dark Continent".

The Duke described Rwanda as "a land flowing with milk and honey, where the breeding of cattle and bee-culture flourish, and the cultivated land bears rich crops of fruit. A hilly country, thickly populated, full of beautiful scenery, and possessing a climate incomparably fresh and healthy," (p 44). With a population estimated at one and a half million the Duke wrote: "Ruanda, in conjunction with Urundi, is the most thickly peopled region of Central Africa" (p 51). Explaining why the Germans had not exercised the same administrative control over Rwanda as elsewhere, the Duke again wrote, "Ruanda is doubtless, with the exception of Urundi, the last Sultanate or Kingdom in Central Africa which is governed today, as in centuries gone by, by a prince clothed with absolute and illimitless powers.

There is only one ruler and no rival sultans are allowed" (p 45). References to Roman Catholic "White Fathers" and quotations from a report of the Urubengera Evangelical Mission at Mecklenburg Creek (Lake Kivu), hinted at missionary activity in the area. The interest of the doctors was further aroused and they continued to enquire about this, to them, little known part of the world.

In December 1916, while serving as military medical staff at Mengo Hospital, Kampala, the two doctors obtained permission to visit Ruanda-Urundi during a three weeks' leave from military service. Due to an error, this permission was granted by the British authorities in Uganda without either the knowledge, or the approval, of the Belgian authorities. The two men were "arrested" at one point, but, dressed in British Army officer's uniform and accompanied by the Rev. Harold B. Lewin, a missionary of the CMS in Uganda, they could hardly be charged with spying or secretly seeking a British takeover of the country! They returned to Kampala without causing any major political incident and with their original conviction increased to certainty: that this was where God would have them work.

Further support was given to them by the young Church of Uganda which, at a meeting of the Synod in January 1918, urged that moves be made to evangelise Rwanda.

Their resolve was further strengthened by reading a booklet written by Bishop John J. Willis, then Bishop of the Diocese of Uganda, entitled *Uganda 1919*. In this the Bishop summarised the missionary work of the CMS in Uganda and pointed to regions needing medical help. Among these, underlined in red ink by Len Sharp in his copy of the booklet, was: "Ruanda, one of the largest native kingdoms in Africa, with some 2,000,000 people (to which Len added 'Urundi 3,000,000'), can best be entered by a Medical Mission. There is, therefore, a pressing demand for four new doctors" (John J. Willis *Uganda 1919* King and Jarrett p 18).

The Great War ended in November 1918, and in 1919 the doctors returned to the UK for leave. There, to quote Dr Stanley Smith, "we first sought and gained the whole-hearted support of the Africa Secretary of CMS, the Rev. G. T. Manley and of the Medical Secretary, Dr Jack Cook. Then we placed before the Society the urgent need for the Gospel of the five million inhabitants of Ruanda-Urundi and told them of the assurance we had that God was calling us to take the Gospel there."

The following February they were tentatively accepted as missionaries but the society's insufficient funds prevented it undertaking full responsibility for this new area of work. However, the Society agreed to support the new venture providing the doctors raised their own funds. That seemed an impossibility and no further plans were made.

Then the impossible happened! A woman in Tunbridge Wells decided to go to church one Sunday morning in September 1920 after an absence of some weeks. The speaker was Canon Stather Hunt who was a member of the CMS Africa Committee. He referred to the challenge that central Africa presented to the Doctors Stanley Smith and Sharp. She sent a gift of £500 towards their work, requesting that its donor remain anonymous. This represented a large amount in those days. Amazed at God's working, the two doctors interpreted this as a divine seal to their call. Soon they were both married, Len Sharp to Esther Macdonald and Algie Stanley Smith to Zoe Sharp, Len's sister.

The two doctors then visited Belgium to seek permission to work in the Belgian mandated territory of Ruanda-Urundi. Here again they recognised that God had gone before them to prepare the way. Encouragement came from an unexpected quarter.

Soon after the Berlin Conference of 1884–85, the German Government had realised that there was no missionary organisation in the Congo or Ruanda-Urundi which could engage in the "civilising" task that Christian missions – Roman Catholic and Protestant – were undertaking in other colonial territories. In 1886, the German Evangelical Missionary Society for East Africa (*Evangelische Missionsgesellschaft fur Ostafrika*), was formed. However, the spiritual drive of this mission was drawn from its links with the "House of Deaconesses of Bethel" and hence its activities were often referred to as those of the "Bethel Mission".

From the Bethel Mission a team of missionaries entered Rwanda from Tanganyika in 1907 and set up the first Protestant missionary post in Rwanda at Zinga, near lake Muhazi. This did not prove to be a suitable site but, on the 28 August 1907, the first Protestant Mission Station was opened at Kirinda, near Nyanza, the residence of Mwami Musinga, the African King of Rwanda. Two years later, in 1909, another station was established at Rubengera, near Lake Kivu, and, in 1912, a third at Remera, nearer Kigali. In Burundi, two stations were established at Musema and at Kibimba. There was a Protestant outreach around these five mission stations in Ruanda-Urundi but this was small because of the limited resources at the disposal of the German missionaries. In contrast, the Roman Catholic Church invested considerable resources in personnel and finances in their eight mission stations. Furthermore, these stations were strategically placed in or near administrative centres whereas the Protestant stations were in rural areas.

At the time when Algie Stanley Smith and Len Sharp were requesting permission to work in Ruanda-Urundi, the Belgian Society of Protestant Missions in the Congo,

(*Société Belge de Missions Protestantes au Congo*), was planning to send missionaries to work in the territory of which its country had assumed the mandate and to take over from the few German Protestant missionaries who were working there. Finding suitable personnel was, however, proving to be very difficult.

It was at this point that an outstanding Belgian Pastor, Henri Anet, emerged as a powerful spokesman for the missionary needs of the newly acquired African protectorate. As one of the official representatives of the *Société Belge de Missions Protestantes au Congo*, and at the request of the Belgian government, he accepted the responsibility for taking over the German Mission stations in Rwanda. It was a brave undertaking in view of the limited resources of the Society. It led him to contact a number of Christian organisations which might be able to co-operate in the task that was before him in Ruanda-Urundi. Monsieur Anet welcomed the possibility of CMS cooperation and arranged for the doctors to meet Belgian colonial officials with a view to obtaining official sanction. The two doctors often paid tribute to the great encouragement that the Belgian Pastor was to them personally and to the help that he was able to give them in their relationships with the Belgian authorities. Permission for work in Ruanda-Urundi was granted and the doctors prepared to set off in faith, knowing that God had prepared the way for them.

In November 1920, the two doctors and their wives left the UK for Africa. On their way by boat they called in at Marseilles and found there a letter awaiting them from the Rev. G. T. Manley, Secretary of the CMS, informing them that the Belgian Foreign Office had withdrawn its permission for them to work in Ruanda-Urundi. This was a serious blow to the missionaries but so confident were they of God's call to them that they continued their journey.

In Uganda, they reviewed their situation. They were convinced that God had called them: firstly, to pioneer-evangelism, that is, to take the gospel where Christ was not known; secondly, to use their medical skills to draw people to the Gospel; and thirdly, to establish a work in the countries of Rwanda and Burundi.

With what they believed to be their ultimate destination closed to them, they considered a number of other areas as an interim measure. The only one which appeared suitable was the Kigezi district of Uganda. CMS missionaries had been working in the centre and north of Uganda since the 1870's, leaving the south-west largely untouched by Protestant missionary activity.

There was, however, another and even more significant reason. Kigezi was an obvious stepping-stone to Ruanda-Urundi. One fifth of its population was Rwandan, speaking the language of Rwanda. This had come about in a curious way.

Before the border between Rwanda and Uganda had been settled, Belgium had laid claim to this part of Uganda to be added to its territorial boundaries of the Congo. The German authorities could, in fact, have made a more powerful claim for demographical reasons as they already occupied Rwanda. The border along the peaks of the Virunga Mountains was proposed by the great powers, as frequently happened, without any reference to African opinion or location of ethnic groupings.

In May 1909, knowing of these threats to their territorial claims to Uganda, the British authorities despatched a mixed force of soldiers of the King's African Rifles, Sikhs and police to the south of Uganda to establish a British presence there. It set up camp on the shores of a small lake named Kigezi, just north of the Virunga mountains.

"From this place," stated the British District Commissioner on the 50th Anniversary of the event, "the Force did a forced night march to Lake Kivu where they were surprised to find a German post, of which they knew nothing. They, therefore, turned north and marched to Rutshuru, and here they found a force of Belgian troops. A clash was only narrowly avoided. The Force was then ordered back to Mbarara but returned again and established itself in a fortified camp on this very place on which we now stand, on the 14th July 1909. Here they were surrounded by a Belgian force which threatened to attack them, but by good fortune a fight was again avoided and the Force remained here in occupation until the arrival in 1910 of a political officer, Captain Read, who established here the first Headquarters of the District. In 1911 the boundaries were finally settled by the Anglo-German-Belgian Boundary Commission, and this is how the Kigezi District became part of the Uganda Protectorate' (*Uganda Argus* 4 July 1959).

As a result of this action the southern Ugandan border was established along the peaks of the Virunga range of mountains. The region of south-west Uganda, named Kigezi by the British authorities, included two tribal areas, *Rukiga* of the *Bakiga* and *Bahororo* peoples, and *Bufumbira* of the *Banyarwanda* people. The political boundary between Uganda and Rwanda split off from Rwanda some 40,000 Rwandans living in Bufumbira, Uganda. So came about the "stepping-stone" into Rwanda that featured so prominently in the fulfilment of God's call to the pioneers of the Ruanda Mission. Without in any way justifying the political motives of the action taken, it is evident that God used this arrangement of national boundaries in His scheme of things.

With the full co-operation of the Bishop of Uganda, John J. Willis, the two doctors decided to begin work in the very needy and largely unevangelised district of Kigezi, Uganda, within which lay the district of Bufumbira, British Ruanda.

Kabale, the major town of Kigezi, is built on a number of adjoining hills. One of these, Rugarama, had been selected by the Rev. Harold Lewin as a potential site for a CMS mission station in 1914. It was to Kabira, a bluff of this hill, that, on the 24th February 1921, Len and Esther Sharp arrived on motorcycle and sidecar and pitched their tent. Three days later, Algie and Zoe Stanley Smith, accompanied by Bishop Willis of Kampala, arrived on donkeys. Within days a site was measured out, buildings planned and work begun.

Chapter 3

High expectations
1921–1926

"What a thrill it was to be out on the frontiers on our own, building our houses and the hospital, healing the sick, and preaching the gospel throughout that lovely country".

So described Algie Stanley Smith those first days in the district of Kigezi. The beauty of its hills, forests, lakes and rivers seemed to confirm the greatness of the God of the gospel they were called to proclaim. Among people who had rarely seen a white man or woman, they epitomised the pioneer missionary, often standing with open Bible, under a shady tree and dressed in khaki shirts and shorts and pith helmets as protection against the overhead sun.

Initially, while Len and Esther camped at Kabale, Algie and Zoe with their baby daughter Nora lodged at the CMS Mission Station at Mbarara, some ninety miles away.

To the British colonial authorities, Algie and Len were already well-known as a result of their wartime service in Uganda. They were given immediate responsibility for a small dispensary and adjacent ward which was already functioning in the government administrative centre. It had been, until then, the responsibility of an Indian Sub-Assistant Surgeon. Len became, albeit part-time, the first District Medical Officer of Kigezi, a post which he held, with the exception of home-leaves, until 1929.

In May 1921, three months after the start of their work at Kabale, they were joined by a nurse. Constance Watney came with fifteen years' experience as a CMS missionary in Mengo Hospital, Kampala.

Rugarama hill soon began to show signs of the landscaping skills which Len Sharp applied to the planning of all mission stations which he developed. High to the north of the site was reserved for the future church building. The lower, southern end would be the location of the schools and housing, but in the middle, at the heart of a caring community, had to be the hospital.

Six months after their arrival at Kabale, the doctors began work on the construction of Kabale Hospital. It was an ambitious plan, given the limited means at their disposal, both in materials and levels of skilled labour, but they worked with the will and zest that comes from the assurance of being in God's perfect will for them. In June 1922, they were able to receive their first in-patient. Three months later Constance Watney was invalided home to the UK. Her place was taken by Beatrice Martin. The head African medical assistant was a Ugandan, Erisa Mutiaba, who had been trained by Algie and Len at the CMS Mengo Hospital, Kampala. A further African assistant, Yusitasi, from the CMS Toro Hospital completed the small but united team which God used greatly in the first hospital of the Mission. Such were the differences in the tribal groupings of Uganda that Erisa and Yusitasi were missionaries to Kigezi from their home districts of Uganda as Algie, Len and Beatrice were from the UK.

Apart from the two African medical assistants named,

hospital staff were trained "on the job". Typical was a
boy of 16 years of age, the son of a chief, who came to the
hospital in 1923 covered with foul smelling sores. He
responded to treatment and, because he demonstrated
an intelligent interest in what was happening around
him, was engaged as a trainee assistant. His name was
Yosiya Kinuka. Little did the doctors who encouraged
him then know of the powerful way God was going to use
him in later years. Many were the Christian leaders who
began their service in this way.

The early methods of evangelisation, although
simple, were well planned. Their inspiration was drawn
from two sources. The first was a Christian Missionary
Report or series of talks which Len and Algie had read
or heard in student days or later, but certainly before
they left for Africa. "This report or message was of great
importance to my father and uncle who remembered it
for many years," recalled Mary Sharp, daughter of Len
and Esther Sharp. "It became for them part of God's
teaching for their ministry . . . through the years it
proved correct."

The principles outlined encouraged the doctors to
follow the pattern of the commission of Jesus Christ to
the Apostle Paul when he was converted on the road
to Damascus as recorded in Acts 26:15–18. As they
preached the Good News faithfully from the Bible, to
people ignorant of its truths, they could expect God to
"open their eyes and turn them from darkness to light,
and from the power of Satan to God, so that they may
receive forgiveness of sins . . ." (18). They were then led
to expect a gap during which time the Bible would be
translated into the native language. When people could
read its teaching for themselves, the Holy Spirit would
work in power to convince them of its truth and assure
them of 'a place among those who are sanctified by faith
in Me (18). Further biblical teaching would establish

those so indwelt by the Holy Spirit both individually and collectively as "assemblies" or churches.

The second source was the carefully thought-out, five-point strategy of missionary outreach outlined by Bishop J. J. Willis in the booklet, *Uganda 1919*. Starting with the selection of a central station, it included: the planting of "outstations"; the reduction of the vernacular languages into writing and the production of literature; the winning of converts; the selection of evangelists and the gaining of a thorough knowledge of the people and their culture.

In pursuing the principles they had derived from these sources, the pioneers planned a campaign of action. At first they, either together or separately, would select a few African workers to help them and go on safaris. The team would visit groups of African houses on a hillside, offer medical attention to those who requested it and invite everyone around to listen to them talking about their Creator-God, about Jesus Christ and His death for them on the Cross.

It was a simple message. However, it soon became apparent that it was not easily accepted. There was a great deal of opposition, not against the missionaries themselves, whom the Africans welcomed for the care they showed for their physical well-being, but against what they taught. In their superstitious culture, the Africans lived in a different world, culturally and spiritually. For many, the mind was held in a bondage of fear to ancestral spirits and often made incapable of logical reasoning relating to the simplest and most common aspects of life: such as hygiene, agriculture, animal husbandry and human relationships. This does not mean that everything said and done was evil. Far from it! There were many customs and ways of looking at things, often expressed in their many proverbs, which resulted in strong family bonds, high standards of loyalty leading to social cohesion and a body of wisdom relating to traditional forms of cultivation and animal husbandry.

"We doubt if people at home realise what it means to these early converts to come out of heathenism," wrote the two doctors. "It is like going over the top (in trench warfare), facing the great enemy, death, with all their old entrenchments of witchcraft and sacrifice abandoned, and trusting in untried armour. Many a time a man will say, when asked to allow his children to read: 'Wait and let me see if your readers die; then I will send my children.'"

Paul's introductory remarks to the Athenians in the Areopagus could, with one modification, be addressed to central Africa: "Peoples of Africa," he might have said, "I see that in every way you are very religious!" This was, and to a large extent still is, true of the peoples of Uganda, Rwanda and Burundi.

It is, perhaps, surprising that, with so little instruction, from aliens stumbling over seemingly unpronounceable words in a language that was foreign to them, many Africans found themselves desiring this new forgiveness of sins, liberation from evil powers and membership of the family of God. There was a power at work which enabled people to understand in a way that could not be explained in human terms. The evidence of thousands of men and women is that something dynamic happened. Their lives were changed. They experienced a previously unknown peace of mind and a new power for good within. They were not thereby given immunity from the powers of darkness, but they found within them a greater power which could triumph over evil.

As the numbers of church-attenders increased, some men among them would be selected to become evangelists. The first Evangelists' Training Course was started at Kabale in 1924. The evangelists were taught by Algie

Stanley Smith and Len Sharp; this in addition to their medical and other activities.

In that year a notable addition to the team was an African clergyman, the Rev. Azaliya Mutazindwa from Toro, north of Kigezi. Algie Stanley Smith spoke warmly of his contribution to the work centred on Kabale. "He at once took over the pastoral care of the churches, and the personal supervision of 150 teachers, whose needs demanded the whole-time work of one man and the understanding of a native pastor to enter into their temptations, trials, and failures. He came as a very gift from God, a man full of zeal and real spiritual power. After two years he returned to Toro, leaving behind him a fine record of faithful ministry."

During each of the first two years of the Kabale Evangelists' Training School, some seventy teachers were given an initial period of intensive instruction and from them ten were selected each year to complete the year and receive their First Letter. The rest were given one term's training in three batches of twenty men each. In 1927, the number was increased to 100 teachers each year. "They have here," wrote the founders of the school, "a glorious opportunity for the working of the Holy Spirit in their lives, and it is our earnest prayer that, term by term, they may go back to their villages, filled with the Spirit of Pentecost. We look upon this school as being perhaps the most effective agency for evangelisation."

At every church centre, schools were started. The simple school buildings, usually of black wattle or eucalyptus trees daubed with mud, were built as gifts came from friends in the UK. The standard of teaching was rudimentary.

Boys had relatively little difficulty in being allowed to attend school. For girls it was quite different. Many parents considered them too useful at home and, in any case, they would soon be married. Some were disowned because they persisted in attending school.

Culture in Africa, as elsewhere in the world, is male dominated. The place of the woman is traditionally to look after the home, bear and rear children, cultivate the fields and exercise her wisdom behind the scenes. Christian teaching in the Bible maintains the order of men in leadership in the home and in the church, but raises the status of women to equality before God and to an equally important, although different, status in society.

The first visible results of the Gospel appeared to benefit men. Boys were the first to be educated and employment in hospital, school and church was over-whelmingly male. Hence the need to make special pro-vision for the less socially privileged women who were often despised and circumscribed by parents when young and by husbands when adult.

The pioneer doctors were well aware of this situation and, in 1923, welcomed Constance Hornby, to give of her time and energies to work primarily among women and girls. Constance was a short, wiry and indefatigable fighter against the traditional prejudices which pre-vented Africans from letting their daughters attend school. A few years later she wrote home, "I could weep for the women and girls in this country. All this month I have been amongst the cattle people (and their flies DO bite!). They are a fine race of men but CAN I get the girls? My first from this tribe, four in number, have been promised but time will prove if at the last their people will let them come."

In 1924, three missionaries joined the team at Kabale: a pharmacist, Miss Margaret Davis, and two non-medical missionaries, Captain Geoffrey Holmes and the Rev. John E. L. Warren, brother of the better known Canon Max Warren. In that year the hospital building at Kabale was completed and Len and Esther Sharp returned to England to seek further support and more missionaries. The following year, lightning struck one of the wings of the hospital and fire destroyed a considerable part of the wood and papyrus structure. It was a severe blow but reconstruction was begun immediately.

After five years of work in the Kigezi area, despite the many difficulties experienced, there were encouraging signs. Of Rukiga, the central part of Kigezi, Algie Stanley Smith wrote, "In every native government centre . . . and wherever any considerable population is collected, we have now planted our teachers, and we believe we can say that with only very few exceptions, there is no important village in Rukiga out of reach of the sound of the gospel. Do not mistake our meaning. The work is not done, it is only begun; but the teachers, such as they are, are there, and the ark of salvation built, into which all who will may come. Every little centre has its church, built by themselves entirely without help, representing something of the earnestness of the readers' faith."

Encouraging as these facts were, the pioneer missionaries were perplexed. The preaching and teaching of the Gospel had been true to God's Word, yet the spiritual results in people's lives were depressingly low. They wrote home, referring to the work in Bufumbira: "There are some deep shadows, alas, in the picture. Two great evils have confronted us as the work developed; immorality and drink. Not a few so-called Christians from (elsewhere in) Uganda have come to this country and denied their Lord in lives of open sin, and yet, strange to relate, observing the outward forms of religion, and showing considerable keenness on its progress. Their subtle example has borne its inevitable fruit in some of the local Christians following in their steps. Worst of all, in more than one instance, those to whom had been entrusted the care of the flock, have betrayed their trust, and have put Christ to open shame. With such as these, after prayerful and patient pleading, we have felt constrained to deal by following our Lord's injunction in Matthew 18:17 and, through St Paul, in 1 Corinthians 5:11. Thank God several have thus been plucked as brands from the burning. The evil of drink in this country is like a demon which drives its victims into many and terrible crimes. Against this evil we have found that nothing short of total abstinence is of any avail, and we have been backed up in this by the enlightened opinion of all the best Christians."

Add to these two evils of immorality and drink, the curse of witchcraft! All this drove the pioneer missionaries to recognise "that our struggle is not against flesh and blood, but against . . . the rulers . . . of this dark world" (Ephesians 6:12). They were preaching a saving Gospel in enemy territory and they could never forget that. Ground gained in winning lives for Christ had always to be seen as a victory over the Evil One and thereafter the battle was engaged to keep the converts true to their new-found faith. Hours of travelling on foot, listening to accounts of quarrels, judging between rival accusers and counselling often left the missionaries physically, mentally and spiritually exhausted. They drew strength from the knowledge that a group of supporters in Great Britain and an increasing number of African Christians shared with them in praying that God would somehow intervene in power and vindicate the truth of His Word and the honour of His Holy Name.

Chapter 4

Into the promised land
1922–1929

On a clear day the distant peak of Muhabura, the easternmost of the Virunga range of mountains which separates Uganda from Rwanda, can be seen from Kabale. Often, as Algie Stanley Smith and Len Sharp worked at Kabale, they would look up beyond the hills of Kigezi to that peak . . . a reminder that it was to the lands beyond those volcanic heights that God had called them.

Politically that goal seemed unattainable. Ruanda-Urundi was a Belgian mandated territory and the Belgian colonial authorities were suspicious of British territorial ambitions. They had already cancelled, for no known reason, the permission given in Brussels for the doctors to work in those countries. How was God going to fulfil what they believed He had so clearly promised?

"Well, it happened far sooner than we could have dared hope," said Algie Stanley Smith, years later, "and by means we could never have foreseen. News came to us early in 1922, and only a year after we had started

work in Kigezi, that the British Government had requested the transfer of a wide strip of Eastern Ruanda
about 100 miles long and reaching right down to Burundi
for the purpose of surveying a route for a Cape to Cairo
railway. As it was now under Britain, I sent a letter to the
Provincial Commissioner in Tanganyika asking for permission to open work there. He sent me a cordial reply,
in which he said he had instructed the new District
Commissioner to meet me at the border and promising
every assistance in our project."

A three-weeks' safari was arranged into Rwanda. It
proved to be a most stimulating experience. "The administrator turned out to be a man I had known in the war,
and he was a Christian," Algie reported. "He offered
me any site we might like to choose for a mission station,
and he attended the simple service in which we preached
to the assembled chiefs and people the Gospel of
Christ."

In September 1922, nineteen months after the beginning of the work of Kabale, Yoeri, a church teacher from
the Ankole district of Uganda, was posted to Eastern
Rwanda. Six months later, in April 1923, a High School
for the sons of chiefs was opened at Rukira and,
with more volunteer African evangelists and teachers
trained in Ankole, a number of church centres were
established.

That year, 1923, saw the last of the series of political
events which led to the Ruanda Mission, a British
missionary society, being established in Ruanda-
Urundi, a Belgian mandated territory. The plan to build
a railway from the north in Uganda to the south, in
Tanganyika, all in British territory, was abandoned and
Eastern Rwanda was handed back to the Belgians. "The
Great Powers had reversed their decisions, but a
Greater Power had done His work, for the Mission was
now established within the country from which it had

been barred" (Lindsay Guillebaud *Grain of Mustard Seed* Ruanda Mission p 22).

In an interview with the chief Belgian official at Kigali, the administrative centre of Rwanda, Algie Stanley Smith was informed that not only could the work already begun in Eastern Rwanda be continued, but there was no official objection to missionary work being extended to the rest of Rwanda. Unfortunately, this permission, given by the highest Belgian official in Rwanda, was not followed up by an official recognition of the Mission by the Belgian authorities. The freedom and help given to missionaries in the years that followed depended on the personal attitude of the Resident in office. This was to give rise to considerable difficulties until the Mission was granted official status.

At the time when Eastern Rwanda was handed back to the Belgians by the British colonial authorities, there were 14 evangelists and teachers working in the church centres and in the High School at Rukira. The take-over of Eastern Rwanda by the Belgians did not, however, immediately improve the situation. Missionary work, in fact, declined.

Describing the situation there in 1925 when only six teaching centres remained and the High School had almost ceased to exist, Algie Stanley Smith wrote, "The retirement of the British Government inevitably gave the natives the impression that the British Mission would also have to leave the country. In spite of the fact that the Belgian government officials did all that they could by friendly recognition to give our work fair play, this impression prevailed; and there were enemies to our work who fostered this idea; so much so that many natives were afraid to show the friendliness that they felt."

Of the two major enemies to the work of evangelisation – witchcraft and the Roman Catholic Church – it is

sad to record that, at that time, the latter proved to
be the more hostile. In Uganda, the British colonial
authorities maintained a strict impartiality in their treatment of Protestant and Roman Catholic Missions. In
Ruanda-Urundi the situation was very different. The
Belgian Roman Catholic government gave the Missions
of that church overwhelmingly preferential treatment
and the church used that advantage to the full. It is
difficult now, with the changed attitude of the Roman
Catholic Church to Protestant Churches following the
Second Vatican Council, to understand its bitter hostil-
ity to Protestant missionary work in those days and its
flagrant use of political power to thwart it. The situation
is recorded here without bitterness and with gratitude to
God for the change of heart which has transformed
relationships between the Churches.

Hardly started, the work in Eastern Rwanda under-
went a time of persecution. The African teachers who
had come as "missionaries" to Rwanda from Uganda
were threatened with violence or death if they did not
leave. "In one village," recorded Algie Stanley Smith,
"the readers were threatened with a beating if they did
not leave our Church and join the Roman Catholics . . .
The teachers, in the absence of a resident missionary to
guide and encourage them, inevitably began to lose
heart, and the occasional visits paid them could
not really counteract the sense of isolation and the
discouragement of dwindling congregations."

Now that the whole of Rwanda was administratively
one country, under a Belgian mandate, it was possible to
move freely from east to west. Ex-Army Captain, Geoff
Holmes, was posted to Rwanda where he was able to use
his military experience in seeking suitable sites. Geoff
consulted Government officials, Mwami Musinga, the
king of Rwanda and his senior chiefs and the missionaries of the Belgian Protestant Mission (SBMP) who

now occupied the previously German stations. As a result a site was requested at Gahini, a hillside overlooking Lake Muhazi. Permission was granted for what proved to be an excellent strategic as well as beautifully scenic location.

Later that year Geoff moved to Gahini to establish the first Ruanda Mission station in Ruanda-Urundi. In August 1925 work was begun on temporary buildings to house workers, to tend the sick and in which to start a school.

With Geoff Holmes went Kosiya Shalita, a young school teacher who had been born near Gahini but had lived in Ankole, Uganda, since childhood. He and his father were baptised together in a small village church in Ankole. At primary school he had shown exceptional promise and eventually attended King's School, Budo, the leading school of the CMS in Uganda. "He left Budo just when he was needed for the work in Ruanda," wrote Algie Stanley Smith, "equipped with the best education Uganda could afford, with a sound knowledge of English, and with a heart steadily fixed on the ideal of being a missionary to his own people. After one year in Kigezi High School as headmaster, he was set free to accompany Captain Holmes, and found himself stationed a few miles from where he was born. Who planned the life-history of this lad (a man now) so as to prepare him and bring him into the work at the very moment he was needed?" Indeed this was evidence of God's gracious work.

An addition to the missionary team was another worker posted to Gahini in 1926. The Rev. Herbert S. Jackson had spent some time in Brussels before sailing for Africa. There he gained a Belgian medical diploma and this gave him official recognition by the Belgian Colonial Office. This was the first of many later moves by the Mission to adapt to the colonial policies of the

Belgian Government. The energetic efforts of Geoff Holmes, Bert Jackson and Kosiya Shalita revived the spirits of the evangelists in the area.

In June 1926, eleven young Christians were baptised at Gahini. They were the first-fruits of the work in Belgian Rwanda. Among the early converts at this time was a boy named Eriya Kanyamubari. Forty years later, as Canon Kanyamubari, he became the Principal of the Bible School on that very hill!

Opposition from the Roman Catholic Church increased. Its openly belligerent character became so acute that Geoffrey Holmes made the long and arduous three weeks' journey by foot and bicycle to Bujumbura, in Burundi, to lodge a protest with the Colonial authorities. The Governor of Ruanda-Urundi was able to issue orders which alleviated the situation to a certain extent but, although helpful, he was limited in what he could do because the Ruanda Mission did not officially exist in the territory.

It became clear that suspicions still existed in the Belgian hierarchy that the Mission's work represented a political infiltration. These were largely cleared at an International Missionary Conference held in September 1926, at Le Zoute, Belgium, to which the Belgian Minister of Colonies was invited. The way towards full recognition of the Mission by the Belgian authorities was then open but its implementation was slow.

In 1927, the Belgian Government was asked to grant a site for a mission dispensary at Gatsibo, a government post in northern Rwanda. "Gatsibo was a point of outstanding importance where the big chiefs of the district continually attended," reported the missionaries. "Captain Holmes frequently visited there and, with the goodwill of the Belgian Administrator, a building was put up as a dispensary. This was the first place to be occupied outside the boundary of the old area of

British occupation." Once again, a medical opportunity became the spearhead of missionary advance.

The dispensary was placed in the charge of an outstanding Christian, Perezi Senyabatwa. "He came to Kabale hospital as a particularly wretched ulcer patient, and after a long period of treatment was cured," recorded the pioneer doctors, "but he got more than physical healing there for the Lord met him, and he became one of the brightest Christians who have come out for Christ in the hospital. Full of love and zeal, he was taken on as a hospital assistant, and when trained he went down to work at Gatsibo as the hospital's 'own missionary'. He was fervently upheld by the prayers and gifts of the staff and the patients. It was touching beyond words to see those poor, maimed folk coming forward at the Sunday services and taking the wire bracelets off their arms to help to send through Perezi the good news of salvation and healing to those more needy than themselves."

Amidst the many difficulties and discouragements, a remarkably encouraging event occurred at a Convention held in that same year at Kabale. In response to a "missionary call" put to seventy-five Kigezi teachers for volunteers to work in Rwanda, thirty came forward! This was with full knowledge of possible consequences: hardship, loneliness, sickness, hunger, and perhaps death. The Church in Kigezi began to look on Eastern Rwanda as its "mission-field". "Missionary teachers from Bufumbira, speaking Kinyarwanda," reported Algie Stanley Smith, "and those from the Rujumbura area, speaking Runyankole, offered to go to those places in east Ruanda where their languages were understood. The zeal of some of these young teachers was inexplicable apart from the energising power of the Holy Spirit."

Within six years of the Mission's work beginning in

Kigezi the newly-established congregations had become missionary churches, sending their own workers over the border into Rwanda.

Although the Mission was, at first, predominantly medical in character, the two pioneer doctors saw no further additions to their ranks until 1927 when they were joined by Dr John E. Church. "Joe", as he was better known, came armed with a Belgian Tropical Medicine Diploma and with strong backing from the Cambridge Inter-Collegiate Christian Union of which he was an "Own Missionary". He worked at Kabale with the two pioneer doctors before being posted, in June of the following year, to Gahini where he became the first resident missionary doctor in Rwanda. Without delay he started the building of the hospital. Joe shared with Len Sharp a remarkable artistic gift for landscaping and building design. The new hospital was carefully planned to be welcoming, efficient and pleasingly blended to the environment.

Hardly had Joe Church arrived at Gahini and the first ward of the new hospital been roofed when famine hit the area. In early 1928 the rains in northern and eastern Rwanda failed. By June the effects of drought were being widely felt. This, combined with other factors, such as the absence of any grain storage system, led to a severe famine and this, given the poor conditions of hygiene, was soon followed by debilitating diseases such as dysentery. The Belgian government organised food and shelter for the most destitute and this was dispensed, in part at least, through the Missions.

The hospital at Gahini was at the centre of relief activity. Thousands flocked to the Uganda border in search of food and many passed by Gahini on their way there. Algie and Zoe Stanley Smith moved to Gahini temporarily to help the over-stretched staff.

The position became so serious that, in February

1929, Joe Church wrote from Gahini to the Belgian Resident in the capital, Kigali, inviting him to visit the desperate areas. He received no reply. After consultation with Bert Jackson, he drove to Kampala to seek aid. Within a few days a famine appeal was launched and an article, written by Joe, was published in a Ugandan newspaper.

To Joe's surprise, but delight, a full column of his article was published in "The Times" of London on the 16th April 1929. Four days later, questions were asked in Parliament concerning the refugees in Uganda from famine in Rwanda. The Belgian authorities were challenged about the situation and the Belgian Prime Minister replied by making public the measures taken to relieve the suffering by the colonial authorities in Rwanda.

Joe's plea for aid did not fall on deaf ears. Help came from a number of sources. In July the rains fell and the famine passed. Two months later, Joe visited Nairobi, Kenya, where he was officially informed of the thanks of the Belgian Government to the CMS for the missionaries' efforts to relieve the victims of the famine. He received personal letters of thanks from the Belgian Prime Minister and the Minister for Foreign Affairs in Brussels. Nevertheless the horrors of those months lived long in the memories of the missionaries.

The strength of the opposition, satanic and political, and the low spiritual state of the missionary work caused great concern. A "Special week of Prayer and Humiliation before God" was planned for both the field and the home supporters in February 1928. A letter from Jack Warren was quoted in Ruanda Notes: "There are now close on 2,000 baptised Christians but we are only too conscious that the signs of real heart change are very few and far between. Moral lapse upon lapse and tragedy upon tragedy have been following one on top of the other. Only this week has come the evidence that one of our most trusted teachers has been stealing the readers' money, cheating fellow teachers and, to crown it all, obtaining money under false pretences from two old men learning the Catechism, who thanked me so pitifully when I returned the money that had been stolen. Another senior teacher has been drinking heavily and has been dismissed. We plead therefore that every Friend of Ruanda will set aside a time on each of the above ten days to wrestle in prayer as we will be doing here, and then we know that we may indeed expect a wonderful out-pouring of God the Holy Spirit, an out-pouring that will not be limited to Kigezi but in its flood will reach the uttermost parts of Ruanda in the days to come."

The skeleton of God's church in Kigezi and north-east Rwanda was in place, but could these "dry bones" live?

Chapter 5

A foretaste
1930–1933

From its opening in 1922, Kabale Hospital drew patients from all over the district of Kigezi, from other regions of Uganda and from over the border in Rwanda. Among these some were suffering from leprosy. A special ward was set apart for them in the hospital. "Soon it became apparent," wrote Len Sharp, "that throughout the land, in the cattle kraals of the plains, among the hillside villages, in the huts around the lake shores, and even among the scattered families in their flimsy forest-shelters, men, women and children were being marked down and doomed by this dread disease. No wonder that we viewed with deep concern the plight of these pitiful sufferers, so prayerful plans were devised to meet their special need, and to do all that was possible to prevent the spread of this disease and to relieve its worst horrors."

The nature and extent of the disease pointed to the establishment of a leprosarium. With this in mind, the Uganda Government medical authorities were consulted. In response, the missionaries were offered the largest island, Bwama, in Lake Bunyonyi. The nearest point of the lake was a convenient six miles from Kabale.

The setting could hardly have been more beautiful and outwardly peaceful but there were other factors which had not been foreseen!

The lake and its islands had for many years been associated with a heathen cult centred on a female evil spirit named *Nyabingi*. It was claimed for *Nyabingi* that she was the reincarnation of an ancient queen who was also a sorceress. Those who professed to be possessed by her spirit claimed the power to control rain, fire, disease and death. Their followers were assured immunity from spear-wounds and bullets. "So great was their power," commented Len Sharp, "that for several years after Kigezi came under British control, agents of *Nyabingi* repeatedly inspired insurrections, causing considerable bloodshed."

The leader of the last major rebellion was a witchdoctor named Ndabagera who lived on Bwama. In this rebellion Ndabagera was defeated by government forces and his people banished from the neighbourhood. At the time when the island was being considered as a possible site for a leprosarium it was without inhabitants. Ancient trees alone marked the sites of the homes of its former satanic-controlled occupants and it was avoided in great fear by local people.

Work on the settlement began in 1930. The approval of the Government of Uganda was expressed in grants for the building, maintenance and development of the work. A nurse, May Langley, lived on the island and the doctors visited from Kabale.

As the years passed, the settlement grew along carefully worked out plans, bearing testimony to Len Sharp's artistic touch. The island was, in fact, the top of a mountain projecting to about 250 feet above lake level. The slopes lent themselves to the building of a number of clusters of simple houses, called villages, which radiated along the contours from the hospital, church and school in the centre.

The obstacles to be overcome were immense: maintaining a sufficient food supply, discouraging patients from leaving when their treatment was only partially complete, encouraging the regular, very painful, intradermal injections of chaulmoogra oil, and providing a social setting for those up-rooted from their home situations. It became known as the "Island of Miracles", and so it was! Men and women, boys and girls, cruelly infected with the dread disease, found there the love and compassion of God for them as individuals and new life in a living Christ who enabled them to triumph over their grave disabilities.

It had been recognised from the beginning that the medical and evangelistic work would have to be backed up by providing literature, especially the Bible, or portions of it at first, in the language of the people. In 1925, the Rev. and Mrs Harold E. Guillebaud came to Kabale as honorary workers. Harold was a gifted linguist. He devoted all his energies to translation work.

Even at home with his family his mind was concerned with the needs of the people he had come to serve. "It had been our practice in England to sing hymns round the piano on Sunday evenings before going to bed," recalled Rosemary Guillebaud, "and our parents continued with this when we arrived at Kabale in 1925. They called our house-boys in too, and as we sang, our father would give a resumé in *Kinyarwanda*, often singing an off-the-cuff translation made as we went along (which of course did not always scan). At the end of the evening, after prayers in *Kinyarwanda* and English, he would sit down and work at any of the hymns we had sung which he felt would go well in *Kinyarwanda*. During the week our mother would cyclostyle these. She had brought out a roll of heavy wall-paper with her 'in case it came in useful', and this was requisitioned to make covers for some 50 copies of the 'Hymn book'. The pages were held in place with pronged paper clips, so that, like a loose-leaf book, more hymns could be added. Eventually there were enough hymns for it to be worth getting them printed, and a hymn book was made with about 100 hymns."

Harold Guillebaud's priority in translating was given to a Kinyarwanda version of the New Testament. Amazingly, it was completed less than five years after his arrival in Africa. Writing of the dedication service at Kabale in February 1930, he expressed his joy: "There seemed a special thrill as the glorious words of the lesson were read: *All nations and kindreds and peoples and tongues* . . . realizing that here was, as it were, yet another of the *nations and tongues* joining in worship and praise." In November of that year, Harold was able to take to Gahini the first consignment of the translation in print for distribution. It was received with great rejoicing.

It was natural that an Anglican mission should require a service book. Accordingly, in the late 1920's, Harold Guillebaud translated the English Prayer Book services into Kinyarwanda. These were in use until 1933 when a revision of the text was felt necessary. A Minute of the Field Executive Committee of the 8 February of that year contains an interesting note: "With reference to the publishing of the Prayer Book, an element of uncertainty as to its permanence arose from the fact that a strong move was being inaugurated in East Africa to begin the formation of a United African Church on the lines of the Church of South India." In fact, a "United Church" never came into being and the revision then printed remained in use for over 20 years.

Somehow, in his very full life, Harold Guillebaud also translated what was to become the best-loved book next to the Bible: *Umugenzi*, John Bunyan's *Pilgrim's Progress*. The original publication was illustrated by photographs of Ugandans taking the characters of the story.

At about this time a series of articles, written by a Roman Catholic priest, appeared in one of that Church's Uganda periodicals. The statements made by the priest and the arguments given to support them created a furore in the Anglican Church there. The Bishop of Uganda, John J. Willis discussed with Harold Guillebaud a possible reply to the articles and suggested that he should write it and publish it in the Church of Uganda's own periodical. "My father's article," commented his daughter Rosemary, "was duly translated into Luganda and printed and at once it provoked a further reply. For several months fresh articles were written and published in a sort of ding-dong between the two periodicals. My Father, who had written in English for translation into Luganda, then wrote it up as a book in Kinyarwanda."

One of the important points in the discussion related to the claimed position of Mary, the mother of Jesus, as "Mediatrix" between man and God, hence the title of the book, *Umuhuz' Umwe* – "One Mediator". It was to prove of immense importance in giving African Christians a reasoned defence of their faith in the unique Person of Jesus Christ as the "only mediator between God and man".

In early 1928, the Mission was joined by two young ordained men, the Rev. E. Lawrence Barham and the Rev. Cecil B. Verity. Cecil was posted to Gahini and Lawrence was based at Kabale. At the same time, the Rev. Ezekiel Balaba, an ordained Ugandan, joined the team at Kabale. He was "of deep spirituality and genuine humility," recorded Algie Stanley Smith, "whose labours, especially in the Evangelists' Training

School, have been rewarded in a marked raising of the standard of our teachers throughout the district."

A month before the Call to Prayer, in 1928, to which reference has already been made, an incident in a remote part of Kigezi was to have striking consequences. "There is a little village far off the beaten track in a valley ringed round with precipitous hills, which resembles a great cauldron;" wrote Algie Stanley Smith in an urgent request to the UK for prayer, "and there lived a woman, fairly young in years, but who had already sold herself to the practice of the occult arts, and was frequented by the local inhabitants as a witch-doctress of some power. One day, towards the end of January, she woke up at midnight, and said to her husband, 'Let us go and worship God.'

"'Are you mad?' he said, 'What have you to do with the Worship?' In the morning she went off with her husband to the local chief, where she again repeated with great vehemence, that she was going to follow Jesus. 'What do you know about Jesus?' she was asked. 'Was it not He who came to call me at midnight?' she replied."

The witch-doctress used her considerable influence to threaten the people among whom she lived with severe punishment if they did not also go to "the worship of God". Accused of stirring up trouble, she was brought before the District Commissioner. "Are you a teacher?" he asked her. She replied, "We are all teachers. All who know God must tell of Him." So, with a caution that she should refrain from violence, she was released. However, she continued to encourage her people to go to the Christians to learn about God. The effect among the superstitious people of the district was very powerful. Thousands flocked to Sunday services, usually in the open-air, as simple church buildings proved inadequate to contain the crowds.

The great numbers which gathered each Sunday in numerous church centres presented a great problem. There was an insufficient number of church teachers to instruct them. Bands of untrained volunteers, armed with prepared lessons, were sent out from Kabale to teach the basic truths of the Gospel. The mass-movement lasted about a year. Then the crowds began to diminish and there appeared to be no great lasting spiritual results.

In seeking to appraise this movement, Algie Stanley Smith wrote, "There is no doubt that the Spirit of God was moving in the hearts of multitudes of people. It made the Mission believe in the possibility of a supernatural work of God among uninstructed heathen. . . . In the light of future events it can be seen now that there were two fatal defects in this movement; the one was the absence of any true conviction of sin, and the other was that the spiritual life of the church was too low to be usable in the day of opportunity. The church had first to be brought under the judgement of God and cry out for mercy. The world cannot be expected to be conscious of its sins, until the Church is conscious of hers; and the time had not yet come, though there were signs of its coming, when God was to bring His people in broken-hearted penitence to the cross."

As the churches of Kigezi returned to normality many of the problems raised by a superficial spiritual work emerged. For three years Lawrence Barham visited the churches which had experienced this strange phenomenon. He found everywhere a need to emphasise the necessity for repentance and faith in Christ to be genuine.

So great was this desire to purge the church of nominalism that, in 1932, great efforts were made publicly to denounce sin in every form and to name and escort off church premises those who were known to be living in sin while affirming church membership. Commenting on this episode in the life of the Kigezi church, Algie Stanley Smith wrote, "In the light of future experience one can now see that such a policy, though Scriptural, is in its application a human condemnation. The convicting power of the Holy Spirit is far mightier and more melting than the ban of the Church after trial. For those who will not repent, and there will always be such, it is the presence of the Lord in consuming power in His people that makes such hardened sinners withdraw themselves . . . A further defect in this 'Cleanse the Church' campaign is that it concentrates attention on one or two glaring sins such as adultery or drunkenness, as though they were worse than pride or anger, jealousy or deceit."

As the mass-movement in Kigezi began to die down, a seemingly small event, in September 1929, proved to be the seed of greater things. That year Joe Church visited Kampala from Gahini where he was stationed. There his prayer for one really saved African with whom he could have deep fellowship was answered. The African was a well-educated, English-speaking, government officer named Simeoni Nsibambi.

This proved to be a momentous meeting, not only of two men who were earnestly seeking a new and living experience of their God, but of two strands of God's working in Africa.

Joe's thirst for a deeper experience of God sprang from his concern at the relatively low-level of spiritual life and effectiveness of missionary outreach in Kigezi and Rwanda. For Simeoni, it was the desire to see God working in power again in his country. It was known that, on occasions, he would go to Namirembe Cathedral and weep over the spiritual deadness of the church.

For Joe, there was no previous experience of revival in

Africa known to him. For Simeoni, in Uganda, there was!

In December 1893, a "Keswick Convention" had brought together a number of missionaries to Kampala. The Rev. G. K. Baskerville, a CMS missionary in Uganda, set the scene:

> "We had been much cast down by the lack of zeal amongst the Christians, not, indeed in the wish for instruction, for they could scarcely have been keener; but in the wish to pass on what they knew, and, again, many were living such low-level lives.
>
> "It was just then that God showed us that we were the cause of the lack of zeal, of the low-level lives and of the absence of joy. A little book by a black man – David, a Tamil Evangelist from India – in which he spoke of the power of the Holy Ghost as a gift to be claimed and appropriated by all Christians just as they had claimed the gift of life – this little book brought a blessing to one, and he told the others; and others of them were led just to ask themselves, if, perhaps they had not been working apart from this power, and there was conviction, and cleansing, and appropriation, and consequent joy and power . . . The next few days were days of blessing. We went up the next morning to the church, and instead of the usual short service had a mission service. We asked the people to forgive us for having worked amongst them without having claimed the only efficient power for service – that coming from the Holy Ghost being in possession of the heart. . . . From this time of blessing may be dated the great activity of the Native Church both in their country and also in the regions beyond". (G. K. Baskerville *The Gospel in Uganda* CMS p 47.)

Another CMS missionary at that convention was George Lawrence Pilkington. His biographer, Charles F. Harford-Battersby, wrote of him at that time:

"It is true that there were outward and visible signs which betokened prosperity, but was there in proportion the inward and spiritual grace? It was this for which he sought, but the dearth of spiritual results was to him and his fellow Missionaries a keen disappointment. Pilkington himself was so much discouraged, that he spoke of giving up Missionary work altogether, unless some change took place.

"In this state of mind he went alone for a visit to the Island of Komé (one of the Sese Islands in Lake Victoria), and it was there that he learnt the great secret of the indwelling power of the Holy Spirit, which transformed his whole life.

"On December 7th, 1893, Pilkington returned to Mengo from Komé, and everyone noticed the wonderful change in him. His very face told of the reality of the change. His boys noticed it, the Christians of Uganda were conscious of it and all who came in contact with him, and that not only from his words but in a thousand little ways which speak more forcibly than the most eloquent sermon." (C. F. Harford-Battersby *Pilkington of Uganda* Marshall Brothers p 225.)

There was no spectacular sequel to the events of December 1893 but a quiet and deep work followed in the lives of a number of Ugandans in whom God gave a thirst for new things. In quiet and unobtrusive ways, small groups would move among their friends and in churches giving testimony to what God was doing in them. When, years later, the same kind of thing happened again, there were those who recognised the similarities and pointed to the end of the last century when God worked through George Pilkington and others. Revival had begun in Uganda long before this quiet meeting in Kampala!

Although they knew little of each other's background, Simeoni and Joe found themselves at one as, sitting on the verandah of what later became the Namirembe Guest House, and using Schofield's Reference Bible, they searched the Scriptures for its teaching on the fullness of the Holy Spirit.

"I have often referred to this time in my preaching in later years," recorded Joe in his autobiography, "as the time that God in His sovereign grace met with me and brought me to the end of myself and thought fit to give me a share of the power of Pentecost. There was nothing very spectacular, nothing ecstatic; it is easy to become proud if one has received a special gift. The only special gift is the experience of the transforming vision of the risen Jesus Himself" (John E. Church *Quest for the Highest* Paternoster Press p 68).

Later that year, the Rev. Blasio Kigozi, a Ugandan ordained teacher and brother of Simeoni Nsibambi, answered the call of God to serve Him in Rwanda. "So strong was his call," he confided to his brother, "that he was prepared never to come back to his native land of Uganda, but was ready to die in Ruanda and to sacrifice his life in order that the people of Ruanda might be saved." At Gahini he became head of the re-opened boys' school which had been closed since the severe famine of 1929.

Nevertheless, in the following years, the spiritual state of the work at Gahini deteriorated. The missionaries felt impotent to cope with the jealousy and hatred which destroyed any unity between the leaders of the hospital, school and church work. This included the two Ugandan leaders, Yosiya Kinuka, the senior hospital assistant, and Blasio Kigozi, headmaster of the boys' school.

In 1931, Yosiya visited Simeoni Nsibambi in Kampala and there God spoke to him very clearly. With simple directness Simeoni pointed to the sin which Yosiya tolerated in his life and in his relationship with other Christians. On his way back to Gahini, sitting on a lorry at the frontier, in the "no man's land" between Uganda and Rwanda, the burden of his sin overwhelmed Yosiya. "I was deeply convicted," he wrote later, "My sins became like a burden on my back, and I yielded to Christ."

Thereafter the situation in the hospital improved considerably and several of the staff were truly saved. Teams of witness were sent from Gahini into the district around. Yosiya Kinuka and Blasio Kigozi were foremost in the leadership of these teams.

In 1930, the Belgian government granted legal status to the Mission. Until then, Gahini was the only station of the Ruanda Mission in Rwanda. The Belgian Protestant Mission (SBMP), occupied three ex-German mission stations – Remera, Kirinda and Rubengera, in the middle and west of the country.

"By the middle of 1930," wrote Algie Stanley Smith, "a growing conviction spread in the Mission that the 'fiery cloudy pillar' of God's presence was about to move on". Two sites were selected for the opening of new Mission stations in Rwanda and applications made to the Government. Permission was refused, largely because of the militantly hostile attitude of the dominant Roman Catholic Church working through its influence on local African chiefs.

So certain were the missionaries that the time was right for advance that, in November of that year, a reconnaissance party explored further possibilities to the west and south. Requests for sites were again made to the government. Difficulties were again encountered, but objections were recognised by the government officials to be largely politically inspired and permission was granted. In 1931, Jim Brazier left Kabale to establish a site at Shyira in the north and, in 1932, Geoffrey and Ernestine Holmes began work at Kigeme in the south. A year later, Algie and Zoe Stanley Smith moved to Kigeme to take over from the Holmes and the medical work developed rapidly. The needs of the church work also grew rapidly and, in 1934, Jim and

Joan Brazier were posted there to join the Stanley Smiths.

At Gahini, Dr Bill Church, brother of Joe, joined the staff of the hospital in 1931, where he worked for the next four years. During this time the Bible teaching of the two Church brothers proved of particular significance in the movement of God that was to come. It was during these years that Joe hammered out in the *saa munani* sessions (2.00 pm daily teaching for builders, carpenters and other mission workers) the basis of the Bible Study manual, *Every Man a Bible Student*, later published in English. Joe and Bill were joined by Pat Walker, the first nurse to live as well as work at Gahini Hospital.

In 1932, the CMS Executive Committee in London agreed to the constitution of the Ruanda General and Medical Mission as "a separate self-administering Mission within CMS". In the following year, with five Mission centres established, including the leprosy settlement at Bwama, and some thirty missionaries on active service, the Mission was able to take a major step forward. Its work in Africa was, until then, directed from its office in Croydon, England. Some of this responsibility was delegated to a Field Executive Committee in Africa. The first meeting of this Committee was held at Gahini in February 1933 with Algie Stanley Smith as the first Field Secretary.

Later in 1933, a delegation from England, consisting of the Rev. A. St John Thorpe and the Rev. W. A. Pitt-Pitts, visited Kabale to lead a "Keswick" convention for missionaries. It proved to be a time of great heart-searching as the missionaries felt deeply convicted of spiritual barrenness in their personal lives, and of strife and discord in their fellowship. They pleaded for urgent prayer at home and in the mission field.

One cause of discord between missionaries was called

the "parson-layman" controversy. The founders of the
Mission were laymen with very clear evangelical convictions and a strong call to evangelise and so lead converts
to baptism and the formation of churches. They were
more concerned with the Biblical basis and reality of the
emerging churches than with the forms of their structures and services. The supporters of the Mission,
however, were Anglican and missionaries were compelled, therefore, in principle to introduce Anglican
forms of worship and practice.

The clergy whom God called to work in the Mission
were also Anglican and it was natural that they should
adhere to their Anglican roots. These roots, however,
were in the Church of England of the 20's and 30's which
was strongly in the grip of "clericalism" where clergy
authority was supreme. Furthermore, it was a regulation
of the Church Missionary Society that, where an
ordained man was posted to a mission station, he would
be the head of the station, however junior he was to
other missionaries.

The early lay missionaries found it difficult to accept
this imposition of clerical authority. They also dis-
approved of some forms of Anglican services and
regulations which they believed to be untrue to the
Scriptures, or of secondary importance.

Algie Stanley Smith expressed this clearly. "Partly
through the tactlessness of the laymen, and partly
through the novelty of the idea to clergy of the Church of
England, some of the ordained missionaries felt that the
laymen were interfering in matters outside their sphere
. . . The Church of England 'parish system' places
nearly all the authority and initiative in the work of the
Church on the clergyman. It is too great a burden for one
man, and it ignores the immense reserves of spiritual
power latent in the laity."

Joe Church recalled one Easter at Kabale when he

and the Rev. Ezekiel Balaba were working very closely together. The rules of the Church made it obligatory for the Holy Communion to be celebrated on important Christian occasions such as Christmas and Easter, and forbade anyone to preach at a church service who was not licensed by the Bishop. As crowds gathered on that Easter Sunday morning, both Joe and Ezekiel felt that the need of the church was that people should be really saved and that this came before rigidly keeping the rules of the Church. There was no Holy Communion observed on that occasion. Morning Prayer took the form of an evangelistic service at which Joe and Ezekiel preached.

It was symptomatic of the life of the Anglican Church in Uganda at that time as well as of the "layman-parson" conflict within the Mission that that event was reported to the Bishop and the matter taken further, right to the Archbishop of Canterbury. As a result Joe Church was officially disciplined by the removal of his licence to preach!

The matter was later resolved happily but the fundamental issues remained. "All missionaries are on the same level," Joe Church contended. "There is no distinction, nothing special in a person having been 'priested'." Joe used the picture of a three-legged stool. The clergyman, the teacher, the doctor or nurse, were of equal importance in presenting the Gospel as were each of the three legs of a stool in supporting the one sitting on it. The picture of the three-legged stool was later extended to represent medical work as ministry to the *body*, education as ministry to the *mind*, and church work as ministry to the *spirit*. In this way the Gospel met the needs of the whole man, *body*, *mind* and *spirit*. Building up the Church was clearly the primary task, education and medicine were important in so far as they contributed to that end. At that time, however, the point of contention lay in attributing a different status to clergy from that of lay workers. "Team work is a wonderful ideal," commented Algie Stanley Smith in later years. "It calls for great humility and self-effacement on the part of the clergy, and tact and humility on the part of the laity. But it is indispensable to a revived Church."

The "Keswick" convention at Kabale, in 1933, resulted in a humbling of the missionaries, leading to a greater oneness between them. The problems did not disappear, however, and a happy relationship between clergy, most of whom were very strong Anglicans, and laymen, some of whom were very strong-minded doctors, took time, much heart-searching and humbling to achieve. The mass-movement in Kigezi and the renewing power of God in a number of individual lives had given the missionaries a taste of His power in action. The hunger grew for that "taste" to become a "foretaste" of greater things to come.

Chapter 6

The fire is lit
1933–1936

The "Keswick" convention for missionaries at Kabale in 1933 was followed, in the same year, by two conventions for Africans. Of these Algie Stanley Smith wrote: "There had often been meetings for deeper instruction when people came in for baptism, confirmation, and church councils, but it was something new for people to be brought together for no other purpose than to get a fresh vision of God and of their own hearts."

The second of these conventions began on the 27 December 1933, at Gahini. There appeared to be no obvious response to the five days of teaching, so Geoffrey Holmes extended the convention for a further day. At an extra prayer meeting, arranged for the Saturday afternoon, while everyone was bowed in prayer, an African Christian rose to his feet and began confessing some sin he had committed. The effect was dramatic. It seemed as though a barrier of reserve had been rolled away. A wave of conviction of sin swept through all those present. It continued for two and a half hours with as many as three on their feet at once trying to speak.

The fire of revival had been lit! From then onwards, there was a renewed zeal as groups of men and women at Gahini, Kabale, Shyira and Kigeme formed teams to visit outchurches and areas as yet unreached with the Gospel. The zeal of the witnesses was not matched, however, by the results in changed lives. God had begun to work in a remarkable way among the leaders. The spiritual fire was smouldering, but there was not yet that response for which some missionaries prayed.

It would have been natural to assume that this surge of spiritual life together with the church, medical and educational work already in hand in Kigezi and Rwanda, would have provided sufficient opportunities for the energies of all the missionaries on the field and many more. That was, in fact, true. However, Algie Stanley Smith and Len Sharp, supported by the other mission-aries, were very conscious that their call from God, to go to Rwanda *and* Burundi, was not yet accomplished. Accordingly, in early 1934, the two doctors travelled south into Burundi exploring possibilities.

On completing their exploratory tour of Burundi, Algie and Len selected two sites. With the full support of the Danish and American missionaries, who had re-cently occupied the ex-German stations of Musema and Kibimba, respectively, Algie and Len applied for Government permission to establish mission stations at Buhiga, in the north-east and Matana, in the south of the country. This was granted. On the 27 December 1934, a band of seventy Rwandan porters set off from Gahini southwards towards Burundi. "It is difficult to convey in words", wrote Algie Stanley Smith, "the thrill of enthu-siasm and assurance which swept through the Mission as it sent its tiny band of invasion forces across the Akanyaru River into Urundi in the early days of 1935."

Four days later he, Bill Church and Kosiya Shalita set off by car for the same destination – Buhiga. There, in the early part of 1935, was established the first Ruanda Mission station in Burundi. Bill Church immediately set about the construction of houses, hospital and school.

Later that same year the same party of porters which had travelled from Gahini to Buhiga, moved on to Matana, some 90 miles further south. They set up camp on the site which became the second Mission station of the Ruanda Mission in Burundi. The party of porters left Matana to return to Rwanda after a few days, leaving Kosiya Shalita to begin the work there.

The reception of the newcomers in Burundi was mixed. "Immediately the people started coming for medicine," reported Algie Stanley Smith, "but it was obvious that they had been warned against the Protestant teaching."

At Buhiga, Bill Church was assisted by a few Rwandan workers from Gahini who had volunteered to accompany him to Burundi to help him in his pioneer work on the new station. He wrote of them, "Not only do they help me with building, but they are continually teaching the *Barundi*, visiting them on their hills and inviting them to come to be taught. The success of the work depends largely on the quality of our African Christians."

In addition to the Rwandan volunteers from Gahini, John Musoke and his wife Naomi came as missionaries from Mengo Hospital, Kampala, to assist Bill in starting the medical work. John was a Uganda Government trained medical assistant and Naomi a Mengo Hospital trained nurse. Not until eleven years later was there a UK missionary nurse posted to Buhiga. John and Naomi combined a strong, clear witness to Christ with steady dependable service in the hospital.

At Matana, Kosiya Shalita was for some months alone among a strange people. To make things even more difficult, during the first few weeks it was cold and

wet, food was scarce and workmen refused to come. He
persisted, however, built himself a little round hut and
then a mud and wattle church school. There he so
identified himself with the *Barundi* that, in the years to
come, they came to love and respect him.

Towards the end of 1935, Len and Esther Sharp
moved from Kabale to Matana to join Kosiya Shalita.
They were accompanied by a Swiss nurse, Berthe Ryf.
Matana is on a highland plateau and conditions were
particularly difficult due to torrential rains, violent
storms, and piercing cold. A grass-hospital was soon
constructed in which Berthe was able to tend the sick
while Len Sharp concentrated on the construction of a
more permanent building. This was completed in 1937,
and, in July of that year, was officially opened by the
Governor of Ruanda-Urundi.

For some time the pioneer missionaries had been
concerned about the leadership of the growing churches
in Rwanda and Burundi. In Kigezi, the church naturally
formed a part of the Diocese of Uganda. This was
not the case in Ruanda-Urundi. At the request of the
Ruanda Mission, the Kenya Mission of the CMS was
asked to second the Rev. Arthur Pitt-Pitts to Ruanda-
Urundi to lead the growing church there. The choice was
a natural one for Len Sharp and Algie Stanley Smith.
They and Arthur had been students together at Cambridge University although studying different subjects.
Since 1917, Arthur Pitt-Pitts had been Private Chaplain,
first to Bishop Willis of Uganda, then to Bishop
Heywood of Kenya before becoming the Secretary of
CMS Kenya in 1930. He had also been one of the two
visiting speakers at the Keswick Convention for missionaries at Kabale in 1933. It was said of Arthur Pitt-
Pitts that he 'agonised in prayer' for those to whom he
ministered.

Encouraged by Len and Algie, Arthur Pitt-Pitts

accepted the invitation to become the first Archdeacon of Kigezi and Ruanda-Urundi. The appointment, in July 1935, was not, however, without some apprehensions on the part of some missionaries who expressed doubt as to the need of 'importing' a clergy leader when there appeared to be adequate lay leadership already in the work.

As, during these years, the Protestant missions worked together in relation to the government, so grew their sense of interdependence. On social and political issues which concerned all Protestant Christians, co-operation proved effective. But what of their evangelising objectives? The growing trust and co-operation between them prompted the facing of an important issue: What was to be the nature of the Church that was being brought into being in these countries? Was each Mission to introduce the denominational pattern that had given it birth? Was a multiplicity of denominations inevitable? Or was there a possibility of a United Church of Ruanda-Urundi on the broad pattern of the Church of South India, the formation of which was very much in the news at that time?

At the invitation of the Danish Baptist Mission a conference of five Missions working in Ruanda-Urundi was held at Musema, Burundi, in November, 1935. In addition to the Ruanda Mission and the Danish Baptists, the SBMP (*Société Belge Missionnaire Protestante*, usually known in English as the Belgian Protestant Mission), the American Friends Africa Gospel Mission, and the Canadian Free Methodists were also represented. The object of the conference was defined by Arthur Pitt-Pitts: "To consider the question of a United Indigenous Church in Ruanda and Urundi and our relationship to one another as Societies in the same cause."

The conference brought to light wide differences in

aims and outlook. Arthur Pitt-Pitts illustrated this: "No longer is the battle today fought over the matter of views on Inspiration or Baptism, but questions of what to us appear as minor points such as smoking of tobacco . . . On the first day, our conference leader stated that any European or African who used tobacco in any form or for any purpose would, in their Church, be excommunicated from the Lord's Table."

The use of alcohol was also a source of differences in church discipline. It seemed that secondary issues were to pose insurmountable obstacles to co-operation between the missions. On this occasion, a deeply spiritual missionary of the Free Methodist Mission, the Rev. John Wesley Haley brought the conference back to repentance and prayer. The issues which had dominated the conference did not disappear but the spiritual oneness of the missionaries was sufficient to keep alive the aim of a united, evangelical, indigenous church in Ruanda-Urundi.

An important consequence of the conference was the formation of the Alliance of Protestant Missions in Ruanda-Urundi. At the same time the principle of "comity" was established by which defined regions of the country were allotted to each mission and "trespassing" was forbidden by mutual agreement. It required a number of years to agree on the details of this comity decision.

At the same time as the moves into Burundi and activity on a political level in the co-operation of the Protestant Missions, renewed spiritual life centred, in south-west Uganda, on the team of Ezekiel Balaba and Lawrence Barham, both of whom were clergy; and in north east Rwanda: on Blasio Kigozi, Yosiya Kinuka and Joe Church, of whom only Blasio was an ordained minister.

From Kabale, Lawrence Barham reported new signs

of spiritual life among the students of the Evangelists' Training School. For three years he and Ezekiel Balaba had concentrated on teaching the meaning and implications of the Gospel using the typology of the Old Testament.

> "Of course, we have been doing it for years," Lawrence wrote, "but latterly more time for teaching and a better knowledge of the language have intensified this work. . . . All last year we have been burdened with the need of revival, and had prayed much for it, and in that year, the spirit of opposition to the claims of the Lord to full consecration increased, till in the September holidays, conviction of sin came on a number of men separately in their own homes. One and another came back in fear and trembling, because they knew they must testify to the others, only to find that others were the same! They, then, received (quite independently of any help from any of us) a burden of prayer, and met every night for prayer."

Men and women were coming under deep conviction of sin. They would tremble violently and sometimes fall to the ground until the peace of forgiveness was experienced. In one area of Kigezi, the 'saved ones' became convinced that Jesus Christ was going to come back to earth that year although no special teaching about the Second Coming had been given. They wanted to know if they should sow new crops if Jesus Christ was coming again so soon. Lawrence Barham and Ezekiel Balaba travelled many miles and spent many hours in counselling those who were perplexed by strange new experiences.

Ezekiel and Lawrence then did what came to be such a common occurrence in the years that followed, they looked around for others who were likeminded to visit them and together seek whatever God had in store for them. They invited Joe Church, Blasio Kigozi and

Yosiya Kinuka to bring a team from Gahini to share in a convention at Kabale at the end of September 1935.

Parallel with these spiritual stirrings at Kabale, a similar movement was evident at Gahini. "A spiritual fire seems to have been smouldering at Gahini for some years," wrote Joe Church, "every now and again bursting out quietly here and there." One of those in whom the life of God had "burst out quietly" was Blasio Kigozi.

Joe told the story in *Awake! An African calling*:

> "As soon as the term was over Blasio retired into his house, and there he spent a whole week in solitude, hardly coming out at all, eating very little, and spending all the time in reading and pleading with God for the power for which he longed. . . . Some thought he was ill; others, that this first term had been difficult and had rather got on top of him. But one or two of us guessed what was actually happening.
>
> "The crisis came during this week of waiting upon God. Man's extremity is ever God's opportunity. 'Satan trembles when he sees, the weakest saint upon his knees.' And it came to pass according to the promise: 'You shall receive power . . .' That power came upon him. He was the same cheery Blasio, but there was a new zeal, a new sense of urgency, a new abandon, a new assurance." (John E. Church *Awake! An African calling* CMS p 17.)

It was with new vision and power that these two, Blasio Kigozi and Yosiya Kinuka led the teams of witness into the district around. On Gahini station itself, the effects were felt in every aspect of the work. A deep desire for prayer grew until at times it caused trouble in the various departments of the work. Prayer meetings and hymn singing went on, often late into the night, or started in the early morning. This "epidemic of midnight prayer and singing" caused some disruption, particularly in the hospital, but it was evidence of a great desire that God would do something new among His people.

Then came the call to Gahini for a team to share in the convention at Kabale in September 1935. Three of the party from Gahini walked the 90 miles to Kabale. They were joined at Kabale by two men who had walked eighty miles from Shyira.

Joe Church invited Simeoni Nsibambi to join them from Kampala. God had preceded him, as he discovered. "Simeoni had had a dream in which he felt he must go to the Bufumbira Mountains (beyond Kabale on the Rwanda border) for a month and pray there, also to go and preach to the lepers on the island," Joe recorded. "He had told no one of this, but he had begun to lay aside money for it at his home in Kampala. My letter came and he realised that this was his call, and he accepted at once."

As the conference ended the teams from Uganda and Rwanda found themselves as one in their expectancy of seeing God working in a new way.

Joe Church and his team returned to Gahini but before the end of the year they were invited to lead a mission at Mbarara, the nearest major town in Uganda to Gahini. Joe described the way this, as other conventions and missions, were organised.

"We took a party of about ten Africans chosen from several different stations, men on whom God had laid His hand . . . they came primarily to do personal work, but could be asked to speak when necessary. We generally had one subject each day, and arranged to keep to the subject in all the talks and addresses and to hammer it home in whatever way God guided during the day. Remember we are writing about Africa, and here, as in the East, spiritual transactions are made with God in the cool and quiet of the night . . . This is where an African worker is so invaluable. Europeans can never get really near enough to the Africans to sit all night in

their dark, smoky huts. But with a band of those who are
known to be on fire for God, the white man can sit in his
room or tent praying, and resting on the assurance that the
things of God are being talked out and that the Spirit of God
is at work."

The subjects followed were those used in many such
conventions: Sin, Repentance, the New Birth, Separation from Worldliness, the Victorious Life and the
Holy Spirit.

The mission at Mbarara lasted over a week in January
1936. "So great was the sense of urgency," wrote Joe
Church, "that the three leaders decided to add an extra
subject, *kurimbuka*, i.e., to perish, or 'the state of
perishing of the sinner before God'. I could not leave my
hospital again, so these three had to conduct the mission
alone on this much older station. Although they were
welcomed by the European missionaries, it was a difficult and exacting task for them."

The three Africans were Blasio Kigozi, a *Ugandan*,
Yosiya Kinuka, a *Munyankole*, and Paulo Gahundi, a
Rwandan. Blasio, in particular, appeared driven by an
inner urgency. He often sat up all night in huts known to
be infested with ticks which cause relapsing fever and
where malaria-ridden mosquitoes were prevalent.
Shortly afterwards he suffered an acute fever caused
probably by either relapsing fever or malaria. The true
cause was never diagnosed, but Blasio died at Mengo
Hospital in Kampala within ten days of the end of the
Mbarara convention.

At Gahini, Blasio was sorely missed. He had, however, left many who traced their conversion to his
ministry and their zeal to his encouragement. "Although
Blasio was not with us," wrote Joe Church, "his spirit
was still a driving force in our midst."

The death of Blasio Kigozi had a profound effect on

his brother-in-law, William Nagenda. Both had received
a good education, judged by the standards of those days.
William had gained a diploma from Makerere College
before it was raised to a degree-conferring institution
and he held a good post as a government clerk. He was a
truly saved man but he did not have the vision and zeal of
his brother-in-law. He immediately offered himself to
the Bishop of Uganda to go to Rwanda where his
brother-in-law had served. "He was unknown to any of
us," wrote Joe Church, "but when we were asked by the
Bishop at the committees which station would like to
have him, my hand went up because I knew that he was a
convert of Nsibambi's. God was answering our prayer
for one to take Blasio's place." So began at Gahini, a
partnership between William and Joe that was to last for
many years and involved many thousands of miles of
travelling together.

In early 1936, the Bishop of Uganda wrote to Joe
Church inviting him to take a team for a mission to the
Theological College at Mukono, the principal training
institution for ordinands in the Church of Uganda. A
wider mission to Uganda was planned to celebrate the
Diamond Jubilee of the Church in 1937 and students
from Mukono would be taking part. First, however, they
wanted a "mission to the students".

On the way to Mukono, Joe and his team stopped at
Mbarara where a remarkable incident occurred. As
recorded by Joe,

> "Many had gathered to meet us on our way to Kampala and
> a gathering had been arranged in the church for 5:00 pm. We
> all spoke and we made an appeal when a thing happened
> that I had never experienced before. A man began to cry out
> and howl at the top of his voice. I was alarmed and made
> people sit down. The man continued weeping lying on the
> floor. I called him up to the chancel to say what he had
> experienced. He was one of the most trusted Christians, a

government interpreter. He stood beside me weeping and in halting words gave a moving testimony. He said that he had seen a vision of Christ in the church and he saw the awful state of the lost and was overcome with grief for his own past. He asked his friends to help him, but he could not stop crying out. Later some senior Christians came round . . . after supper and said that they too had seen a similar vision in the church . . . We felt the power of God in that meeting that evening and we wondered if God was allowing us to see the literal fulfilment of the promise of Joel 2:28 – 'Your young men shall see visions . . .'"

The Mukono Mission began on the 22nd June 1936. Joe reported, "We followed the same plan as previously, but the chorus: 'Spirit of the Living God,' seemed to become part of the mission, and we sang it as a prayer, before almost every meeting . . . The final testimony meeting on Monday morning before we left was an experience the true value of which will only be known in the eternity which is to come."

The "Mukono mission" was not without its critics. Some senior staff members of the College found the Gospel preached "unlovely" and "unsettling to baptised and confirmed students" and spoke disparagingly of the "*Banyarwanda cattlemen*" and their simple message!

It was during that last week in June 1936, while the Mukono mission was in progress, that the smouldering fire burst into flame in Rwanda as recorded in Chapter One.

Chapter 7

The flame spreads
1936–1939

A month before "the smouldering fire burst into flame" in June 1936, a pamphlet, written by Joe Church, entitled, *Victorious Praying*, was published in England. "God used this to call forth a great volume of prayer, unique in the story of the Mission," wrote Algie Stanley Smith. "The whole Revival movement seemed to surge forward as prayer ascended up on high. From this time onward the smouldering fires blazed out."

Radiating from Gahini in Rwanda, and from Kabale in Uganda, teams of witness travelled, sometimes on foot, to other stations in Rwanda and Burundi. From these centres, teams visited outschools as hundreds of ordinary people experienced the convicting and saving power of God in their lives. The majority of teams were formed of ordinary men and women whose distinguishing features were a dynamic experience of a living Jesus Christ, a burning desire to share with others the truths that had become so real to them and a power in communicating those truths which brought conviction in their hearers.

With forty-four missionaries either on the field, on leave or about to join the work for the first time, the complement of the Mission was larger than it had ever been or was going to be again until after World War II. Some of the missionaries, including the two pioneer doctors and their wives, had been in the work for over ten years, while fourteen new workers had arrived in the country within the previous twelve months. Some of the older missionaries looked back to the times of heart-searching when the gospel they knew to be from God had been preached and taught with some tangible results in changed lives, but rarely had they seen a deep work of the Holy Spirit. Now God was doing something new. The power of the gospel was being demonstrated in startling and unexpected ways.

By the nature of their selection and training, all the missionaries were, in theological terms, strongly "conservative evangelical" – they believed in the absolute and final authority of the Bible as the only true revelation from the one Creator-God. For many of these newer missionaries, as well as for some of the older ones, some of the happenings they observed were difficult to fit into their evangelical understanding of things. It was very upsetting.

Often repeated were scenes of deep anguish over sins committed until there was repentance and a cry to God for mercy. Some of the sins would ordinarily be considered as trivial but they became unbearable in the presence of a holy God. The day before Lawrence Barham set off for a safari visiting the churches in the Kigezi district in November 1936, a gardener came to him "and with great beads of perspiration standing out on his forehead told me of a few small things he had stolen from me. I should have been inclined to think them of no importance, but he told me of how he had lost all peace, and had had to face up to going to prison for theft if he confessed. I realised afresh that even what we should call petty pilfering is sin, and was giving this man agonies of shame and distress of mind. This is not emotionalism; it is stern conviction of sin by the Holy Spirit, and it fills us with awe."

"It has been a deeply humbling experience," wrote Algie Stanley Smith, "for one has been shown something of the poorness of one's previous experience. These men and women, who have been literally 'born again' are, some of them, those whom we looked upon as our brightest trophies, yes and we wrote of them in Ruanda Notes; and yet on their own confession they were stealing, drinking or committing all manner of sins unknown to us. One just cries out with Isaiah: 'My leanness! my leanness!' (Isaiah 24:16). But this sense of unworthiness is no morbid thing; it has been one of the most emancipating experiences in one's life, for it has brought deliverance from the subtle bondage of pride, and now the Lord Jesus fills the picture. He is supreme and altogether sufficient."

Other sins were related to witchcraft, satanic practices and sexual activities, which were strange to those not familiar with African culture. Then there was the explosive joy of sins forgiven and liberation from the stranglehold of Satan. Often emotions ran high. Very high! Singing would go on well into the night and, on occasions, continue until morning. Open confession of sin, sometimes very personal, embarrassingly so to some missionaries, would be mingled with testimonies of triumph over evil powers and highly animated prayers to God whose presence was powerfully felt. Sometimes there were what some felt to be unintelligible mumblings which, seen with the experience of hind-sight, were probably "speaking in tongues". On one occasion a man informed Lawrence Barham that he now spoke Hebrew! Lawrence asked him to speak in that language. On hearing him Lawrence replied, "I have studied Hebrew and what you are saying is not Hebrew!"

There were many remarkable dreams, in many of which people were pointed to statements in Scripture which particularly applied to them or to some sin or sins they were concealing. On occasions, people would fall to the ground in a seemingly trance-like condition. These more unusual expressions of revival were not condemned nor repressed, as some have claimed, but they were not considered as important compared with the expressions of conviction of sin, assurance of forgiveness and power to witness boldly.

On his arrival back at Kigeme after leave, Jim Brazier wrote:

"There is a great deal to praise God for although some things are a sorrow and a disappointment. There is a spirit of revival on the station among the Christians and a number of backsliders have been restored and every evening the station rings with fervent singing. This singing is something new. The African spirit seems to have broken through the 'tempo' of our English tunes and instead of the drag we have always struggled to defeat in their singing they have the fire and rhythm which I suppose was the spirit behind 'jazz' and 'swing'. It is strongly emotional, of course, and it will be interesting to see how the spiritual perception, which our African leaders have in large measure, will direct it."

At Buhiga, Ruth Pye-Smith was working at the beginnings of an educational work, there and in the district around. There were no school buildings and skilled workers were few. It was tough going.

"As on the spiritual side, so in the material," she wrote home, "labourers are so very few that one is unable to get on with the work quickly, whether it is spreading the Gospel or putting up buildings." But, she went on, "as in the last Ruanda Notes almost every letter contained a song of praise for the wonder-working power of the Holy Spirit dealing with so many of us, Europeans as well as African friends; so the joyful story must be continued in this letter, too. One only marvels at the love and patience of the Lord with us over so many years of professing to be truly His, when that was only so in part.

> *Pardon, peace and power,*
> *Mine this very hour!*

That is the message which the Lord has sent during these last few months, with glorious assurance."

As God worked in power among the men at Gahini in 1936, so He began to change the women. Christ in the home proved to be the greatest transforming influence in family relationships, particularly in the standing which women enjoyed when their husbands found that they could live in the "light and love" of fellowship with Christ and with their wives.

What did all this mean? That God was working in power was very evident, but so was Satan. This was spiritual warfare! An initial view saw "revival" as drawing a sharp dividing line between "light" and "darkness" – those "in the light" recognised and accepted the blazing purity of God's holiness contrasted with the awful sinfulness of anything and everything that did not correspond to God's holy character; those "in the dark" refused to face the truth of sin in their lives and repent of it wholeheartedly. As time passed it became clear that things were not as simple as that. "Light and darkness" also contrast "reality and unreality" and the discernment between these was much more difficult.

Those whose transformed lives showed such distinctive new life were nicknamed *abaka* by an African sub-chief near Gahini and this name became accepted widely. The root meaning of the African word is "to set alight" and hence, the *Abaka* were "those who had been set alight" or "the burning ones".

The understanding that everyone was either *in the light* or *in darkness* led to those who had experienced the new *light* of complete openness to God and to each other, seeking to bring others into that same experience. Tragically this led to the creation of two groups. Soon mission stations, outchurches, families, even missionaries became divided into those who aligned themselves with the *Abaka* and those who did not. As time passed it became evident that among those who called themselves the *Abaka* there were some whose publicly pronounced experience of God was either very superficial, largely emotional, spurious or non-existent. As always, when God is working, Satan was too, and there were tares among the wheat.

From Gahini, Geoffrey Holmes wrote:

"Here there are two 'camps' – those who are in with the *Abaka* and those who are not in with them. Actually here at Gahini most of the native Christians are in with this new group. There is no real fellowship between those who are in this group and those who are not. Those who are in it are continually seeking to convert those who are not to their way of thinking, and every means of persuasion and moral coercion are employed. This new group have their good points and I think the chief of these is perhaps their keenness to spread the Kingdom of God in these parts. But it is a misguided keenness which leads to a result the opposite from that which is intended. Some of the Christians are so taken up with their own spiritual struggles that they have very little time for the heathen round about and no real message for them."

Among those who did not align themselves with the *Abaka* there were some who supported wholeheartedly what God was doing in revival power, but did not approve of the divisions caused by the distinguishing fences that the *Abaka* appeared to put round themselves. Equally, there were many who stated publicly later that they did not at first align themselves with the *Abaka* because they were not willing to face up to sin in their own lives. It was only when God put the searchlight of His Holy Spirit into their lives and they were willing to repent of their sin, that they entered into the joy and liberation of sins forgiven and unclouded fellowship with God Himself.

All this was brought into stark relief by a powerful characteristic of this work of God – the breaking down of human and spiritual barriers leading to deep fellowship where there was previously discord or misunderstanding. Barriers were revealed between missionaries, between African workers, between "black and white", between the ethnic groups of *Hutu* and *Tutsi*, between feuding families and between inhabitants of adjoining districts.

> "Fellowship is becoming one of the marked results of the blessing that we have had," wrote Lawrence Barham. "Tribal distinctions are being swept away in a way we have never seen before. Kabale is in a different language area from Gahini. The *Bakiga*, over the border, were once sworn enemies of the tall *Batutsi*. Even last year there was still fear and mistrust between the Christians of these our two first stations, but it seems that under the hand of God, that barrier has absolutely vanished. A deep and dangerous thousand foot gorge separates the people of Ruanda from those of Urundi. A new thing has been seen here. Bands of Christians from Ruanda have gone over into Urundi to tell of the Brotherhood of Christ."

Expressions of spiritual experience are very personal, those of "fellowship" are very inter-personal. It was found that the stark distinctions made between what was "in the light" and what was not, could militate strongly

against the grace and gentleness needed for true
fellowship.

The *Abaka* became characterised by a very strong
aggressive: "putting people in the light" for all manner
of reasons. When this kind of challenge was made in a
spirit of gentle and loving concern, there was often a
humble acceptance leading to a putting right of wrongs,
the clearing of unwarranted suspicions and the recognition of unconsciously-given impressions of despising,
superiority and criticism. The deep fellowship which
resulted from this kind of "light" and "bending the
neck" to truth, lovingly presented, was new indeed and
powerful in its witness to the power of the Gospel.
Where the "putting in the light" challenge was made
without a spirit of gentleness and loving concern, the
reactions provoked were often very harmful – harmful to
fellowship between those concerned, but equally harmful to their testimony to what God was really doing in
many lives.

Bill Church, the doctor at Buhiga, was one who
received a devastating challenge.

"The Revival, which has swept over other stations in
varying degrees left Buhiga superficially touched only until
July," he wrote in 1938. "Before we left for the Conference
at Gisenyi all our Christians were cold and depressed,
almost to the degree of being morbid. There was, however,
one hopeful sign. They were deeply concerned and convicted about the state of the station and gave themselves to
much prayer. While we were at Gisenyi, when no European
was on the station, revival came. As soon as I returned I
sensed the new atmosphere by the look of joy on people's
faces, and the enthusiastic hymn singing which went on in
various places throughout the day. The senior Christians
soon arrived to tell me of many remarkable happenings and
finished by saying that it was their sins which had held up
revival at Buhiga."

The intense reality of all that he saw impressed Bill greatly and he welcomed wholeheartedly the expressions of God's reviving power in their fellowship at Buhiga.

"The blessing continued for some weeks," he went on. "There were a few excesses but nothing which was not easily controlled . . . Then, however, Satan launched an attack from the effects of which we have not yet recovered. It was an humiliating experience for me, but that should not deter me from telling you briefly and honestly what happened . . . Three evangelists came from Gahini to hold meetings. During a conversation with me they stated that in their opinion I was not born again, indeed I was still in the way of destruction.

"To my surprise four of our leading Christians at Buhiga supported them. They gave several reasons for this opinion, among others that I had never confessed my sins in public with tears and that I did not know the meaning of a broken heart. I thought they had mixed up salvation and sanctification, but it became quite clear that they meant exactly what they said. As they persisted in this opinion I sent for Archdeacon Pitt-Pitts who, after a good deal of talk and prayer, was used by God to reveal to them their mistake and now peace is restored . . . These senior African Christians desire a deeper spiritual fellowship with us and that type of fellowship is hard to achieve and easy to lose. How hard it is to achieve at home, and how much harder here with differences of race, language and culture."

Wherever there were outbursts of revival there were many who entered into the new liberating power of God. Equally, there were some sincere men and women with a genuine experience of salvation but who seemed untouched, spiritually or emotionally, by what they saw happening around them. For many of them, including missionaries, this was a time of deep heart-searching. Was their conversion experience not genuine and were they still, in fact, "unsaved"? Was there something in their lives which prevented things happening in them which they saw happening in others? Had all this something to do with temperament? Did they not have the right disposition to experience what others experienced? This was very puzzling and it did not help to be told, as they often were, that they needed to "repent!" Repent of what?

Among the missionaries who could not accept the harshness of the challenges made by the *Abaka* and the divisive "fences" they appeared to erect around themselves was Algie Stanley Smith. He recognised and supported what God was doing in people's lives but he refused to align himself with the *Abaka*. This led to him being considered as being "against revival"! The facts spoke otherwise.

"Algie came to Buhiga with a small team while we were there," recalled Godfrey Hindley. "As the team was preaching suddenly people began trembling and falling to the ground in conviction of sin. Algie called to a senior African saying, 'Just take them outside' and there they explained the Gospel to them."

As a founder of the Mission, Algie was in a very senior position. Many looked to him for leadership. He saw that a unity between all believers, based on a reality of inner experience, was of greater importance to the work of God than were the sharp distinctions between "light" and "darkness" that many of the *Abaka* made, based on the way people expressed themselves outwardly.

"Looking back on the events of the past few weeks," he wrote in his diary, "the Lord seems to have given me new light and a new hope which is already being realised . . . First, I am convinced that among the leaders of the *Abaka* movement, there is no fear of doctrinal differences. Second, that we ought to be profoundly thankful to God for the *Abaka* movement and for these leaders. It has been through them and not through the more prosaic people that God has brought about the spiritual awakening in Kenya and Uganda. This doesn't mean as some unwisely say, 'They are always right'. Third, these differences between us will never be cured by argument or lukikos (committees or courts) or memoranda. Fourth, it is only Christ who can do it. I think it is to drive this home that He has allowed all previous efforts of both sides to fail. We must really believe that He can do it. Fifth, the only way for us is to get to a new place of surrender or self-abandonment before Him, pleading to know our worthlessness and getting a new conception of the meaning of faith. Our only concern is to be continually in fellowship with Him. Sixth, therefore I abandon controversy or argument. It is no solution to our problems to join the *Abaka*. This obscures the real essential of being more deeply united to Christ and would only perpetuate divisions. Seventh, people do need correction, but I want to learn how to move them by prayer, not by authority or argument, so that their convictions are based on what Christ has shown them, not on what I have ordered or argued. Eighth, towards all, love. So I long for the 'rivers of living waters' to be flowing and this doesn't mean an attempt to be 'hearty', but spontaneous effortless living under the control of the Lord Jesus Christ, and in the continuous consciousness of His presence."

The visit to Gahini of a tea-planter from Uganda was to give a new depth to God's working. William Turner-Russell worked at Namutamba tea-plantation where there was a strong Christian witness through its owner, Leslie Lea-Wilson. William Turner-Russell came from a Calvinist background and was well-versed in the Scriptures. He pointed out to the missionaries that their teaching of the Gospel was not complete. They were, so he insisted, only preaching that the Cross brought forgiveness of sin but not full deliverance from the guilt and power of sin. What they were teaching, he insisted, was the "repentance of John the Baptist". The missionaries and African leaders at Gahini, including William

Nagenda, accepted this challenge. A new dimension was added to the truths being proclaimed.

Writing from Gahini, in June 1937, Cecil Verity referred to this new element in what was happening.

> "Last year many got their first awakening to what a life in Christ Jesus was meant to be, but although many then got in at the Wicket Gate, like Christian in *Pilgrim's Progress*, few got to that place where they saw the Cross and their burden was rolled away. Then, also, as many have admitted, confessions of sins were made, especially sins which were known to others, but there were left in the life other things known only to God and the individual himself or herself which were unrepented of and the consequence was that many did not get into a place of peace or power and so went back into sin.
>
> "Now, at last, God is bringing home to us all, we white people as well as our native Christians, what the real meaning of repentance from dead works and faith in Christ really involves. God has been searching us out and there is hardly one of us who has not been found wanting. When God starts to show a man what he is really like, the process is often acutely humiliating and we begin to see ourselves as we really are, miserable sinners. All the props seem to fall and respectability that so often masquerades as Christianity is shown to be hollow until the soul in desperation cries to God for forgiveness and deliverance."

The three years from the outbreak of revival in June 1936 to the Missionaries' Conference at Gisenyi in July 1939 were turbulent indeed. Diaries and letters written at the time indicate the depths to which missionaries' understanding of their missionary task was shaken.

Len Sharp was one who found it difficult to accept that all the expressions of revival, as it was being experienced in Rwanda, were from God. He was a keen student of the Bible and a staunch defender of its truths. He refused to accept as Scriptural any expression of Christian faith and experience which could not be supported by the Bible.

In a booklet entitled, *Great Truths from God's Word*, he included sections which reflected his concern for a truly biblical basis for what was being so strongly emphasised. One of the chapters, headed "False Repentance", gave biblical quotations illustrating "Remorse but not prayer for forgiveness", and "Public Confession and Restitution, but without prayer to God for forgiveness". Another specified the "Danger of seeking signs of the Holy Spirit". It was typical of him that, when confronted by a young evangelist at Matana who, full of enthusiasm for his new-found experience of Christ, asked him if he was born again, he replied quietly, "Young man, I was born again before you were born!"

In July 1939, the annual missionaries' conference was held at Gisenyi, on Lake Kivu. It proved to be a time of much heart searching. Areas of conflict within the Mission, particularly relating to the expressions of revival, were faced. All agreed that God was working in powerful ways in convicting men and women of sin, of leading them to repentance and faith in the cross of Christ, of giving a liberating release from the guilt and power of sin by cleansing in the blood of Christ and by creating a great fellowship of "light" and "love" between Africans and between Missionaries and Africans. But conflict centred on a number of issues. Particularly strong opinions concerned the nature of open confession of sin, especially where this involved mentioning names and giving details of sins, among them sexual sins confessed in the presence of those of the opposite sex, which could cause harm by shocking sensitive people and introducing ideas not already there.

Other points of conflict included the extent of "being in the light" about faults in others, the need for discipline in fellowship meetings, particularly where these involved singing far into the night, and the place of emotional outbursts, notably in large meetings. The Minutes of the Executive Committee which followed the conference recorded a "resolution and suggestions for fellowship". These included a four-point definition of fellowship, eleven principles applicable to the experience of fellowship and seven "hints on fellowship meetings and the way to run them".

The Conference was a memorable one for Archdeacon Arthur Pitt-Pitts. He had gained a reputation as a caring pastor, but also a strict and efficient organiser, with a determination to see a church brought into being which would be true to the Scriptures and also part of the wider Anglican fellowship. This sometimes brought him into conflict with both African and missionary colleagues, particularly those who saw freedom in revival as transcending all other forms of relationship. At the Conference he was "put in the light" in unmistakable terms. He was told bluntly that he was hindering revival by the way he discussed missionaries and by his ambition to be Bishop when he was not fit for it because of the unconfessed sin in his life!

Behind the harsh manner of the challenge was a genuine concern for the Archdeacon and for God's work in which they were involved. It was a typical challenge from the *Abaka* missionaries. Instead of replying in anger, as he might well have done, Arthur Pitt-Pitts was devastated! "Do you here believe that I am hindering revival? If so I must go," he pleaded humbly with his fellow-workers. "Do deal faithfully with me. I trust you to help me." This humbling of himself before his colleagues led others also to recognise and confess faults in their relationships with him and with each other. "Brokenness", a term which became associated with revival, reached very deep levels of meaning as the missionaries were "broken before God". Joe Church wrote of the Conference: "We met in a time of crisis in world affairs as well as in the history of our Mission. But we all met the Lord face to face again beside this African 'Sea of Galilee'".

Referring to Arthur Pitt-Pitts, Algie Stanley Smith recorded, "The Lord gave him . . . a new vision of the Cross. He went from that conference with a new and deeper power of leadership and the last two years of service still left to him were probably the most fruitful of his service in Ruanda and Urundi".

As the experience and perception of those in leadership positions developed, so did the recognition of the divisive powers of the name *abaka* and it slowly went out of use to be replaced by *abakijijwe* in Rwanda and Burundi, and *abalokole* in Uganda. Both words mean "saved ones".

In Burundi, the growing work made it urgent for a translation of the Scriptures to be available in *Kirundi* as it was in *Kinyarwanda*. The two languages are similar so would one translation be adequate for both countries?

In 1937, Harold Guillebaud moved to Burundi to study *Kirundi*. He soon became convinced that the differences between the two languages were sufficient to warrant separate translations. An incident which confirmed this view was recorded by his daughter, Rosemary.

"The Ruanda Mission had only just started work in Urundi, and there were as yet almost no converts, so the men given to my father as his linguistic informants were all non-Christians. He had recently translated the hymn, 'The Lord's our Rock, in Him we hide' into *Kinyarwanda*, so he read this to them and asked if they could understand it.

'Yes, we understand it', was their reply.

Knowing that they were not Christians, my father decided to delve further. 'What does this word *igitare* (rock) mean?' he asked.

'It's a white one', was the answer.

'A white one! A white what?'

'A white cow, of course!' His informants looked at him as though astonished that he should betray such ignorance."

It became quite clear that although a *Kinyarwanda* word might be recognised in *Kirundi*, it did not necessarily convey the same meaning!

With a team of four or five *Kirundi*-speaking Africans he was able to translate the remaining Gospels and some Epistles and these were published shortly before the outbreak of the Second World War by the British and Foreign Bible Society.

In August 1938, a team of eight, seven Africans and Joe Church, comprising one clergyman, three evangelists, a Headmaster, a Head Hospital Assistant, a musician and a doctor, visited Kenya. "God had to deal with us first before we went, and it was a humbling time," wrote Joe. "He convicted me of 'bossing' my African brothers, so these five weeks together were spent in absolute oneness with Christ as our Leader, as never before. About a hundred Europeans met for the Annual Kenya Keswick Convention. God broke through our European reserve there when, on the Saturday night, a new thing was seen in Kenya. In the crowded lounge these African men of God were called on to speak to the Europeans of the victorious life, and revival. Many Africans broke down in public and testified to what God had done . . . the Ruanda Mission now has a permanent and real link of fellowship with Kenya."

Amazingly, God was working in power in other parts of Africa too. In early 1939, Joe Church was requested to take a team to the CMS stations of Southern Sudan and those of the African Inland Mission in Eastern Congo.

"We were invited to go and link up with those who had had similar revival experiences as ours . . . I cannot say more in a short letter like this than that the Spirit of God is sweeping through the Sudan, and hundreds are seeking Christ. As one travels along the road, village after village has its hastily built open-air Church placed under some central big tree, put up in the last few months by the people themselves. There is nothing inside except a lectern and rows of forest tree trunks that form the pews. We met the leading Christians and held meetings at Lui, Loka, Yei and then went home via the AIM stations Rethe, Arua, and Oicha . . . the signs and manifestations accompanying these movements of His Spirit have been similar in many ways."

Revival did not come to a vacuum! There was intense activity on and around every one of the six mission stations of Rwanda and Burundi, particularly those which had been recently started. On each station primary schools were started, staffed, for the most part, by teachers who had had no training whatever for their work. There was no state aid except for institutions of which the head was a Belgian, and this excluded all schools of the Ruanda Mission. There were, therefore, no specified requirements laid down as qualifying for grants, as was the case in Uganda. And there were no text books. The first book available in the language of Rwanda was the New Testament.

It was 1937 before the Mission appointed a Board of Studies, "to standardise and supervise the educational work and institutions of the Mission and especially the standardisation of Teacher Training." On this Board were three clergy, two doctors and one missionary involved in education, Dora Skipper.

The first Educational Conference of the Mission was convened by one of the doctors at Shyira in 1938.

"Dr. Norman James," recorded Peter Guilleaud, "with his genius for organisation, was deeply interested in the question. He took the pains, with the help of the recently published Congo Protestant Council report on Protestant Education in the Congo, to prepare some notes on what to teach in the different subjects for five years of primary school as recommended by the Belgian colonial authorities. He called together the senior teachers of the different mission schools for a conference lasting several days, at which he outlined the syllabus and gave information on useful books obtainable in French, English and Swahili. He even instituted a lending library of educational reference books, which functioned for some time. This was a real step forward and was a great help to our teachers and schools."

At the Gahini girls' school in which God had worked and was still working so powerfully, the first efforts were made in the training of pupil-teachers, after the pattern common in the UK. Writing in 1937, Dora Skipper referred to Abisagi, who had been trained at the Gayaza Normal School in Uganda, one of the three teachers from Toro in Uganda. "She has been the greatest help. She is very reliable and undertakes all the training of pupil teachers for the other schools. With her help we have this year started a Normal School for teachers . . . As the new schools are started in different stations, Gahini is called upon to supply teachers."

As these teachers were posted to other mission stations so they took with them the example of their African teachers such as Geraldine and Abisagi, whose shining testimony attracted many children as well as adults to the living Christ within them.

Despite the great need for developing the work already started, Algie Stanley Smith, Len Sharp, and the missionary team were sure that God was leading them to open a further station in Burundi. So, in 1936, a further search was made and a site requested at Buye (at first wrongly named *Ibuye*), in the north of Burundi, near the Government centre of Ngozi.

The opening of the mission station at Buye in 1937 marked the end of the period of occupation. It also heralded a new organisational structure. The station was situated near the geographical centre of south-west Uganda, Rwanda and Burundi and near the important north-south road linking Rwanda and Burundi. Despite poor roads, it could be reached in one day's car travel from every station of the Mission. It was to be the administrative centre both for the Mission and also for the growing church. To this end, the first building to be undertaken was a house for the Archdeacon which included a large room for meetings and conferences. This was followed by more houses, a hospital and a school.

In Kigezi, the Rev. Thomas Gregory Smith was posted to Kabale in 1939. Within a week he had taken over the responsibility for the whole educational work of the church there. In 1941, Lilian Clarke joined Constance Hornby and Greg Smith to form the trio which led the missionary work in Kigezi for many years.

The years from 1936 to 1939 were eventful indeed. Looking back, Algie Stanley Smith wrote:

"I think that the chief lesson to me in these past years has been that the Holy Spirit is in actual fact (not pious theory) the Master Workman. Take the outstanding characteristic of the revival, namely, Conviction of Sin. When we try to bring home to a man his sin, the result is sullen defiance and a flat denial of guilt. But when He does it, the result is a broken and contrite heart, and the joy of pardon and peace. One questions . . . whether there can be any true work of the Spirit without this overwhelming sense of personal unworthiness. Nor is this extraordinary but is, as I believe, God's normal way of working. I can't help feeling that God leaves us to carry on in our ineffective energy, actually unable to help us, because we think we must run it all. And then in His own good time, He comes, and pushes us puny creatures aside and works. And when we see these wonders, we say 'How extraordinary.' But I believe they are His normal and invariable way of working, when unhampered by our unbelief."

The work in all three areas – south-west Uganda, Rwanda and Burundi – had reached the limits of geographical expansion. Time and workers were now needed for consolidation. It was at this time that momentous events on the political scene in Europe cast their shadow on Africa as elsewhere in the world. In September 1939, Great Britain declared war on Germany.

Chapter 8

The shadow of
World War II
1939–1946

S everal thousand miles separate Central Africa from
Europe. Nevertheless, the effects of the outbreak of
World War II in Europe in 1939 seriously affected
missionary work in Africa. Travel to and from the
UK was rendered virtually impossible and postal
communications were disrupted.

In that same year the Mission faced a serious financial
crisis. The final instalment of a gift of £30,000 promised
some five years previously, in annual amounts of £5,000,
was withheld. This gift had been of great help and
encouragement at a time of rapid expansion into
Burundi. "Owing to differences of view between the
donor and the mission committee," recorded Algie
Stanley Smith, "it was withdrawn on more than one
occasion. It made clear what Hudson Taylor used to say
of large bequests, that they gave him cause for real
anxiety lest they diminish the sense of daily and hourly
dependence on the Lord."

In addition, the Mission found that its normal income
had not kept pace with its development. It was faced

with the necessity of drastically reducing expenditure. Serious economies were made, including the reduction of Kabale Hospital to a dispensary.

In the month before the outbreak of World War II, it was announced that "the Council has regretfully been forced to the decision that it would not be justifiable to maintain in the field, workers for whom we have no support, and consequently for the present a number of valuable missionaries at home on furlough and some who are shortly due to arrive, for whom we have very little support, will be unable to return to their work until such time as we have adequate financial support for each of them."

The outbreak of war sadly found Rosalind Pitt-Pitts in the UK with their three children while her husband was in Africa. Archdeacon Pitt-Pitts died in Africa without seeing his wife and children again. Several missionary families did not return to Africa until the end of the war.

The financial restraints affected the Mission's work at every level. Until then the wages of church teachers, albeit very small, had been paid from Mission funds. These were cut by twenty per cent and everywhere this was accepted without complaint.

"At Gahini," recorded Algie Stanley Smith, "the Church council met, and decided to close twenty-two churches where no real response was being made to the Gospel, and nearly ninety paid teachers were discharged. At the same time it was decided to urge on the whole church the vital importance of self-support. The immediate result has been remarkable. At one church which was to be closed, the members immediately bestirred themselves and promised to collect all the teacher's pay and, in practically every instance, those who had been told to leave the work have refused to leave their flock, and are going to carry on without pay. It may well be that this crisis will prove one of great blessing to the Church . . . I am quite certain that, but for the revival, this crisis would have meant disaster. But the Lord gave the spiritual blessing before He allowed the material testing, and so it has found the main body of the Church firmly established on the Rock of Ages."

Writing in 1942, Algie Stanley Smith reported that two districts – Kabale and Gahini – were fully self-supporting and the average for all the churches and outchurches was 50 per cent. The churches were moving in the right direction faster than had been anticipated.

Soon after Buye was established as the Field centre for the Mission, the church suffered two serious blows in rapid succession. Archdeacon Arthur Pitt-Pitts was posted there soon after its opening. He saw as his first task that of calling together a tentative Church council which met in 1939. In May of the following year, he chaired the first meeting of the Diocesan Council for Kigezi and Ruanda-Urundi in the unusual circumstances of a government rest-camp at Gako, near Kigeme, because the flooding of the river Mwogo made further movement impossible. For some time he had been suffering greatly from arthritis in the spine and, immediately after the Council, he went to Kenya to recuperate. However, complications set in and he died peacefully from a rare blood disease on Good Friday, 1940.

Later that year Harold Guillebaud was appointed to succeed him as Archdeacon. Within six months of his appointment he became ill and died at Matana in April 1941. Thus, within twelve months the Mission and Church were deprived of two senior clergy.

As Algie Stanley Smith was standing at Harold Guillebaud's graveside with Margaret, his widow, and Lindsay and Rosemary, his two daughters, who were themselves first-term missionaries, he said to Rosemary, "You will

have to take up the translation work your father has laid
down.''

Rosemary had been posted to Kigeme expecting later
to start teaching. "Now there was this new challenge,"
she recorded, "and as yet I knew no *Kirundi!*". Soon
after this she was moved to Matana with the intention of
teaching in the girls' school, but this was not to be.

Stefano Ndimubandi who had, latterly, been her
father's chief helper in translation was in hospital. In
July 1941, she visited him there "armed with a note-
book, Greek, English and *Kinyarwanda* New Testa-
ments, and tackled the introduction to Acts with him."
At the suggestion of Algie Stanley Smith, Rosemary
took the first twelve chapters to the Rev. Hans Jensen
(he later changed his name to Emming) and Emanueli
Sibomana of the Danish Baptist Mission who were also
engaged in translation work. "In spite of numerous
arguments over vocabulary, necessitating many
changes, they commended us both to the Lord to continue the translation. Lindsay was able to relieve me of
my school work so I took up translation full time." That
was, for Rosemary, the beginning of over a quarter of a
century of translation work.

In 1938, the centre for clergy training moved to Buye
in Burundi with the transfer there of Lawrence and Julia
Barham. The training of evangelists continued at Kabale
under the leadership of Ezekiel Balaba. Until then the
only African clergy in the Mission, Ezekiel Balaba,
Kosiya Shalita and Blasio Kigozi, had been educated,
trained and ordained in Uganda. Under the leadership
of Lawrence Barham, six ordinands, with their wives
and children, began a two-year course at Buye in 1939.
Three of them, Yosiya Kinuka, Semu Ndimbiirwe and
Erenesti Nyabagabo, were ordained in February 1941,
and Nikodemu Gatozi and Zefaniya Rwenduru, a year
later. One of the ordinands died during the course. They

were posted to mission stations with the result that, with Kosiya Shalita at Matana, only one station, Buye, was without an African pastor.

While Lawrence Barham was concerned principally with the training of church teachers and clergy, his wife's influence was wide indeed. The counsel of *umushike w'a Yesu*, (sister of Jesus), as Julia was affectionately known, was sought by many, given freely and greatly valued. She was able to explain and recommend to many women, especially the wives of senior church teachers, the principles which motivated the Mothers' Union organisation – the importance of the woman in maintaining the sanctity of marriage and in the bringing up of children. Great were the problems of some women; particularly acute was that of the woman who, having come to Christ for new life, had to live out that life as one of several wives of a non-Christian, unsympathetic husband.

Although Buye was the centre of the Mission and Church work, the church building there was only a temporary thatched one. On the 24th December 1939, while the church was crowded for the Christmas Eve service, the structure gave an alarming lurch in the wind and there was a stampede to get out. "The church did not quite fall then," wrote Lawrence Barham, "and fortunately no one was hurt, but it has since toppled over like a wounded elephant." During the next thirteen years and with the help of gifts from the UK a new, large church was built to become the first Cathedral church of the Diocese of Ruanda-Urundi.

Until 1940, with a few exceptions, each hospital had trained its own African medical personnel. The training was "on the job" in the specific tasks required. Exceptions were a few promising girls who were sent to the Maternity Training School, CMS Mengo Hospital, Kampala. In 1940, at Gahini Hospital, Mildred Forder began the first two-year course in the Mission for the training of midwives. A second course began two years later. From these two courses ten midwives were trained. They proved to be of inestimable value as they were able to be in complete charge of uncomplicated cases and so relieved the pressure on missionary nurses.

In the last quarter of 1943, serious, widespread famine hit not only the whole of Rwanda but also Burundi, Uganda, Kenya and Tanganyika. In addition to the failure of the rains, a disease attacked the sweet-potato crop, a staple diet in Rwanda. There were no reserves. The Belgian Government requested the Missions for assistance in tackling the grave epidemics of typhoid, typhus, dysentery and smallpox, and it was swift and generous in supplying necessary drugs.

Both missionary and African staff rose magnificently to the occasion. Commenting later, Godfrey Hindley wrote, "It has been a most wonderful chance of putting to the test the depth of fellowship God has given us Europeans with the Africans. When we were asked to take on this work, it was immediately divided up into sections, under keen men with teams under them. Many leave their homes at dawn and return at dusk, but nearly always with news of fresh contacts, hungry souls satisfied or someone having been born again."

God used the compassion and love demonstrated by the relief work carried on in these centres to change for the better the attitude of many Africans, particularly those high in the African administration: chiefs and sub-chiefs, who had been suspicious of Protestant activity in what they felt was Roman Catholic territory.

Around the Mission stations in Kigezi, Rwanda and Burundi, the "fires of revival" continued to burn. All through the World War II years, when links with the outside world were difficult and specialised supplies limited, the hospitals maintained their healing and evangelising work; and the development of schools progressed slowly. Every aspect of the work was touched by revival as God raised up leaders in each branch of the work.

Some African leaders were outstanding. Of these William Nagenda was prominent. It was felt that his ministry would be more effective if he were ordained. Accordingly he entered the Church of Uganda Mukono Theological College in 1939. "He had been at Mukono six months or so before me," recalled the Rev. William H. Butler, a member of staff of the College. "At first I found him abrasive, frightening and challenging!"

At that time Mukono suffered from what William and a number of other students felt to be a subtle infiltration of liberal theology. William resisted this fiercely and was bitterly resented in consequence. "The impact of liberal theology was absolutely shattering," recalled Bill Butler, who had recently been ordained and was a relatively inexperienced lecturer in theology. "It was William and a few others who were radiantly walking with the Lord who held me firm and who challenged me when they saw me going astray."

William and a number of other students were in the habit of meeting for fellowship and prayer at 4:00 am each morning. The aim was not primarily to denounce what they believed to be unscriptural in the College's theological teaching but rather to encourage each other and pray for the other students, especially as there had been stealing and immorality among them. The example and testimony of those students was powerful indeed and attracted many of their fellow students but it incurred the wrath of the senior College staff. The Rev. Bill Butler was posted away from the College.

In order to limit the students' activities, the Mukono authorities imposed strict rules including a ban on the early morning meeting. The students pleaded earnestly that these rules be revoked but this was refused. A half-term holiday was spent in prayer and fasting, then the following morning, twenty-five of them attended the 4:00 am prayer and fellowship meeting in defiance of the rules. They were expelled and forbidden to preach or take up any function or even appear in any church in the country. The government was informed and they were classed as "a dangerous native movement in time of war". Among the expelled students were William Nagenda, Yohana Bunyenyezi and John Musoke.

At a meeting of Missionaries and Africans convened at Kabale in December 1941, a minute stated: "We are unanimously convinced that the 'Mukono Incident' was unwisely handled and that the students were not in any true sense 'rebels'".

The "Mukono incident" received wide publicity. William Nagenda was welcomed by Leslie Lea-Wilson, dairy farmer and owner of Namutamba Tea Plantation. In a way that was reminiscent of Old Testament history, the presence of William and a small nucleus of saved workers and their wives brought great blessing to the plantation. It became a centre of witness to God's working in revival. William was never ordained but he, with Joe Church, shared in many missions in Africa and beyond.

During the years from 1938 to 1945, two types of convention were held. The first was for missionaries and the medium of communication was English as most missionaries were English speaking. Even those of the French speaking Belgian Protestant Mission and of the Danish Baptist Mission knew enough English to take an effective part. Such conventions were held at Gisenyi in 1938 and 1939.

The second type of convention was convened for Africans. The first of these to be arranged in Ruanda-Urundi was held at the Danish Baptist Mission station,

Musema, in 1939. It proved to be a memorable occasion both for the outworking of God's power in revival and also for the co-operation of the Protestant Missions, particularly in Burundi. Algie Stanley Smith wrote of that convention,

> "It brought great blessing to the Baptist Church there; the real beginnings of Revival were seen. Only a few months later, when Denmark was overrun by the Nazis, the Danes found themselves one of the 'orphaned' missions cut off from all visible means of support. The effect of the new life in the Church showed itself at once. Full self-support was undertaken by the African community; they immediately began to advance into new districts, and the Mission opened a new mission station. Funds began to come in later and all through the war this gallant mission went ahead. But its finest hour was surely when, utterly without resources, Europeans and Africans faced the future with high courage and faith and immediately planned for advance. It was the power of God in Revival alone which made this possible."

Conventions were held at Buhiga in 1941 and at Muyebe, a station of the American Free Methodists, in 1942. The Muyebe convention was notable for several reasons. It was the first occasion when an Alliance convention for missionaries was held simultaneously with a convention for Africans. The result was dramatic. For the first time scenes of "wild ecstatic joy" were witnessed by the American missionaries and their reactions varied greatly. Some were able to understand and even share the exuberance. Others were shocked, accusing the Africans of hysteria and the missionaries of doing nothing to control such extravagant behaviour!

African conventions were held in Burundi in 1943 and in 1944. So great were the crowds that two were arranged in 1945.

In the years 1944 and 1945, missionary conventions
were held at Mutaho, Ruhororo and Mweya, stations of
the Friends Africa Gospel Mission. Their American
form of Camp Meetings was novel to non-Americans but
they were occasions of great reconciliation between
missionaries.

In Rwanda, a different situation prevailed. At that
time relationships with the Belgian Mission were difficult for a number of reasons. There was not, for
instance, that happy agreement about the evangelical
fundamentals of the faith which existed among the
Protestant Missions in Burundi. A convention was
arranged in 1942 at the Belgian Mission station,
Remera, but this did not take place. However, in 1944,
the convention held at Shyira proved to be a momentous
one for the work in Rwanda.

Describing the Shyira convention, Joy Gerson wrote,
"People from all our stations and from the Belgian
Mission met and knew themselves as one Church . . . At
this Convention there were many reconciliations and a
new certainty that we are all in one team at this great
time of Revival . . . One son of the county Chief (who is
in prison) came to the Convention to see what it was like,
and while there was convicted. He repented of, and
produced for burning, the tip of a horn he had bought for
400 francs with which to bewitch and kill his cousin
whom he thought might be attending the same Convention. Only the power of the living Saviour can deal with
the feuds there are in Ruanda. There were many other
spiritual victories among us all."

It was natural that the oneness that these conventions
brought to the Christians in Ruanda-Urundi should be
reflected in relationships between the growing churches.
An Advisory Church Council was formed and its first
meeting, at which Africans formed the majority, took
place at Buye in February 1943. It was chaired jointly by

Pastor John Wesley Haley, the honoured and respected senior missionary of the Free Methodist Mission and the Rev. Kosiya Shalita of Matana.

"It was wonderful to see the emancipating power of spiritual oneness in Christ," commented Algie Stanley Smith. "Our people found it difficult to conceive of a Church which had no Bishop, used no Prayer Book nor, like the Friends, practised no Sacraments. But the manifest signs of the Spirit's working made such differences appear trivial and our oneness in Christ the supreme fact. The meetings were remarkable for frank speaking and love for each other and much misunderstanding was removed." A number of representatives of all participating Missions urged that the possibility of a United Church for Ruanda-Urundi be pursued with vigour.

Within the Ruanda Mission, the possible formation of a United Church was linked with the burning question of Anglican churchmanship. Fears were expressed in the UK as to where this move towards a United Church might lead. A minute of the Executive Committee at its meeting at Buye in February 1943, reflected the views of the missionaries on the field. "The Executive wish to assure the Bishop as well as the Home Council, that they have no intention of departing from the Church of England in its Protestant and Evangelical tradition, except in so far as they wish to press toward the ideal, shared by all the great Protestant Communions, of merging our denominations in a wider Union, framed on lines similar to that of the South India Scheme, which will have the sanction of the Home Authority and will maintain our Communion with the Home Church as well as the Church of Uganda."

In a strongly worded paper on "The Churchmanship of the Ruanda Mission", Algie Stanley Smith wrote, "It is the cry of the indigenous Church in every country when they get sufficiently advanced, 'We don't want your European divisions, we will probably have divisions, but let them be our own.' It is the cry of our hearts, 'Why are we separated from our friends whose evangelical faith we share, because we are bound by an alliance with a ritualistic and modernist Church with whom we have practically no sympathy?'"

If there had been a moment of opportunity for merging the churches of these missions into a United Church it was in the mid to late forties. The great weakness of the movement lay in the fact that the initiative was almost wholly missionary – European or American. By the time African leadership was sufficiently advanced to participate effectively in the discussions, links with the various home denominations had become so strong that it was virtually impossible to break them.

While questions concerning the future character of the church occupied the minds of the missionary leaders, the major outreach was in the hospitals. Of the missionaries in Africa during World War II, four ordained men were engaged in the training and support of evangelists in starting new church centres, nine educationists were developing central schools on mission stations and outschools in the districts around them, but the majority of specialised missionaries – twelve doctors and seven nurses – were concentrated in the hospitals of the mission. Fourteen others, including wives, were involved in women's work and other activities.

The early hospital buildings were primitive indeed by modern standards but so were the homes in which people lived. Africans felt, if not welcomed, at least less threatened in recognisable circumstances.

From the beginning, the mission hospital was the focal point of regular medical safaris to the district around. A safari team would include bearers to carry the equipment, medicines and dressings needed. Later a car or pick-up replaced the bearers. The medical staff were also the evangelists. After a morning treating queues of patients, the same doctors, nurses and dressers would, in the afternoon, teach the way of salvation and add their own testimonies to the living Christ whom they proclaimed. As the medical staff were also evangelists, the medical safari was a powerful witness to the "wholeness" of the Gospel.

The safaris usually lasted two or three days in one area and often resulted in sick people being referred to the hospital. Great efforts were made to integrate into the local church those who came for treatment. It was not unusual for such safaris to lead to the opening of a local outschool and the appointment of an evangelist.

"The impact of a mission hospital depends entirely on the staff," reflected Ken Buxton after seventeen years at Buye hospital. "You can preach until you are blue in the face but if the dressers are stealing on the quiet or taking bribes, it undermines the whole message."

A large part of the missionary doctor's and nursing sister's time and energies were devoted to training African staff. For many years there was no other source of trained medical personnel. It was not, however, only qualified dressers and nurses that the missionaries had in mind. Harold Adeney saw "the medical side of the work as a training for leadership . . . a large number of medical workers have taken an important part in the church. Yosiya Kinuka is the outstanding example of this."

"One of the greatest impressions we still have," commented Ken Buxton many years later, "was of boys and girls coming out of very primitive surroundings, with totally illiterate parents and an utterly heathen background, coming into hospital, learning, coming to Christ and becoming utterly trustworthy hospital workers. This was a wonderful evidence of the grace of God and I think that, in the long run, those men and women were the lasting effects of our medical work."

Each day the hospital staff met for morning prayers. This was a time for teaching, praying together, testifying of experience gained and growing together as a team for Christ. Then there was the teaching given to the waiting outpatients usually by hospital staff but sometimes by the local evangelist or school teacher. Ward services provided opportunities for all leaders on the mission station to take part.

Morning prayers, teaching outpatients and ward services in the hospitals, could be dull and lifeless. At other times, the convicting and liberating presence of God transformed them into vibrant, dynamic expressions of the joy of sins forgiven, reconciliation between repentant sinners, triumph over the satanic powers of evil and a united concern to proclaim Christ to those who came within their influence. The effects were felt throughout the hospital.

There, as in other outreach activities, the picture of the three-legged stool was an excellent one when there was a harmonious and effective working together of medical staff, school teachers and church workers. When these were truly saved and living in fellowship with one another the witness was powerful indeed. At other times there was rivalry and jealousy between church workers, whose incomes were often pitifully small; the African medical staff, who had the more assured salaries (hospitals charged fees, albeit very small); and school teachers, particularly when their salaries were subsidised by the State. Repentance of envy of others' possessions and jealousy of others' gifts is costly to pride and sense of status.

At times the doctors would despair at the apparently infinitesimal impact of their efforts on the total medical scene. "What on earth are we doing here?" they would

ask. "We give people pills and medicine and then a
month later they come back with just the same disease!"
Viewed medically, curative medicine achieved only
short-term results. Nevertheless, however limited the
medical results may have been, when seen against
the seemingly limitless extent of illness and disease, the
spiritual impetus of the healing ministry in opening
people's hearts and minds to God was immense. It was in
changed lives where the clearest evidence of the value of
medical work lay.

The newest mission station, Buye, in Burundi developed rapidly. In addition to the Theological College
and the Hospital, it was here, in 1941–1944, that two
two-year training courses were organised by Peter Guillebaud, for men teachers drawn from Rwanda and
Burundi. On one occasion, the Holy Spirit moved
powerfully among the students.

One Friday evening in April 1944, an overwhelming
sense of the presence of God came upon the students in
their dormitory. All through the night they were deeply
convicted of sin, confessed their sins and put things right
with one another. In the morning it was raining and so
they could not go into the school garden to hoe as was
usual on a Saturday. Peter, unaware of these events, was
working on his car. Then, at midday, Peter went out to
meet them. "I did not know what had hit me," Peter
remembered. "There these students were, burning the
blankets which they had stolen, and destroying bad
letters from girls and much else." Something remarkable was happening. These young men were overcome
with the awfulness of their sin, they were repenting of it
to God and confessing it to each other. There was
testimony to forgiveness and a new sense of the reality of
the presence of Christ.

And there was singing! The story of John Bunyan's
Pilgrim's Progress in its Kinyarwanda version,

Umugenzi, had been an inspiration to many Africans. Now it came to life in a new way. "God gave us a new hymn that day," said one of the students, "about the way in which 'Christian' came to the cross and his burden of sin rolled away for ever, and of the certificate he received at the cross, which was worth so much more than any certificate you could get from the church or school." Verse after verse was added to the hymn in the picture language of *Pilgrim's Progress* but drawn from the students' immediate experience of God working in them. And after each verse came the chorus:

> *Bless'd Cross, bless'd Sepulchre, bless'd rather be*
> *The Man who there was put to death for me.*

Almost all the students experienced the convicting power of God in their lives. Some of them were saved then and immediately entered into the reality of a living experience of Christ. "Out of this time of blessing," remembered one of the students, "there sprang a new bond of oneness and light between us who were saved, African and European, and a new co-operation in and out of school, worked out through the Blood of Christ."

By far the largest convention until then was held at Kabale in September 1945, ten years after the very significant one of 1935. "Fifteen thousand people gathered in a great open-air amphitheatre. Over a thousand visitors came from Uganda, Tanganyika, Ankole, Zaire, Rwanda and Burundi. Sam Sindamuka, later Archbishop of the Province of Burundi, Rwanda and Zaire walked some 300 miles from Matana, in Burundi, to Kabale! The theme of the conference was 'Jesus satisfies'".

As often happened, the convention was not without a satanic attack. A Quiet Day was arranged just before the Convention for the team of about fifty Africans and missionaries from which the speakers would be drawn. It became immediately evident that a serious rift divided the team. "The cause of the trouble," wrote Joe Church, "arose out of reports of a time of blessing that we missionaries of the Protestant Alliance of Ruanda-Urundi had experienced at a recent convention."

The previous occasion to which Joe Church referred was the Annual Missionary convention at Mutaho in 1944. There great pressure had been brought to bear on the *Abaka* missionaries, all of whom were of the Ruanda Mission. Because they appeared to deny fellowship to fellow missionaries who, in their view, compromised with sin, they were considered to be rebels, not only by colleagues in the same mission but also by those of the other participating missions, some of whom were from a "Holiness Movement" background. The latter found it hard to fit into their theology these fiery missionaries who talked about repentance and walking in the light without any mention of a "second work of grace". They were known by some as the "sin and say it" brigade! One senior American missionary said to some of them, "I can see the way God is working through you but your experience is way beyond your doctrine".

At the convention, unity in the Spirit was felt to be so important that missionaries from both sides of the divide knelt together in an act of repentance and reconciliation. The *Abaka* missionaries confessed to hardness of heart and asked forgiveness of those whom they had hurt in this way. "When we repented of hardness," remembers Elisabeth Guillebaud, "we asked the ones whom we had been hard against to lay hands on us. I remember Dr Len Sharp laying hands on me. It was a very moving experience." Together they prayed for a fresh fullness of the Spirit.

The report of this reconciliation quickly reached Cyril Stuart, the Bishop of Uganda, who, unknown to the

Rwanda missionaries, used it to attack what he felt to be the hard (*Abaka*) attitudes among the Uganda *Balokole* (saved ones).

At the Quiet Day before the Kabale Convention, the Rwanda *Abaka* missionaries were faced by adamant Ugandan leaders who insisted that they repent of compromise. "Many of us found this very hard," stated Peter Guillebaud. "It had seemed so right at the time, how could we go back on it? The Ugandan leaders felt that we had joined up with those from whom we were divided by deep issues related to sin and repentance, had 'papered over the cracks' and sought a fullness of the Spirit that bypassed true repentance. I and some others went into deep spiritual darkness and were useless at the convention."

In this situation, Joe Church's deep sense of spiritual priorities gave him freedom where others felt bound by an apparent rift in fellowship. They were in a battle, he insisted, they may have made a mistake at Mutaho but that should be dropped for the time being so that they could proclaim unitedly the message God had given them. The Ugandan leaders recognised and accepted the spiritual authority of Joe.

Not until after the convention and after much pain and heart-searching was peace restored. The distinction between true reconciliation and "papering over the cracks" is sometimes a fine one. Reconciliation which involves compromise on matters of principle is never genuine reconciliation. The issues for which the *Abalokole* in Uganda and the *Abaka* in Rwanda stood, particularly the uncompromising stand against sin in any form and the completeness of the work of Christ on the Cross, were fundamental. How could there be full fellowship with those who did not appear to accept these truths? They must stand firm in them and, in the right spirit, challenge those who did not appear to accept

them. Light invades darkness; it is when light is covered
or dimmed that it ceases to be effective. Yet this does not
justify the use of harsh or unloving words or actions.
Grace and truth meet in Jesus.

Despite the rift, temporarily shelved, between the
leaders, God worked amazingly in that convention.
"Miracles happened," wrote Joe Church. "Fairly
heavy rains were falling on September 19th to test
our faith. The great open-air arena was useless and
flowing with muddy water. We claimed, in prayer, that
God would give us the most perfect weather. He
did! It suddenly changed. There were lovely warm
days with moonlit nights, from the moment people
arrived."

The theme, *Jesus Satisfies*, was introduced on that
Friday by an address on Psalm 22 and the words, "I am a
worm, and no man". Joe Church took the vast crowd
"back to the place where the need of the world was met,
where Satan was defeated and where Jesus cried out in
the words of the Psalm: 'My God, my God, why have
you forsaken me?'" So that sinners may be satisfied,
Jesus was, "willing to be 'a worm, and no man' for us . . .
So we have to be willing to be as 'worms'; we have to be
humbled, to 'die', in order that rivers of living water may
flow through us to a thirsty world. Only if we lose our
life, our reputation, our rights, our prestige, do we find
life . . ."

On Sunday, before the great crowd of some 15,000
people the team of speakers focused their addresses on
Psalm 23, "My cup overflows". "I saw many weeping,"
wrote Joe Church. "There is no thrill in all the world
greater than seeing hearts melting before the love of
Calvary. Faces relax, peace pervades, abandon comes in
and men yield to the pleadings of their Saviour. Many
times we have seen this as the Spirit of God descends
upon a gathering . . . People who have really seen it

cannot speak lightly of the movings of the Holy Spirit and Revival. It is too sacred."

Many were the moving testimonies which followed as, one after another, Africans told of their situations: "I have twelve children, I cannot afford to educate them . . . but *Jesus satisfies!*"

"My wife and I have been married for ten years and we have no child . . . but *Jesus satisfies!*"

"I am not young now and I cannot find a husband . . . but *Jesus satisfies!*" God used in a remarkable way such simple testimonies and praise to God in song echoed round the Kabale hills.

When Godfrey and Phil Hindley were posted to Shyira, Yohana Bunyenyezi, one of the expelled Mukono students, was the headmaster of the boys' school. A few weeks before a convention held at Shyira in 1944, Godfrey and Yohana had travelled to Bujumbura, the capital of Burundi. As they were driving along a road overlooking the valley of the Ruzizi river towards Bujumbura, Yohana asked Godfrey to stop the car. He got out and as he looked down into the valley he said, "Look at all those banana trees! The place must be flowing with beer. We want those people for Christ."

At a meeting in that Convention, Peter Guillebaud felt strongly compelled to speak on the Bible story of the four men with leprosy at the gate of Samaria during the siege, as recorded in 2 Kings 7. Taking the words, "We're not doing right. This is a day of good news and we are keeping it to ourselves," he applied it to the situation in Bujumbura. There, some American missionaries had started work but lacked African helpers to develop it. Though somewhat distrustful of the Anglican church, they had appealed for a worker to help them. Following the challenge given, Yohana Bunyenyezi offered to go to Bujumbura.

At the same convention a young school teacher, Yona Sekimonyo, was desperately ill with bronchiectasis. He had to be carried on an iron bed to attend the meetings. Hearing of the appeal for workers Yona asked Godfrey Hindley, "Why, when there are all these young men here, does no one offer? I feel that I should go!" And he was bedridden at the time! Although no miracle was prayed for, within a month he was completely healed. Yona followed Yohana to Bujumbura and for some years took a leading part in building up a school there. Another young man, Abel Bizuru, joined Yohana and Yona, and very soon a remarkable movement of revival began among a group of Zairians working in Bujumbura, some of whom were later used by God in Zaire and other surrounding countries.

During the Second World War years the hostilities in Europe prevented any missionaries returning to the UK for furlough. Some were able to break their service by a visit to South Africa. Among such were Ken and Agnes Buxton. As a result of their testimony there to what God was doing in revival in Rwanda, Burundi and Kigezi, supported by that of a few Mennonite missionaries working in Tanzania who had been equally blessed, a call came to Joe Church to take a team to visit churches and ministers' gatherings in South Africa.

Due to the racial situation in that country, three missionaries – Joe Church, Lawrence Barham and Godfrey Hindley – answered the call in October 1944, but no Africans. "There was warmth, personal talks and decisions," wrote Joe Church, "but we felt a deep undercurrent of resistance against the insuperable barriers of colour-bar and sectarian exclusiveness . . . The committee in their farewell to us asked us to be frank and we shared this delicate subject with them saying that we cannot envisage revival in South Africa with our African brothers separated from us. But we couldn't help thinking, what would have happened if William and Yosiya *had* come!"

In 1946, a year after the end of the war, the Ruanda Mission celebrated its Silver Jubilee. It was a time of great thanksgiving and stocktaking. In that year Jim Brazier was appointed Archdeacon of Kigezi and Ruanda-Urundi. There were nine mission stations, forty-eight missionaries, nine African clergy, over 2,300 lay mission workers, over 25,000 baptised members of whom around 7,300 were communicants, meeting in nearly 1,100 churches. There were 142 students in the Evangelists' Training schools. On the medical side, there were 354 beds in seven mission hospitals with a total of around 9,600 inpatients and 196,000 outpatients that year. At Bwama Hospital there were 547 leprosy patients. In education, well over 3,000 children attended different levels of church schools.

Looking back at this time, Algie Stanley Smith spoke of the "crowning mercy to the Ruanda Mission and Church in bringing to us through the power of the Holy Spirit the unspeakable blessing of revival. The Church through God's blessing had been growing fast; but though it had been doctrinally sound, there had been very little deep conviction of sin. But when the Spirit came, He began with great power to convict of sin, of true righteousness not our own, and the terrible certainty of judgement to come. Through His dealings with us in ever increasing power the whole life of the Church has been transformed."

After the end of World War II, communications with the UK began to improve and there was the hope of new recruitment to the Mission. A socialist government was voted into power in Belgium, replacing the Roman Catholic one, and it promised to redress the overwhelming imbalance of government support for Roman Catholic mission work in the Congo and in Ruanda-

Urundi, to the exclusion of almost all Protestant activity.

It was time for advance, particularly into service which would develop spiritual leaders, consolidate the church, provide teaching for the growing Christian communities, and cater for the needs of young people.

Chapter 9

The flame reaches Europe 1946–1952

The end of World War II, in August 1945, brought a sense of release not only to the war-torn countries of Europe but also to the mission fields which looked to them for support. The missionaries in Kigezi, Rwanda and Burundi were encouraged to believe that the prospect of expanding the work established in the pre-war years would be matched by increased support from home. God had brought the Mission into the "promised land". He would not fail it in the conquest that remained. The boundaries were set but there remained the task of reaching the many thousands who had not yet had the opportunity of hearing the Gospel, of educating the illiterate to the point where they could at least read the Scriptures for themselves and then of training a leadership of both clergy and laymen for a strong indigenous church, and all this in fellowship with other Evangelical missions.

At first there were serious manpower problems because most of the missionaries had served much longer than their usual term of five years. Those returning to the UK for furlough in 1946 to 1948 included Joe and Decie Church, Lawrence and Julia Barham, Harold and Isobel Adeney, Peter and Elisabeth Guillebaud, Greg and Irene Gregory Smith, Godfrey and Phil Hindley and Kenneth and Agnes Buxton, none of whom had been home to the UK during the war years.

In 1947, the Worldwide Evangelisation Crusade sponsored a visit to the UK of William Nagenda and Yosiya Kinuka. They joined a team of missionaries on leave headed by Joe Church and including Bill Butler from CMS Uganda. The testimony of these together, black and white, missionary and African, reached many churches, university and college Christian Unions and conventions in the UK. Missionaries and Africans spoke of what they had seen and experienced in Africa, describing in simple terms what God had done there and what they were convinced He could do anywhere.

As in Africa, so in the UK, the response was mixed. There were two matters which led to disagreement. The first arose from an attempt to simplify what had been learned in revival. In response to earnest pleas for ways to bring about revival, missionaries tried to express their experience of God in ways which could be more easily assimilated by sophisticated listeners who were used to orderly, carefully planned sermons.

"We took the message of revival as we had seen it in East Africa," reported Lawrence Barham, "in the form of five steps up to calvary: prayer with a hunger, brokenness as we see the blood of Christ, the fullness of the Spirit, openness as we walk in the light and the resulting oneness of the revived family. Both in the crowded public meetings and in the special gatherings for pastors there was evident a sense of hunger and desperation which we have not noticed before in England. There still seems to be in some evangelical circles a complacency which will have to be replaced by a heartbroken sense of need and repentance if revival is to come."

Similarly, at the 1947 Keswick Convention Young People's meeting, Joe Church used the same phrases as five stages in "the walk along the highway of holiness". It was not long before they came to be interpreted as a "formula for revival". William Nagenda and Yosiya Kinuka refused to be limited by what appeared to them to be a kind of jargon.

The second criticism arose from the emphasis that was placed on the unusual yet very meaningful deep fellowship experienced through an openness about their sins and weaknesses which led to great praise and glory to God and power in witness. As in Africa, the place of confession of sin in public became a contentious issue.

Typical were the comments of a clergyman, who expressed his strong fears of the consequences when people tried to implant in a church something that worked elsewhere, however successfully.

"This happened with the Ruanda revival through which God brought such blessing in Africa," he said, "and then people came back to this country and tried to do the same thing here. You simply can't do it. Not in those terms. Because God had done it in Ruanda, people could not pick the system up and say, that over here it's all going to be revival if we all confess to our wives, you know, 'we had bad thoughts while we were frying the eggs at breakfast this morning!' That was literally what was happening over here . . . Here were loving people, who loved Christ, who had seen wonderful things happen in Ruanda and who tried to transplant the system rather than do what God wanted to do there at that time and to meet with his people."

Bill Butler visited one Ruanda Mission supporting church with others of the missionary team including William Nagenda and Yosiya Kinuka. It was the kind of church, Bill recalled, where "there had to be an 'after-meeting' whatever had happened in the service. William was not allowed to preach because he was not ordained. Yosiya did preach but the Vicar announced that William would speak at the 'after-meeting'. When the leaders met for the after-meeting William said, 'I am sorry but I have been asking the Lord and He has not given me anything to say.' Yosiya added, 'Me too!' The Vicar was furious!"

In 1947, Peter Guillebaud, Lawrence Barham and Bill Butler attended a Young Life Campaign conference arranged by one of its evangelists, Roy Hession. Among those who entered into a new experience of God's power of which the visiting team testified was Roy himself. It was the beginning of a very fruitful fellowship between a number of UK Christian leaders and those who were active in the East African Revival, as it came to be called. For many years there was a testimony to the truths highlighted by revival, in annual Christian Holiday Conferences at Abergele, Clevedon, Southwold and elsewhere.

Despite the weakness and inadequacies, keenly felt by both missionaries and Africans alike, there were many in the UK to whom God gave a new, transforming understanding and experience of the cross and of the indwelling Christ in daily life and service.

During the brief history of the Mission three missionaries had died in service: Jack Warren had been forced to return to the UK, Arthur Pitt-Pitts and Harold Guillebaud had died in Africa. The Spring of 1950 saw the passing of the fourth, Dr Catherine James in the UK. She had served from 1935 to 1938 with her doctor husband, Norman, at Shyira. During this time, through the revival, she came into a new experience of God and it was with a burning heart that she, with her husband, returned to the UK on leave in 1938. Wartime financial restraints prevented them from returning to the field in 1939.

"In 1947, she and her husband returned to the field," wrote Algie Stanley Smith in a moving tribute to her, "and for nearly two years the flame of love for Christ and for the people burned more and more brightly. Family reasons took them back to England in 1949 and it was in November of that year that the blow fell and she received with real joy the verdict that she had only four months to live. Those who saw her on the last stages of her journey home, spoke of her room as the antechamber of heaven. Her letters to the women of Rwanda, bidding them farewell, were deeply moving and were circulated all round the churches. In her last few months many hearts in England were set on fire as she gave her simple and radiant testimony."

In the years that followed, Joe and Decie Church, William Nagenda and others were able to answer calls for visits to North America, France and Switzerland, Palestine, India, Pakistan, Australia and New Guinea. The testimony of the team as they worked together and with others was clear, as Joe pointed out: "There was no need to talk about fellowship, or the victory God was giving over race hatred. William was there to demonstrate that oneness."

Chapter 10

Priorities challenged
1946–1965

"Within the last twenty-five years, advance has been almost unbelievably rapid," commented John J. Willis, former Bishop of Uganda, in a report which appeared in the Silver Jubilee Ruanda Notes of February 1946. "And it may be doubted whether any other Mission Field can record so large an advance within so short a time . . . Where European and Native staff alike are relatively young and inexperienced, where converts are so quickly made, before qualified leaders can be trained, the danger of a landslide cannot be forgotten."

The nature of that landslide soon became apparent. At some time around the mid-forties in Kigezi, and nearly a decade later in Rwanda and Burundi, a radical change in missionary educational activity occurred almost unnoticed. From being an instrument of evangelisation which its missionaries controlled, education became a state-subsidised, church responsibility in which missionaries, as part of the local Church, were called to play an increasingly larger administrative but smaller spiritual role.

There were two causes of the educational explosion: firstly, Africans increasingly realised the benefits which

education could bestow, and secondly, governments
were willing to make educational grants. But the type of
education the young Africans sought was not necessarily
that which the community needed most, for they were
intent on well-paid, white-collar jobs, few though they
were, despising the agricultural and manual skills which
their country needed most.

Under these social forces, the momentum of education began to overtake initial African reluctance and
missionaries were pressed into organising more
educational facilities than they had either financial or
personnel resources to provide, or for which they could
assure a sound spiritual foundation. The educational
work would probably have become an almost entirely
secular movement if its spirituality depended on the
missionaries alone. There were far too few of them to
exercise any far-reaching influence.

When God began to work in a new way in Kigezi, from
1936 onwards, many of the teachers were untouched and
the schools began to drift away from their church foundations. The school teachers, with their better education, despised the church teachers and their simple
congregations.

The breakthrough came in 1941 with the conversions
of Festo Rwamunahe, headmaster of Kinyasaano
School in North Kigezi, and of his second-in-command
and friend, Festo Kivengere. In the years that followed,
nearly half of all the school teachers in Kigezi were
converted, and even where the leadership was untouched spiritually, there were 'saved' boys who gave a
clear witness before their teachers as well as to their
fellow-students.

Within the local church a deep spiritual work was
going on, not everywhere, but sufficient to permeate the
whole. In Kigezi, more so than in Rwanda and Burundi,
teams of witness composed of pastors, hospital workers,

teachers, and ordinary church members, independently of any missionaries, visited schools and testified to a living Christ and a saving Gospel. The impact of this indigenous church outreach, coupled with the daily influence of committed Christian teachers, was revolutionary. It was from this background that leaders such as James Katarikawe, Festo Kivengere and many of the present clergy and Bishops emerged.

From 1946 onwards the original primary aim of missionary endeavour to evangelise the unreached was equalled if not superseded by the urgent need to provide an educated and trained leadership for the church, for the schools and for the community. The need for missionary involvement at the secondary level became pressing.

In all three territories, all primary and most secondary education was in the hands of missions – Roman Catholic or Protestant. Otherwise the colonial policies of Britain and Belgium were different. In Uganda, the language of government was English, in Ruanda-Urundi, it was French. Whereas the churches in Kigezi and Ruanda-Urundi had been organised under one leadership, this was not so in either education or medical work. Uganda followed the British pattern and was subsidised from the capital Kampala. Ruanda-Urundi followed the Belgian pattern and received grants through the capital Usumbura, later to be renamed Bujumbura.

In Kigezi, Greg Smith had served as Supervisor of boys' schools during the World War II years while the girls' schools were cared for by Constance Hornby and Lilian Clarke. When Greg returned from leave in 1952, he took over the responsibility for the integrated supervision of all the church schools.

The administrative demands of the rapidly expanding work became so great that Greg Smith spent nearly all his time and energies in the education office. "I begin to wonder," he wrote, "how long we shall be able to administer this huge organisation. On my last two-days' safari I disposed of nearly £2,000 in cash as salaries to teachers in eighteen schools." There were no trained office staff, and the only course open to him was to add further to his workload by training personnel to take over some responsibilities. Of those so trained the most notable was James Katarikawe.

Throughout the 1940's and 1950's, there were outbursts of spiritual life. A typical instance was reported in 1955.

"At our chief centre in British Ruanda, 50 miles to the west of Kabale, there was a sudden moving of the Holy Spirit in the boys' and girls' schools. The blessing began when a saved master apologised to a boy during a singing class for getting angry with him. Thereupon the boy stood up and confessed that he had hated him for it, and both of them accepted the Lord's forgiveness and were reconciled together. A wave of conviction then spread through the school. A day or two later, another master who had backslidden for several years was taking religious instruction in the girls' school when he suddenly said, 'I am going to give you my testimony', and then and there he came back to the Lord. There were some thirty children in those two schools who were blessed at that time . . . from the start they became the enemy's special target."

Elsewhere, hints of what was happening appeared in unusual ways. "One evidence of what the Lord was doing," wrote Greg Smith, "was that books, pens and other things stolen from the schools were returned. In the accounts of the schools I frequently had to start a column headed 'Conscience money' for refunds by teachers and pupils, sometimes after a long period.

Repentance always involved putting things and relationships right."

When the Diocese of Uganda was divided into five sub-diocesan areas in 1957, to become full dioceses in 1960, it was planned to have an Educational Secretary for each area as well as a Bishop and an Archdeacon. With the approval of the Ruanda Mission, Greg Smith was appointed Educational Secretary, Western Province. Lilian Clarke became the primary schools' supervisor leaving Greg with the oversight of church secondary schools.

"In 1960," recorded Lilian Clarke, "I was the Primary Schools' Supervisor and Festo Kivengere was my assistant. In 1961, Festo was the Schools' Supervisor and I was his assistant."

The Uganda government took over the supervision and administration of all church schools in 1964. Greg Smith returned to the UK and Lilian carried on in her church girls' schools' supervisory role, assumed in 1962, until 1970. Direct missionary involvement in primary education in south-west Uganda ceased then and missionaries served only in the Kigezi High and Girls' Junior Secondary Schools at Kabale and at the Bwerenyangi Girls' School in Ankole. From 1963, Joan Hall was headmistress at Bwerenyangi assisted by other missionaries as well as African staff.

Unexpectedly, in 1961, the headship of Kigezi High School, was again assumed by a missionary, the Rev. Dick Lyth, an ex-Government District Commissioner in the Sudan. The school had been under African leadership since 1949. "Under Dick with his agricultural background," reported Greg Smith, "KHS developed into a Secondary Modern School with an agricultural bias and a school farm was started at the bottom of the hill below the school. It was the only 'upgrading' of that school which the government would allow. Though Dick's enthusiasm and personality carried this through and made it a success, it was not popular with the Africans to whom anything other than a straight academic course leading to a senior secondary school was regarded as second-rate and despised."

After Independence, Kigezi High School combined with the Girls' Junior Secondary school to form a co-educational establishment under an African head-master, Zabulon Kabaza. Dick Lyth came to the UK in 1964 then, after leave, returned to Kabale to develop the Christian Rural Service.

During these years there developed one educational institution which was unusual – Kabale Preparatory School. The need for a school for the children of missionaries had become apparent during the war years. In 1938, Joe Church had arranged for his children to be taught by Eileen Faber in an unused garage at Kabale. Two years later, under her leadership, Kabale Preparatory School (KPS) was started in temporary buildings. The staff consisted of "governesses" – English women like Eileen – who had accompanied missionary families to look after their children. The son of the local British District Commissioner became the first of many children of non-missionary parents to attend the school. It had remained a private venture, organised by parents, until 1947, when it became a Mission responsibility.

When World War II ended, there was a sharp drop in school numbers as missionaries and their families returned to the UK for long-overdue leaves. However, with new missionaries going to the field in the post-war years and more government officials taking advantage of the school for their children, the number of pupils rose steadily reaching a total of 30 in 1950.

The approval of the Uganda Government was shown in 1952 by the granting of a subsidy to cover two teachers' salaries. Two years later, a further £4,000 was received from the same source for rebuilding part of the main building and the addition of bathrooms, isolation rooms and new dormitories. The upgrading from "tubs" to "baths" was particularly appreciated!

In 1962, two African children joined the school as boarders. It was the beginning of a new era. English was still used exclusively throughout the school, a difficulty at first for the African children, but later to be an advantage. One of the first two Ugandan pupils later gained a degree at Makerere University and, later still, studied at Oxford University.

The arrival of Mary Hayward in 1952, as nurse and matron, and, a year later, Nan Read, as teacher, began a partnership which was to last until 1979 with Mary's departure. Muriel Martin joined the team in 1960. Nan, Mary and Muriel formed the backbone of the staff for many years. Nan's headship, the longest in the history of the school, ended in 1980, when she returned to the UK.

KPS was handed over to the Ankole-Kigezi Diocese in 1962 and a Board of Management was appointed with Bishop Kosiya Shalita as Chairman.

The ethos of the school continued to be that of a family, with the missionary teachers being called 'aunties'. "At KPS", wrote Nancy Chase, "I saw my job to be making as happy and homely and educationally good as possible a boarding school for children to come to at such an early age, and to continue the Christian education that most of them had at home . . . and to enable their parents to be on the mission field, knowing that their children were in good hands. When it was reported that one child from a non-missionary home had written home, 'This is a Jesus school and it is fun', I felt that the school was achieving its purpose."

Many children of missionaries retain happy memories of the "Aunties" and African domestic staff who created a "Jesus-centred", happy, homely atmosphere for their early school years.

On the medical side of the Mission's work, the first hospital at Kabale had been closed in 1939 and had been replaced by a dispensary with some beds available for patients. A number of Church leaders felt, however, that the gap left was more than a medical one, which could be filled by the dispensary and nearby Government hospital. Pleas were made that the Hospital be reopened.

In 1955, an unexpected possibility was explored. At Kisiizi, some 30 miles north of Kabale, a flax factory, built for a government financed project which failed, was left vacant. The Mission requested the site to develop it into a hospital. Three years later permission was granted.

The site and existing (ex-factory) buildings were dedicated by Bishop Kosiya Shalita at a service which was attended by a very large crowd on the 30th March 1958. Len and Esther Sharp camped on the site and construction work began. Len's landscaping skills were again evident as old buildings were converted for hospital use and new buildings were planned.

Dr John (son of Len and Esther) and Doreen Sharp moved into the existing, ex-flax factory's, assistant manager's house. In one room, John examined patients while a dispenser handled the medicines and an assistant gave injections and dressed ulcers! Rarely has a 'new missionary' brought such an immediate understanding of his missionary doctor role. "Africa was his home," wrote Ken Buxton, reviewing his life, "and he could understand the yearnings, the frustrations and the fears of the African mind. The language, too, came readily to him."

During the next seven years the hospital developed steadily. It provided a focal point in the area, not only for medical care but also for evangelistic outreach. Towards the end of 1965, John was taken ill and the symptoms were sufficiently serious for him to be flown home for medical investigation. He died in October 1966. His broad, welcoming smile as well as his medical skills were greatly missed.

In retrospect, the years from 1921 to 1965 had witnessed a remarkable educational and medical trans- formation from the traditional, cultural initiation into adult society and treatment of ills, to a largely western, educational pattern of instruction and health welfare. Had this transformation been a purely secular one its consequences would have been explosive indeed. The extent to which this was achieved peacefully and with willing co-operation rather than in a violent disruption of traditional cultural patterns of life can only be attri- buted to God working in Africans far beyond the abili- ties of any missionaries to achieve.

For men and women in whom God had done a deep work of conviction of sin and who experienced the living Christ, the transformation was deep. In others, edu- cation and the knowledge of health care were fine until there was a crisis, the resurgence of an old family feud, or a death despite the best hospital care. Then the old cultural patterns of thought and behaviour would often rise quickly to the surface. The Church of God in Kigezi was still under attack but it had been established and even the powers of hell could not prevail against it!

The pains of progress 1946–1965

A year after the end of World War II, a change of government in Belgium brought dramatic new developments in its colonial territories. The newly elected Socialist government broke the virtual monopoly of aid to Roman Catholic institutions. Financial support for medical and educational work was henceforth offered to both Roman Catholic and Protestant missions on the same basis. Grants were subject to signing a *Convention* (legal agreement) which required government inspection of staff and premises, staff qualifications and conformity with Belgian standards and acceptance of Belgian syllabuses. These stipulations required expatriate staff – doctors, nurses and teachers – to have a good working knowledge of French and to have spent a specified time in Belgium to orientate them to work in a Belgian administered system.

The *Convention* was signed by the Congo Protestant Council in 1947 and this extended to the Alliance of Protestant Missions in Ruanda-Urundi. In Brussels a *Bureau des Missions Protestantes* was set up with the

Rev. Wakelin Coxill as Secretary. He provided a very diplomatic and inspiring leadership, appreciated by missionaries of many nationalities and societies who, destined for the Congo or Ruanda-Urundi, pursued their language study, and Colonial and Tropical Medicine courses in Belgium. The *Convention* came into operation in 1948. Five years' grace was allowed for the Missions to bring their medical and educational work into line with Belgian standards.

In Rwanda and Burundi there were, in 1946, 6 hospitals and 7 central schools on Ruanda Mission stations and 716 outschools with some 2,000 pupils. Where the missionary doctor was recognised by the state, small subsidies for medicines were received, but for education there was no state aid nor official recognition.

The offer of grants from the government was accepted enthusiastically by Africans. For a time, however, many missionaries were very hesitant about contracting into a system which appeared to be promising material benefits, but which also seemed to hide a number of pitfalls which might divert the Mission from its God-ordained task. Only after much prayer and heart-searching was it considered right to accept and use for God's purposes all the provisions that were now being made available to them. Later it became clear that not to have accepted the help offered would have been to deprive the developing church of important resources.

The first missionary educationist to Ruanda-Urundi after World War II, Doreen Peck, reached Africa in 1946. Four years later, in 1950, Mabel Jones and Heather Masterman and, in 1951, Nina Putman, joined the education team. Mabel and Heather were the first educational recruits to complete their French language and Colonial Course requirements in Belgium before going to the field. It was two years later still that the first post-war men educationists, Ken Kitley, Ted Sisley and

Bert Osborn arrived on the scene, the latter two having satisfied the Belgian orientation requirements. All three had seen war service. The number of educational missionaries in Rwanda and Burundi grew steadily from the 7 in early 1946 to a peak of 22 in the early 1960's.

Following the signing of the *Convention* with the Belgian authorities, and in consultation with other member missions of the Protestant Alliance, it was decided that the Ruanda Mission should be responsible for the main teacher-training institution in Rwanda and other missions would be responsible for a similar one in Burundi.

Permission to develop a new mission station at Shyogwe, in Rwanda, was granted in 1944. As soon as temporary accommodation was available, in 1946, Peter and Elisabeth Guillebaud began a course for teachers. They selected some Africans to help them from among those who had been trained at Buye, chosen both for their teaching ability and for their qualities of spiritual leadership. At the time Peter wrote,

"We actually began on the 28th June 1946 with 75 boys, all boarders . . . we have had to make do with unfinished buildings and lack of equipment at the start, but the Lord has been with us and has met the needs. Best of all, the Lord has given us a good start from a spiritual point of view, better than my faith, for one, had thought possible. One day, some of us went off to a convention for a week-end, leaving a master in charge, and when we got back we found that Revival had broken out in the school during our absence. And ever since then, there has been a growing group of saved boys going on with the Lord. It is a wonderful evangelistic opportunity to have all these lads from all over Ruanda and Urundi, from every one of our stations as well as two of the Belgian Mission stations. How we praise God for the saved masters He has given us!"

In 1948, a Protestant Alliance combined secondary (*Ecole Moyenne*) and four-year, teacher-training school, (*Ecole de Moniteurs*), was started at Shyogwe. Aid from a Belgian Welfare fund, the FBI (*Fonds du Bien-Etre Indigéne*) was granted to enable class-room accommodation, kitchen and dormitories to be built. In Burundi, a similar school was started at Kibimba, a station of the Friends' Africa Gospel Mission.

Also at Shyogwe, a senior primary class (*école préparatoire*), was started, which prepared students for the entrance examination to the highest level secondary school in the country, the *Groupe Scolaire*, run by the Roman Catholic *Frères de la Charité* at Butare (then known as Astrida). In 1947, five candidates passed the examination. At the school there were no Protestant staff to supervise them, so Algie and Zoe Stanley Smith moved to a house and hostel, provided by the Government, which became known as the *Home Protestant*. There Algie Stanley Smith combined his duties as Warden of the *Home Protestant* with that of Field Secretary and, at the same time, devoted as much time as possible to the translation of the Old Testament into *Kinyarwanda*. This combination of tasks proved to be an impossible load to bear and, in view of the importance of the translation work to the growth of the churches, Godfrey Hindley took over as Field Secretary in 1949.

In 1947 Joy Gerson and Doreen Peck started an elementary, two year teacher-training course (*Ecole d'Apprentissage Pédagogique*) at Shyira for both young men and women. The inclusion of women was due to the insistence of Joy despite the pressure of both Africans and other missionaries that men should be given priority.

This was the first missionary, educational activity to be visited by a government official before aid was granted. After the Belgian Inspector had inspected the school, he complained to Joy Gerson, "You have not worked enough days to qualify for the grant! You will have to alter your figures". Joy replied that she could not do that. "Then your candidates will not be able to receive their certificates!" he retorted. Joy pleaded for a night's grace in which to think and pray about it. "So we did," recalled Joy, "and we decided that we would work much longer into the holidays to make up the days. The certificates were granted and the subsidy came in due course with a special addition for great honesty!"

Contrary to expectations, the girls proved themselves well able to hold their own with the men, and the stimulus of competition was valuable to both. Soon co-education was adopted throughout the Mission's primary schools, not as the ideal, but to use teaching personnel to the fullest advantage.

In April 1955, the school at Shyogwe, under the headship of Ken Kitley moved to Remera, a mission station of the Belgian Protestant Mission, but returned to Shyogwe in 1958.

The first African headmaster of a primary school appointed by the Mission in September 1953, was a remarkably able and energetic young man, Silas Majoro. His high abilities and integrity of character were recognised by the King of Rwanda, Mwami Ruda-higwa, at whose invitation he was appointed a member of the highest African, political council of the country, the *Conseil du Pays*. The Belgian Governor of Rwanda, seeing his potential, was instrumental in obtaining a grant for him to study in Belgium. As the first Protestant student from the Mission to study overseas, he began his studies in 1956, but, sadly, died of a serious kidney infection in Belgium, on the 31st May 1958.

Until 1955, the organisation of primary schools cen-tred on a missionary, usually a woman, on each mission station. On returning from leave in 1955, Bert and

Dr Algie and Zoe Stanley Smith

The Founders

Dr Len and Esther Sharp

Drs Joe and Decie Church

Rev. Yosiya Kinuka and Mr William Nagenda

Bishop Lawrence and Julia Barham

Bishop Jim and Joan Brazier

Drs Harold and Isobel Adeney

Top left: Miss Constance Hornby and Miss Lilian Clarke

Centre left: Dr Godfrey and Phyllis Hindley

Bottom left: Dr Kenneth and Agnes Buxton

Rev. Greg and Irene Gregory Smith

Peter and Elisabeth Guillebaud
d Rosemary Guillebaud

p left: Pastor Yona and Mary
namuzeyi

ntre left: Pastor Paulo and Dorotiya
we

tom left: Bishop Festo and Merab
engere

Miss Mabel Jones

r Kenneth and Wendy Moynagh

Dr Joe Church's cards:

Not "I" but Christ

Yes, Lord

Heather Osborn were posted to Buye where Bert, with Charles Mutanganwa as assistant, was asked to co-ordinate the primary education of the Mission in Ruanda-Urundi with a view to bringing it under one organisation, with common syllabuses and uniform rates of pay, so submitting a unified system for government grants.

It was at this time that the demands of education began to outstrip missionary ability to provide them. Some missionaries questioned whether they were called to such a vast amount of institutional and administrative work. Writing home in 1957, Joan Nicholson articulated her thoughts as well as those of her colleagues: "Often I ask myself if I am really touching at all the work for which the Lord called me here. But as I thought it through, I became convinced that the fault is rarely in the 'set-up', but almost always in the heart of the missionary . . . It will be some time before our African brethren here can take over full responsibility for schools and hospitals, so, for the present, part of our job is to do what they cannot do. But as far as direct evangelism is concerned the opportunities in our institutions here are unlimited – except by the coldness and lack of vision of the missionary."

When Bert and Heather returned to Shyogwe from leave in 1960, Bert was recognised as an official Inspector of Schools. An assistant was appointed, Modeste Mudaheranwa, who showed exceptional ability in handling the growing volume of paperwork related to government grants for staff and equipment. A system of School Supervisors (*Directeurs d'Ecoles*) was introduced. These became directly responsible for the primary schools. Among them were some men who later became leaders in the Church – André Kayizari, Samuel Sindamuka, Justin Ndandali, Faustin Rwagacuzi.

In the late 1950's, the Rwandan government

introduced a system in primary schools called *double vacation* by which every teacher was responsible for teaching two classes, one in the morning and the other in the afternoon. Its advantages in the increased numbers of children who could be given a primary education by the teachers available was countered by its disadvantages. Shorter hours in school led to a lowering in children's levels of achievement. One of the subjects which suffered was that of religious instruction. In some schools there was compensation in the testimony of genuinely Christian teachers.

The rapidly growing educational organisation not only resulted in less contact between missionaries and African teachers and pupils, but also between church leaders and their own schools. Often less well-educated than the teachers and certainly less well-paid, the African clergy often felt out of their depth in ministering to some of the more educated members of their congregations.

Missionaries and teachers met at conferences and, from time to time, God intervened in power. Joan Nicholson recalls such an occasion at Buye.

"The closing meeting was a time of testimony. We praised as one and another told how the Lord helped them. But as I heard them tell of how Satan had been tempting them, of the lies he had been whispering, it seemed that my eyes were opened as never before. Some of these young schoolmasters are our very dear brothers in the Lord. I know I personally depend upon them tremendously in school here. Often they have far more to give spiritually than I have. But since that testimony meeting it has almost seemed to me that I have seen the Evil One standing behind each of these young people and lashing them with a whip as he whispers his accusations and lies. 'Of course,' he says, 'it's all right to be saved, but it is not really possible for an African to *seek first the Kingdom of God*; it's another thing for the European, he has so much already; you must seek first wealth and education, and then the Kingdom of God.' . . . Can the young teacher possibly stand the whirl of it all – the uncertainty, the insecurity, the newness, the fears and doubts, the mistrust? . . . these young people here will not stand the strain unless they are held by One who is stronger than the prince of darkness."

Attempts were made to raise the level of the two-year teacher training schools. The first success was in 1962 at Buhiga from where Nina Putman wrote: "In September, the long awaited day arrived when we should raise the standard of this school and turn it into a secondary level teacher-training school for girls. There are still very few girls in Burundi ready for this but we started with a class of twelve . . . The difficulties are enormous – no buildings of our own, no equipment, no money to date, but the Lord has wonderfully helped us – girls and staff alike."

The major Alliance educational establishments at Shyogwe, in Rwanda and at Kibimba, in Burundi, were still largely staffed by missionaries but some French-speaking non-missionary, and sometimes non-Christian, teachers were joining the staffs, funded by European technical assistance programmes. Students at Shyogwe discovered for the first time that Science was not part of the Biblical Gospel! The confusion is not surprising when both Scripture and Science were taught by the same teachers!

It is difficult to summarise the life in these schools. Shyogwe was staffed largely by missionaries of the Ruanda Mission, but at Kibimba, the staff was drawn from a number of missions. Shyogwe passed through the ordeal of the political revolution. For Kibimba, the time of trial was in the future. In both of these institutions, young men and women were presented with the claims of the Gospel and an encouraging number responded.

Many of the Protestant leaders in church and secular life passed through these schools and only God knows what was achieved in their lives during their time of training.

In 1965, 42 years after the first Mission school was started at Rukira, near Gahini, all the Church-subsidised schools of Rwanda and Burundi came under direct government control while remaining institutions of the Church. Freedom to teach the Scriptures existed in all the schools, but the effectiveness of this teaching depended on the teachers. Although the number of those living a truly God-centred life was probably relatively small, all had been taught during their training the important biblical truths and when God worked, as He did from time to time, in the same convicting power as in the past, there was an understanding of what God was doing. Missionary involvement at the primary level ceased.

In that same year, the Protestant Hostel at Butare was taken over by the Government. Missionaries in education were concentrated in secondary schools – seven on the staff at Shyogwe; one, Doreen Peck, at a new school for primary teachers at Kigeme; five on the staff at Buhiga; one, Pat Brooks, at Matana and Ken Kitley at Kibimba.

Parallel to the expansion in education due, in part at least, to the new regime of grants introduced by the Belgian socialist government from 1946 onwards, there were important changes in medical work.

At first the shortage of medical staff entailed cutbacks. Kigeme Hospital was closed temporarily in 1946 as there was no missionary doctor to put in charge. As Jim and Joan Brazier were located there it was possible for the hospital to reopen later that year under the supervision of Dr Joan Brazier and nurse Beatrice Louis. Only with the arrival of Dr Ken and Wendy Moynagh did the hospital have a full-time doctor again.

In 1949, Buhiga Hospital was officially opened by the Deputy Chief Medical Officer of Burundi in the presence of the King of Burundi, Mwami Mwambutsa. This was a significant public recognition of the Mission's medical work in Burundi, but it also marked the peak of pioneer medical out-reach.

The *Convention* between the Belgian Government and the Missions which revolutionised the Mission's educational work in Rwanda and Burundi also affected the medical scene. It brought with it strict regulations concerning which medical staff would be recognised and whose salaries would be subsidised. All expatriate doctors and nurses were required to conform. This included undergoing a period of practical training in tropical medicine in a French-speaking environment in Africa.

Government recognition of staff and subsidies towards their salaries brought both opportunities for the better staffing of hospitals and problems in managing them. The years 1954 to 1960 were, according to Harold Adeney, "the heyday of our medical work".

In 1949, Mildred Forder moved to Buye in Burundi to initiate an Alliance Maternity Training School (*Ecole d'Aides-Accoucheuses*). The buildings and equipment were financed by grants from the Belgian Welfare Fund, the FBI (*Fonds du Bien-Etre Indigène*). Students were drawn from all missions of the Protestant Alliance in Rwanda and Burundi. "There is no doubt about the need for this work," wrote Mildred Forder; "for the women of the country still suffer unspeakable horrors at the hands of the 'old women' and coming here for help is often their first chance of hearing the Gospel."

At the examination for the state-recognised diploma after the two year course, ten of the twelve students passed. The Government examiners agreed to test fifteen other students from various stations, including those who had passed the much earlier course at Gahini.

Twelve of these were successful. The 22 midwives with state diplomas were a welcome addition to the country's mission medical staff. Equally encouraging was the fact that many of these women testified to the power of Christ in their lives. "One, who passed her midwifery and nursing course quite well," commented Mildred Forder, "comes from the filthiest pagan home you ever saw. It astounds me what a change Christ makes to these girls in every way." The instruction given was not solely hospital-centred, for it was Mildred's vision for those under training to become not only efficient, caring midwives but also effective evangelists on the hills from where they came.

In 1954, Dr Pierre Babel started a Mission school for hospital orderlies (*Ecole d'Aides-Infirmiers*), to teach students from Protestant mission hospitals in Rwanda and Burundi. The one-year course was recognised by the Government.

A notable medical workers' conference was held at Kigeme at the end of October 1955. Thirty participants included doctors, nursing sisters, African dressers and nurses from the Mission's hospitals. It proved to be an outstanding occasion, both spiritually and for medical work in general. From the conference there emerged a new pattern for medical mission work within the Church.

While located at Shyira, in 1963, Maureen New took a brave, new step forward when, for the first time in Rwanda, she cared successfully for premature babies. "I used an orange box with a mattress filled with dried grass, two hot water bottles, and kept a pan of water simmering on a primus stove to give warmth and humidity. A gastric tube was used to feed the baby and baby clothes from parcels sent by women's groups in England to clothe it."

Maureen met ridicule and incredulity from the nurses

who held the common belief that it was God's will for such babies to die. For the sake of the premature babies, all-night duty was enforced for the first time. "It was costly for me", wrote Maureen, "as I often had my suspicions confirmed when I visited the premature baby and mother at 11:00 pm to find the nurse had gone off to bed! The greatest reward was to say farewell to the proud mum taking her baby home at the end of a long, uphill struggle. Then the nurses admitted that it was worthwhile and they would willingly stay awake all night to care for them. Before long we had premature babies being brought to us from wide areas of the district . . . So from the early 60's, this speciality has continued through the Mission hospitals."

In less than ten years, the mission's educational and medical work had been transformed by government recognition and grants. This was progress indeed, but it was not without its pains. Leadership, once in missionary hands, was rapidly passing to the African church and this was only slowly being equipped to assume that role. Furthermore, State grants and assistance from Aid Agencies tended to force progress in a secular direction.

In 1965, the Ruanda Mission ceased to exist as a legal entity and all its material assets were handed over to the newly formed Dioceses of Rwanda and Burundi. Schools and hospitals came under Church control. Adaptation to the new regime in the schools was easier than in the hospitals. One African Bishop commented: "Over everything in my diocese I have authority except in the hospital because the doctor knows more about medicine than I do. How can I tell him what to do?" The relationship of doctor to Bishop led to some difficult situations but the overall picture was one of co-operation.

Chapter 12

The outcasts
welcomed
1946–1970

'Mission to the outcasts' is a good description of leprosy care. There can be few more demanding forms of service. At least, that was true until the 1970's. Prior to that everything physical about the care of leprosy patients was distressing – the horrific disfigurements, the foul-smelling sores and, in the earlier days, the very painful injections of chaulmoogra oil into the skin. Equally distressing was the sense of rejection felt by the sufferers, from relatives, friends and society. It was a testimony to the compassion of Christ that missionary and African staff willingly served such 'outcasts on the island of Bwama, in Lake Bunyonyi in south-west Uganda.

Throughout the war years, the responsibility for the leprosy work at Bwama, including that of the hospital during two years when it was without a nurse (1943–45), fell on Grace Mash. Having been a "governess" to the Sharp children while the family was young, she had found a new and much more demanding calling when that service came to an end. She gathered around her a number of remarkable men and women from among those who had been treated for leprosy and together, "we managed until Marguerite Barley and Janet Metcalf (both nurses) came in 1945 and I went for my furlough. There were waves of revival. How much we praised the Lord for such times."

Over many years, a cycle developed at Bwama with numbers of new patients being admitted every year. Equally every year there were some who were able to return to their homes "healthy and strong once more, and these spread a good report throughout the country, thereby inspiring others with fresh hope." For over twenty years the average number of patients on Bwama was around 900.

About 1949 the situation began to change due to the advent of sulphone drugs. Dr Bob Parry was then in charge of the Leprosarium and he made energetic use of them. During the next fifteen years the number of leprosy patients at Bwama began to dwindle steadily.

During this time, the fires of revival flickered.

"Years ago," wrote Meryl Parry, "when God brought Revival to Uganda and Ruanda-Urundi, He visited Bwama too, and many hearts were set on fire with love for the Saviour, and a desire to bring others to Him. Then, as time went on, the fire began to burn low, and as an African woman said rather wistfully, 'In those days we had the fire, but now we have only the smoke.' This was sadly true for many years, and we wondered whether God would ever revive His work again on Bwama. Then, in 1961, the fire of the Holy Spirit began to sweep through Kigezi again and many people, old and young, repented of sin and trusted the Saviour, turning 'from darkness to light, and from the power of Satan to God'. One weekend a few of us from Bwama were at a big Convention 50 miles away, and there we saw ourselves and saw our Saviour afresh, and returned to the Island aglow with the joy of His salvation. At once the Holy Spirit began to work on Bwama, and many were convicted and repented of sin, getting right with one another and with the Lord.''

When the work had started at Bwama in 1930, it was estimated that there were some 3,000 people suffering from leprosy in the Kigezi district. A Government survey in 1962 had estimated the number of such sufferers at 175. Clearly a reassessment of the situation was required.

Dr Norman Green took over the medical responsibility for Bwama in 1965. Two years later he reported, "Today, through the goodness of God, and the use of modern, sulphone drugs, our total population numbers 450, of whom 228 are patients under treatment, and over 60 are no longer active, but badly crippled or blind who will always need care."

The Uganda government was, at that time, organising rehabilitation centres in different parts of the country for the physically handicapped. As the number of resident leprosy patients decreased on Bwama so it was decided to convert the buildings which were no longer needed, to rehabilitation purposes while retaining a few houses to serve as homes for the old, crippled or blind, "burnt out" (no longer infectious) patients.

Muriel Vaughan moved to Bwama in 1967 to undertake the supervision of this new work. During the next seven years, she, with a team of African workers, developed a range of crafts so that each handicapped individual might find an occupation which suited his or her disabilities. The services of Muriel were recognised officially when she was honoured in the Queen's New Year Honours Overseas List by being awarded the MBE. Bwama, as a leprosarium, had accomplished its first mission; now it assumed another.

Meanwhile, in Ruanda-Urundi, no proper treatment of leprosy was available anywhere. A considerable number of sufferers crossed the Rwanda border into Uganda to go to Bwama. This created problems for the Government of Uganda which gave grants for the treatment of Ugandan patients, but did not accept responsibility for the care of patients from Belgian administered territory.

In 1946, the General Secretary of the American Leprosy Missions Inc, Dr Eugene Kellersberger, visited Ruanda-Urundi and saw the great need that was evident there. In consultation with representatives of the Free Methodist Mission, the Danish Baptist Mission, the Friends Africa Gospel Mission, the World-wide Grace Testimony Mission and the Ruanda Mission, he was able to propose to the Belgian Government a joint initiative to establish a leprosarium under the auspices of the Alliance of Protestant Missions of Ruanda-Urundi. The Government approved the project and offered help in addition to granting a suitable site.

Agreement was reached, in 1950, on a tract of bush country at Nyankanda, in Burundi. The area was almost devoid of habitation because it was overrun by lions and leopards. Elsewhere the country was thickly populated and intensely cultivated. As with Bwama, the prospect of beginning a leprosy establishment on virtually uninhabited land appeared attractive to both the Government and the missionaries. The local inhabitants, however, relatively few though they were, regarded the intrusion with great apprehension.

Work was begun by the American Friends Africa Gospel Mission with the generous help of the Belgian Government. Grants were made for buildings, road-making and for the initial supply of food. Further aid was forthcoming from American Leprosy Missions. The Friends Mission also seconded a doctor, Floyd Muck, who lived temporarily at the nearest Mission station, Kwisumo.

Here also came Simeoni Ngiringubu. He had been working at Kigeme Hospital in Rwanda when, in 1948, he was diagnosed as having leprosy. He crossed the border into Uganda for treatment at Bwama. His wife, Edurida, insisted on accompanying him despite many attempts to dissuade her. She said, "Have I not married him for better or worse?"

"He came into great blessing," wrote Marguerite Barley, "and he was used greatly by the Lord in blessing to others. He had a great sense of humour and was always very encouraging to the other patients, understanding as he did, the suffering so many of them went through." When he was cured of leprosy he returned to Kigeme, but, because of the great fear of leprosy in those days, people were afraid of him and he was not allowed to work in the hospital. He offered to join pioneer staff at Nyankanda.

On the concession itself work was about to be started but there were problems. The Africans who laid claim to the land refused to accept the agreement made by the government with their chief. Dorothy Lowe, the first Ruanda Mission missionary at Nyankanda, takes up the story: "They made no plans for moving elsewhere, and they cast their spells in *Kirundi* fashion to drive out the intruders."

To their great disappointment the doctor returned but not Simeoni who was seriously ill. Simeoni's friends had advised him to consult the witchdoctor but he had refused. "Four of my children have died, but it was not because of spells," Simeoni had replied. "The Lord took them, and I shall see them again one day." Simeoni recovered and returned to Nyankanda to the dismay of those who had trusted in their sorcery to banish him.

Even before the hospital building was completed, patients in a pitiable state began to arrive. Soon fifteen patients settled in grass huts and resources were strained to cater for them. Many of them were fearful of their strange, new surroundings and of the lions roaring in the vicinity. This was something they had not heard before.

Work progressed and Government aid in the supply of food helped to establish the centre. The Danish Baptist Mission provided Pastor Filipo to be the chaplain and also an expert builder in Knud Dahl whose wife Ruth, an American nurse, was able to work part-time in the hospital.

In the first year of the leprosarium about 70 patients were admitted and, in the following year, 400 more. It was not long before the leprosarium became known throughout Ruanda-Urundi. The government took patients there in its own ambulances.

In 1954, Dorothy Lowe was seconded to Nyankanda from Bwama as a laboratory technician, and, a year later, a nurse, Betty Gray, joined her. It was still dangerous country, so much so that for a time after they arrived they were not allowed to walk outside the bounds of the leprosarium because there was a lion at large which had killed three people in one week. Numerous leopards and hyena roamed the countryside.

There were then around 800 people on the station – staff and patients. Dr Bob Parry and Meryl, his wife, served for a few months at Nyankanda in 1954. From there he commented on the desperate state in which some patients arrived: "I have heard some of them describe the state of despair they got into when they knew they had leprosy, and remembered the native way of treating a man who was ill and enfeebled with leprosy – they would tie him up in his grass mat and leave him in the bush for the animals to dispose of!"

In August 1959, Drs Alan and Barbara Bapty were posted to Nyankanda. During the nearly two years that they were there, they experienced many difficulties. The isolation of Nyankanda added to the problems. When

they left Nyankanda for Kisiizi in July 1961, their place
was taken by Dr and Mrs Wayne Meyers, of the United
States. They, a physiotherapist, Miss Shultz, and
Dorothy Lowe, formed the missionary team until 1962.
In November of that year Dorothy Lowe was taken
seriously ill. The diagnosis showed that she did not have
long to live. "She accepted this with great peace," wrote
a fellow missionary, "and her radiant witness in the last
weeks of her life at Mengo Hospital in Kampala, helped
many to a clearer faith in God."

In the late 1950's, when the work at Bwama was
beginning to diminish because of the introduction of the
new sulphone drugs, that at Nyankanda was growing.
This was largely due to the many leprosy sufferers in
Rwanda and Burundi who had not been able to benefit
from modern treatment.

In Uganda, there was still a significant number of
leprosy sufferers living in their homes and requiring
treatment. However, although the new drugs were
proving to be very effective, they required the patient to
complete a course of treatment, otherwise there was a
serious risk of building up a resistance to the drugs.

From about 1967, the World Health Organisation
changed its international policy from one of isolation of
infected cases to that of the integration of leprosy sufferers with other patients, recommending that wherever
possible, patients should remain in their homes and
attend local clinics for treatment. Accordingly it
modified its advice to governments. The Uganda
Government accepted this policy but had no one to put it
into practice in the south and west of the country.

Pat Gilmer, a nurse, was posted to Bwama in 1966.
The following year she moved to Kabale and from there
she began a safari service to the Kigezi area, which
consisted of regular visits to church and government
dispensaries. Meanwhile a leprosy centre was being built

at Kisiizi. This was completed in 1969 and, from then onwards, Pat made this the base for her leprosy treatment safaris.

Over the course of the following years, with a team of workers, she was able to build up a register of leprosy sufferers, diagnose new cases and offer treatment on a regular basis, ensuring as far as possible, that all courses of treatment begun were completed. The nature of the terrain, the roughness of many of the tracks which served as roads, the primitive character of some of the dispensaries where she held clinics and the unpredictable behaviour of vehicles, often made these safaris gruelling tests of physical endurance! Even more demanding were the spiritual challenges which the itinerant service offered. Leprosy was still a dreaded disease which rendered sufferers unacceptable to the community. Even Christians often found it difficult to welcome leprosy sufferers.

"'Adventuring for Christ'", she wrote in 1968, "would sum up the past year: adventuring into a show ground with a teaching exhibition, into hospitals, dispensaries, mud-and-wattle aid-posts, a new district and an out-of-the-way village in a game reserve. It has not been without mistakes or misadventure and often the days have been fraught with frustration. The battle to have leprosy treated as any other chronic infectious disease is no easy one; we are fighting years of prejudice and fear. The team is constantly reminded that the weapons we use in our fight are not the world's weapons but God's powerful weapons, as we meet a drunk medical assistant, an indifferent district health inspector, or a man sincerely baffled by 'so many religions'. There is also the adversary's attack on the team itself as we face constant travelling and the danger of a busy but barren life."

The battle against leprosy, and the powers of darkness which often surrounded it, continued.

Chapter 13

Towards
independence
1946–1965

The Silver Jubilee of the Mission in 1946, provided
the occasion to review what had been, twenty-five
years previously, nothing but "hopes, dreams and
prayers". "This," Len Sharp observed could be "seen
not merely in the appearance of numerous native ad-
herents, nor even of an apparently prosperous and
well-organised native Church, but, through and in the
midst of these happy signs of missionary success, in the
calling out of a living Church. By this I mean men,
women and children, who have come to know the Lord
Jesus Christ as their own Saviour, freed from the guilt
and stain of past sin and from its power day by day: men
and women who are growing in grace, in fruitful service,
and in likeness to Christ."

The influence of the strong medical leadership of the
Mission supported by the working of God in revival, led
to a view of the church which concentrated on Christian
character, holiness of life and effectiveness in spiritual
ministry; rather than on church organisation and leadership. In neither of the two Bible study manuals used in

the Mission, *Every man a Bible student*, by Joe Church and *Great truths from God's Word*, by Len Sharp, is there any section dealing with the Church.

The "well-organised native church" to which Len Sharp referred above, comprised one organisational centre at Buye, where Lawrence Barham and Ernest Nyabagabo staffed the Canon Warner Memorial Theological College.

In the rest of the three territories, a total of 9 African clergy, 1979 men and 322 women lay workers in the churches, hospitals and schools; 25,105 baptised members of the church, 7,362 of whom were communicants. Added to this was the appointment, in the Jubilee Year, of Jim Brazier as Archdeacon of Kigezi and Ruanda-Urundi.

Five years later, in 1951, Jim Brazier was consecrated in Westminster Abbey as an Assistant Bishop to the Diocese of Uganda, responsible for the archdeaconry of Kigezi and Ruanda-Urundi.

In an article which appeared in *World Dominion* in the year of his consecration he wrote, "To us on the mission field, revival is the only hope for the growing Churches of Africa. Christianity is now fashionable. To be called a heathen is almost to be insulted. Education, progress, high standards of living: all are closely connected with Christianity because missions have introduced all these things as part of our western civilisation; and European governments still depend on the missions for the greater part of their work of cultural development."

Conventions provided focal points for spiritual challenge, fellowship and evangelism. Increasingly, small conventions, involving a few local congregations, were being organised, mainly during the dry season from June to August. The larger conventions drew people from a wide area including neighbouring countries.

On a height in Uganda overlooking Lake Victoria is the church centre called Kako. In 1950, it was the venue for a memorable convention. "There had been no invitations," wrote Joe Church, "but the word was passed through the Revival fellowships that there would be a convention, primarily for leaders, at which all who longed for revival would be welcome."

The theme of the convention, "Set free" was focused on a simple picture: a prisoner, sitting on his little stool in a prison cell, tired after pacing up and down, shaking his clenched fist as he protested against his punishment. His name, crime and sentence were written clearly on a charge sheet pinned to the wall of the cell. Then the door opened and Jesus Christ entered and invited the prisoner to come and be free, for his sentence had been settled on the Cross. Many were convicted of the sins which kept them prisoners: pride, jealousy, fear, impurity, bitterness and self-seeking. When, in deep repentance, they responded to Christ's invitation, they found peace and freedom.

Gahini celebrated its Jubilee in 1952 with a convention which brought visitors from as far afield as Tanzania and Malawi. At one meeting, those present included the Mwami, then King of Rwanda, the Belgian Assistant Resident and many leading chiefs of the country. It must have been a tense moment for Joe Church as he rose to greet the large assembly and so many notable people. Never a very good linguist, the occasion was made memorable by his confusion of French and Kinyarwanda as he addressed the crowd: "Mes amis *bose*"! (My friends *all*.)

Even more memorable was the way God used William Nagenda to present the simple picture of the learner-driver in Uganda, displaying the L for Learner sign. "In God's kingdom," he pointed out, "we never stop wearing that L, for Jesus said, 'Come to Me . . . learn of Me

. . .' That sign speaks not only of a heart that is willing to be humble and accept from God what He wants to teach, but it also indicates that here is someone who is learning. Furthermore, it is a warning to fellow-travellers that the one wearing the L is not perfect and needs love, light, fellowship and encouragement."

Ten years after the 1945 convention at Kabale with the theme, "Jesus satisfies", another one at the same place brought together similar crowds from Uganda, Rwanda, Burundi and beyond. Of the theme, "Jesus satisfies?". Joe Church wrote "I have never seen so much power reside in that little question mark, lit up as it was by the Holy Spirit. Day by day we saw the Lord Jesus calling to us, with His arms outstretched, and saying, 'Do I really satisfy? Is your cup running over? Am I your first love?"

Around 50 missionaries and some 3000 to 4000 Africans met for the Convention at Mbarara, in Uganda, in April 1959. Ken Moynagh gave the Bible Readings on the book of Ruth. As often in conventions, a Bible story formed the background of a central theme. In his gentle yet penetrating way Ken took the old story of Ruth and applied it to the present. "Through the tragedy of Elimelech (the name means 'My God is King'), who left God's chosen land to go down to Moab in search of the things of this world," recorded Joe Church, "the Lord showed us that the great need for us each one is to return, like Naomi, to Bethlehem, the 'House of Bread' for the bread of life. Ken reminded us that Naomi and Ruth found in Bethlehem one of their own kinsmen, Boaz, who loved Ruth, and redeemed and cared for her, and blessed her – a picture of the Lord Jesus who took upon Himself our flesh that He might be made like us, and has done as much and more for us. During the Convention and since many have been talking of coming out of Moab and returning to Bethlehem."

No one in the Mission's Silver Jubilee Year could have

foreseen that in twenty years' time there would be an independent diocese in each of the three territories led by its own bishop, two of whom would be African. Neither, it must be added, did the colonial powers imagine that they would be called on to grant independence to these territories in the same time span! The training of an educated leadership was seen to be important but it was not pursued with great urgency.

At Kabale, the buildings of the Evangelists' Training School were taken over in 1948 for a Vernacular Teacher Training Centre and the training of Church teachers was suspended. It reopened in 1954, with Canon Rwamfizi as Principal but it was to be another decade before the training extended beyond that of church teachers to clergy.

The training of clergy for the three areas was centred at the Canon Warner Memorial Theological College at Buye, Burundi. On their return from leave, Lawrence and Julia Barham began a course for ordinands selected from experienced "Third Letter" men. In February 1949, five men were ordained at Kabale and four at Gahini.

In 1952, the Rev. Alan and Catherine Lindsay joined Lawrence and Julia Barham at Buye. At the beginning of 1953, a new course for sixteen ordinands and their wives and families was started. This was the largest number that had ever been accepted for one course. Eventually 14 men were ordained on the 7th November 1954. These nearly doubled the number of African clergy in Kigezi, Rwanda and Burundi, bringing the number to 31. Among those ordained were the two future Bishops of Rwanda and Burundi, Adoniya Sebununguri and Yohana Nkunzumwami.

In the years that followed, until 1962, the Warner Memorial Theological College trained clergy for the three territories and senior Church Teachers for

Rwanda and Burundi. Alan and Catherine Lindsay were joined, in 1959, by Albert and Joan Brown with the Rev. Gideyoni Kabano as assistant.

"The pace of life has been quickened considerably here at Buye," wrote Albert Brown in 1960, "by the founding of an Alliance Theological Seminary – which is of course in addition to the ordination course already running. This new Seminary is for men of good education who feel the call to serve in the ministry of the church. It serves both our own Anglican church and also the Baptists (in origin a mission from Denmark), and the Presbyterians (in origin Belgian), and the Methodists and the Friends (both American). So far only the Anglicans and the Methodists have produced men and they compose the first class of six. All of them are ex-schoolmasters and we are enjoying teaching them. It is, however, something of a strain to have to try to teach in French."

An important element in the training of clergy at Buye was the emphasis placed on provision for clergy wives. The small houses which formed "Deacons Row" allowed for one or two children in addition to the ordination couple and, for some, this was limiting.

Julia Barham, Catherine Lindsay and Joan Brown worked together to instruct the wives of ordinands in a wide range of skills. Some of the wives presented special problems. "It's true that most of them are grand-mothers. It's true that eight out of the twelve never went to school before," reported Joan Brown, referring to the group of wives then in session. "What we desire most of all for them is that their two years here will draw them into a closer walk with the Lord Jesus. We hope that they will go out from here with not only the desire to be co-workers with their husbands in the Lord's work, but with a vision for work amongst other women and for passing on to them what they have learned." The course included practical subjects such as cooking, sewing, hygiene and writing, as well as Scripture, preparation of talks and the running of women's meetings.

The special needs of women had been recognised in the past and women's meetings were regular features on many mission stations from the early days. Often, however, special activities for women were organised to make use of opportunities presented by other events. Children's clinics in the hospital offered a good opportunity to talk to the mothers who attended them for the care of their children. Much depended on the availability of a missionary wife to take advantage of the opportunities presented.

On every mission station, teams, consisting of missionaries, or their wives, and the wives of African church workers, visited nearby Christian and non-Christian homes. Elisabeth Guillebaud and Gwyneth Weston describe a typical situation at Shyogwe, in Rwanda.

"There is a good team of Christian women, wives of mission workers, living on the station, and together we go out on Wednesday afternoons visiting the women of the neighbourhood. We go to those whose names are on the register of the women's meeting, particularly to any who are ill or who have not been to the meeting recently. People always seem to appreciate being visited and we usually find at the meeting the next day a group from the place to which we have been; then the following week they are often away again! Sometimes, instead of going visiting, the wives living on the station gather for an afternoon's learning – a cookery demonstration or a discussion on baby welfare. At present we are sharing ideas on teaching children to pray and read the Bible. We long for there to be available in *Kinyarwanda* books of Bible stories and simple prayers, such as those which are published in English."

At Matana, in Burundi, Margaret Guillebaud was able, in the 1940's, to obtain some help from the Mothers' Union in the UK to enable the very capable and spiritual widow of a Pastor, Mrs Eseri Serubibi, to run a Brides' School at Matana for fiancées and wives of church workers.

A similar course for fiancées was run by Isobel Adeney at Buhiga. "This last course (1951) was a particular joy to us," Isobel wrote, "as all the girls were keen Christians and, at the end of the course, they all gave their testimonies as to what a help and blessing it had been to them to come here and learn. The girls come in by the day, and most of us Christian women on the station share in the teaching."

Also at Matana, Joan Nicholson became so concerned for the needs of the girls who were not able to continue their training at the Buhiga teacher training school that, in 1958, she started a simple domestic course for ten of them. "When the way began to open for this course, the Lord seemed to say to me," Joan wrote, "'Yes, you want to give these girls something to do, and you want to help them to have better homes later on, but the real aim of this course is that some among them may be really saved and take their places uncompromisingly on My side.'" Such was the thinking behind a number of similar ventures in the history of the Mission.

In Kigezi, Margaret Clayton returned from leave in 1958 and, to her great delight, was invited to change her role from that of school teacher to that of Mothers' Union worker for the Ankole-Kigezi Diocese under Bishop Kosiya Shalita. Margaret immediately set about her major tasks, those of training women in leadership, in improving standards in nutrition, hygiene and general health care, in teaching skills in sewing and cookery, and fostering handicrafts.

When Dick and Nora Lyth were posted to Kabale in

1960, Nora was able to work with Irene Gregory Smith in helping leaders of the women's groups already meeting in the district. They taught health improvement, crafts, knitting and "home and spiritual leadership' to about 60 women. Nora wrote a book called *Knitting made easy* which was printed in English and Swahili. This is still in print.

With the approval of the Church leaders, Nora began to give instruction in Family Planning. At her request a midwife was trained in this specialism in Nairobi and together they set up a Family Planning clinic in the Kabale town centre with the aim of advising women and their husbands but not unmarried girls. The clinic was continued by the mid-wife after Nora left in 1972.

Also at Kabale, Nora was able to co-operate with wives of leading Church and Government officers in starting a non-denominational club in Kabale town centre for girls who failed entrance into secondary school. The club became more like a school where crafts, health and secretarial subjects were taught, as well as knitting, Nora's special interest. The club ran for about two years.

On two occasions, Nora Lyth organised clergy wives' conferences while the clergy looked after the children! It was quite an innovation. "We taught all the usual Christian Rural Service type of courses, as well as the special relationship of being a clergy wife. Bishop's wives Geraldine Sabiti and Beatrice Ruhinde came for these and were wonderful leaders for them. I remember on one occasion, having written down on a blackboard all the problems of life they could think of, we found that heading the list was 'husbands'! But thankfully the Lord met us all in convicting power, and many husbands praised Him later for the 'new' wives they had received back from the conference."

Youth work in Uganda had been focused in the Boys' Brigades which were formed in several church centres.

The success of this movement was demonstrated at a great gathering of the Brigades organised for an evangelistic week-end in October of its Silver Jubilee Year. It closed with a gathering of about 3,000 officers and boys on the Sunday morning.

The UK Headquarters of the Boys' Brigade took a special interest in Uganda and, in 1960, appointed Geoffrey Hewitson to be the Organising Secretary for the whole of that country. His first year was spent in the Kigezi district where there were then 11 enrolled companies, and some 15 more at various stages on their way to enrolment. In early 1961, Geoffrey wrote: "The work is now increasing rapidly and the Lord is opening many new places and presenting many new opportunities for advancement, not only in Kigezi, but in other widely separated parts of Uganda: in Ankole, Busoga, West Nile and in parts of Buganda. There are people in all these districts who want the Boys' Brigade . . . Thank God that He brought the Boys' Brigade to the church in Kigezi, and that there are now many men who have a vision of what it can achieve; and pray that the Brigade may develop in the whole of Uganda into a great and mighty force that is able to show boys the way to their Saviour and to eternal life." In the 1960's the Boy's Brigade was adopted as the official boys organisation of the Church of Uganda.

The 1st Kigezi Girls' Life Brigade Company held its Enrolment Service in July, 1962. There were then 29 Boys' Brigade Companies in Uganda of which 18 were in Kigezi.

It was easier to introduce the BB and the GLB to British Uganda than to Belgian Ruanda-Urundi. As in Uganda, it was Lawrence Barham who started the first Boys' Brigade Company at Buye, in Burundi. By 1967, Keith Anderson and Ted Sisley reported that "the Boys' and Girls' Brigade Companies are continuing and new ones being formed. We are longing to extend this work before the young folk are absorbed with other movements as it is now compulsory for all young people to belong to a recognised one.''

First the revolution in Rwanda in the early 1960's, and then the violence in Burundi in 1972 led to the dissolution of both the Boys' Brigade and the Girls Life Brigade companies in Rwanda and Burundi. The political climate in both countries was not conducive to foreign-based, religious youth groups which included activities, such as marching and the formation of bands. These could be misconstrued as being "military" in character. Even the secular Scout organisation suffered the same fate.

The first major change in church organisation took place in 1957. Linguistically and socially, the district of Kigezi was closely linked with that of neighbouring Ankole. It was natural that the two church areas should merge to form the sub-diocese of Ankole-Kigezi. From that time the Kigezi Church sent its delegates to the Diocesan Council at Mbarara in Ankole.

The pressure for *amajyambere* (progress) which affected education so strongly, changed the status of the church teacher on whom fell the greatest load of Christian teaching, evangelism and pastoral care of the local congregation.

"The position of the village evangelist has changed a good deal in recent years," wrote Bishop Jim Brazier in 1958.

"Ten years ago he was a privileged village leader, educated more than most, secure and reasonably well provided for, and free from the multitudinous labour duties imposed by chiefs. Today most of the old labour duties have been replaced by higher taxes which the evangelist has to pay like anyone else. An ordinary labourer receives more pay than he does, and the fact that often he is working away from his home village means that he has less oportunity for helping himself by extending his cultivation of cash crops such as coffee, beans and other marketable products. A probable development will be to find a local Christian to take charge of the church, and this may lead in time to a system of unpaid lay readers, so that money can be made available to pay senior evangelists and clergy a reasonable allowance."

The church teacher had two major tools for communicating and teaching the *readers* in his care – the Bible and a hymn-book. Probably the only other source material available to him were the notes he wrote by hand when in training at an evangelists' training school.

In Kigezi, a hymnbook of 212 hymns in *Lunyoro*, published in 1935, was in use until after World War II. During the late 1930's and 1940's many new hymns appeared as those who were saved and revived expressed themselves in new and vibrant words and music. Largely through the initiative of Festo Kivengere the Twale (Deanery) Council decided that the new hymns should be collected; some added from the UK, notably from the Keswick Hymnbook and others from *Luganda* and *Kinyarwanda* sources. Largely through the hard work of Greg Smith a *Rukiga* supplement of 100 hymns was published by the SPCK in 1951. Those two books remained in use for many years.

In the post-War period the need for an up-to-date hymn book which catered for the needs of all the Protestant Missions became pressing in Rwanda.

Peter Guillebaud was occupied in teaching until 1952 when he and Elisabeth returned to the UK for leave. On returning to Africa, Elisabeth again became involved in the training of primary school teachers at Shyogwe, leaving Peter free for literature work. Peter set to work compiling a *Kinyarwanda* hymnbook which would be acceptable to all the missions of the Protestant Alliance.

In Burundi, Rosemary Guillebaud had compiled 333

hymns in *Kirundi* drawn from the Protestant Missions working in that country. In Rwanda, there had been two editions of the first hymnbook produced for the Mission by Peter's father, Harold Guillebaud, with about 100 hymns. In addition there was the hymnbook of the Belgian Protestant Mission which consisted of about 100 hymns, translated into *Kinyarwanda* from German before World War I, and from French by the Belgians. The Methodists wanted some of their hymns of American origin, which had already appeared in the Kirundi hymnbook. There were also a few hymns, originally in Danish, contributed by the Danish Baptist Mission. Further research led to some very good hymns in *Rukiga*, from south-west Uganda, and some from *Ruhaya*, the dialect of Bukoba in Tanzania. In addition to those from recognised sources there were the newer hymns, written at times of great spiritual movement with the words written in rough exercise books, some going back twenty years to the 1930's. After a considerable amount of work over four years, the hymn book was finally printed in Kinshasa, Zaire, in 1958.

The hymn books produced in *Kinyarwanda* and *Kirundi* are still in use for general service in all missions in these countries today. They represent the core of hymns which are still very meaningful to many Christians, particularly the older ones. Later, many new hymns were added as, in times of renewed spiritual awakening, new songs emerged as testimony to the reality being experienced.

As more Africans became literate and more Bibles became available, so grew the need to help individual Christians to read and understand their Bibles. Printed cards which gave the Scripture Union reading for each day had been available from the 1930's, first for the New Testament only (when that was all that was available), then later for the whole Bible.

For some time both Peter Guillebaud and Dorothée de Benoit had sensed the need to go a stage further and provide Bible reading notes which would give comments on the daily passages, to provide teaching which was so much needed. In 1959, they worked together to prepare a set of notes on one book of the Bible. "Don't ask me why," commented Peter, "but we chose a most extraordinary book – Ecclesiastes! It strikes chords with African wisdom. Those original notes have now completely disappeared."

The first Scripture Union Notes, called *Umusomyi* (The Reader), were printed in 1960. They were translated from the French "Daily Bread" notes, called *Le Lecteur de la Bible*, which were used throughout French-speaking Africa. At first, notes on some books were printed in *Kinyarwanda* and on others in *Kirundi* – both were understandable by speakers of both languages. However, after two years, the nationalism of both Rwanda and Burundi made this arrangement unacceptable, and separate editions had to be produced for the two countries. It would be hard to assess the value of *Umusomyi* to thousands of young Africans in helping them to read the Bible daily and apply it to their lives.

It had been clear for some years that the churches in British Uganda and Belgian Ruanda-Urundi could not continue for ever as one organisation. God had worked the miracle of giving deep fellowship between Christians from the three areas, clergy had been trained together and conventions had provided opportunities for meeting and a sharing of what God had done for them. However, the political and geographical divide, particularly as the granting of independence to the territories loomed nearer, made a break inevitable.

In 1960, the training of clergy for Kigezi was separated from that for Rwanda and Burundi. The Rev. Amos Betungura was appointed Principal of the Kabale

Normal School which served the Kigezi-Ankole region.
One of his first tasks was to change its name to that of
the Canon Barham Divinity School. Amos Betungura
came from Bishop Tucker College at Mukono and the
Divinity School became a kind of "over-flow" from
Mukono. The students came from all over Uganda. The
church in Kigezi ceased to be linked directly with the
churches in Rwanda and Burundi.

Less obvious at first, but with increasing force, it
became clear that a similar break would come, sooner or
later, between the church in Rwanda and that in Burundi. From 1962 onwards the Dioceses of Rwanda and
Burundi undertook the responsibility for the training of
their own church teachers and clergy, at Gahini in
Rwanda, and at Buye in Burundi.

Although political independence was granted to
Rwanda and Burundi in 1962, movement and communication between them was completely free. However, restrictions on travel began to be imposed, partly
at least, due to the political upheaval in Rwanda and the
problem of refugees. Towards the end of 1963, restrictions were intensified and by the end of 1964, the border
between the two countries was closed and only passable
with special permission.

In 1963, Bishop Jim Brazier returned to England. He
had served God in the Mission for thirty-five years, the
last twelve of which had been as Bishop. Jim was a very
sensitive pastor of men and the last few years, with the
severe strains that ethnic-orientated, political pressures
brought into the church proved very difficult. "The
division of his diocese on racial grounds," wrote Major-
General D. J. Wilson-Haffenden, Chairman of the
Ruanda Mission council, "with all that that division
involved of hatred, murder, destruction and bitterness,
weighed heavily on the bishop, but throughout it all he
has continued to serve his people to his utmost."

In February, 1964, Leslie Brown, Archbishop of the Province of Uganda, with the approval of the Diocesan Council of Rwanda and Burundi, invited Canon Lawrence Barham, then General Secretary of the Mission, to succeed Jim Brazier as Bishop. Lawrence had already served thirty-one years in Africa, but his choice was an obvious one in view of his experience and the confidence placed in him by the clergy and people of Rwanda and Burundi. He was consecrated on the 8th March 1964, in Namirembe Cathedral, Kampala. As Bishop of the Diocese of Rwanda and Burundi, he was charged with the mission of serving the churches there as their Bishop until African bishops were consecrated for the future separate dioceses.

In preparation for that event, five African clergy from Rwanda and Burundi were selected and, in September 1964, began a period of training in England, sponsored by Inter-Church Aid. Two of them, Revs Yohana Nkunzumwami and Adoniya Sebununguri, later became the first bishops of the dioceses of Burundi and Rwanda.. The others were: the Revs Festo Gakware and Festo Mpangaza from Rwanda; Yohana Gahenga from Burundi; together with the Rev. Emmanuel Sibomana, a Baptist minister sent by the Danish Baptist Mission. He was Secretary of the Protestant Alliance of Burundi and well-known in Ruanda Mission circles as the author of the hymn, *O how the Grace of God amazes me*.

At the end of 1964, the last joint Diocesan Council of the Diocese of Ruanda-Urundi met at Buye. At this council representatives from Rwanda and Burundi met separately to select the names of the African clergy to be submitted to the Provincial House of Bishops in Kampala, for the election of an assistant bishop for each country. The elections duly took place and Canon Adoniya Sebununguri was consecrated Bishop of Rwanda at Kigeme on the 6th June 1965 and Archdeacon Yohana

Nkunzumwami was consecrated Bishop of Burundi at Buye on the following day, the 7th June 1965. The consecrations were conducted by Archbishop Leslie Brown, assisted by Bishop Erica Sabiti and Bishop Lawrence Barham.

On the 6th March 1966 the dioceses of Rwanda and Burundi became independent and their Assistant Bishops raised to Diocesan level. Lawrence and Julia Barham returned to the UK, their mission accomplished.

It was forty-four years since the first African teacher sent by the Ruanda Mission had started work in northeast Rwanda, in September 1922. The Ruanda Mission still retained the old spelling of its name, but its work as a pioneer, church-planting mission in the areas to which its founders were called, was over. This did not mean that its work as a Mission was wholly accomplished. The emerging churches needed and, indeed, pleaded for help in finance and in technical skills and training. This, however, was to be under the authority of African church leaders, with the aim of establishing the churches and enabling them to fulfil their God-given mission to their own people.

The churches in SW Uganda, Rwanda and Burundi were now independent of Mission authority but willing to work in partnership with any who would help them, and in this task the Ruanda Mission had a vital, although delicate role to play.

Chapter 14

Revolution in Rwanda 1959–1964

In 1946, Uganda and Ruanda-Urundi came under the United Nations Trusteeship Council. Indirect rule was to be replaced, in stages, by limited self-government under the authority of Britain in Uganda, and Belgium in Ruanda-Urundi. Institutions were set up through which the countries would, eventually, govern themselves.

The leisurely pace of development was shattered by the violent uprising in the Belgian Congo. It became clear that independence would have to be granted earlier than had at first been anticipated.

Of the three territories in which the Ruanda Mission worked, Rwanda was the first to be affected. On 24 July 1959, the king of Rwanda, Rudahigwa, Mwami Mutara III, died in mysterious circumstances in Usumbura (later changed to Bujumbura), the capital of Burundi. No explanation was given as to the cause or manner of his death. In the absence of a successor nominated by the late king, Jean-Baptist Ndahindurwa was appointed to be the new Mwami Kigeri V, following the traditional

African process and without consulting the Belgian authorities.

Reports differ as to who initiated the political moves. After the installation of Mwami Kigeri V, there were a number of brutal political assassinations of prominent *Hutu*. This was followed by a violent uprising of the *Hutu* against the *Tutsi* which went far beyond those directly involved in government. In the months and years that followed, thousands of *Tutsi* were killed or brutally mutilated and driven from their homes. Refugees flocked to temporary reception centres or crossed the borders into neighbouring countries. Final estimates gave the figures for those killed at between 10,000 and 14,000 of both *Tutsi* and *Hutu*. Over 100,000 *Tutsi* fled into Uganda, Tanzania, Burundi and Congo (later changed to Zaire).

The situation presented a great challenge to the missionaries. A protest was made to the Belgian Vice-Governor General in Bujumbura, at what appeared to be a "standing aside" of the armed-forces, mainly Congolese soldiers, and doing little or nothing to stop the violence. It was difficult to know what could be done officially which would not appear to be siding politically with either the *Tutsi* or the *Hutu*.

The churches established in Rwanda included *Tutsi* and *Hutu* members. Both ethnic groups were represented in the Church leadership. The missionaries found themselves straddling the divide. For nearly three years the "troubles" overshadowed everything else.

Mission stations, Protestant and Roman Catholic, soon became refugee centres. At Shyogwe, Peter and Elisabeth Guillebaud and Mabel Jones found themselves at the centre of the violence which had first erupted not far from them. The country around became the scene of burnt houses, slashed banana trees, devastated coffee plantations and, in places, there arose the stench of rotting flesh. On occasions, hordes of men and boys, shrieking and brandishing spears, knives, machetes and other weapons, attacked the houses of African workers, while the fear-stricken families found refuge in missionaries' houses. Was this protection of the hunted "*Tutsi*" a political activity? For the missionaries the question was simply answered: they had a commission to deliver the oppressed and protect the powerless. But that was not the way that politically motivated Rwandans – both outside and within the Church – looked at it. Soon missionaries came to be categorised as pro-*Tutsi* or pro-*Hutu*!

At Shyira, on the 4th November 1959, Doreen Peck and Josephine Stancliffe found themselves surrounded by an ever approaching circle of burning houses and crops and an increasing flow of refugees, including some *Tutsi* leaders who were particularly wanted by the invading hordes. Following a hurried consultation between the church leaders, Josephine accompanied by two Mission workers set off to seek help at Gahini, while Doreen remained the only missionary on the station. The situation was resolved when, as a result of the intervention of Harold Adeney, the refugees at Shyira were transported over the border into Uganda.

In Rwanda a refugee centre was set up at Nyamata, in the Bugesera, a region to the east of the country. A church teacher and, later, a Pastor were posted to a church centre, Maranyundo, a short distance from the refugee camp. Doreen Peck worked tirelessly to help those whom the Rwanda government transported there. Godfrey and Phyllis Hindley also visited the refugees regularly, working with the local evangelist, James Kayinamura.

Many of the refugees came from church centres elsewhere in the country. As they poured in Phyllis wrote, "As women and children came out of their so-called houses to greet us, those whom we had known in such different circumstances, I just couldn't keep the tears back. I suppose refugees and refugee camps are much the same in all parts of the world but this place certainly makes one very sad."

At Kigeme, the violence in the district around was so great that very few *Tutsi* remained – most of them were killed or fled as refugees to a neighbouring country.

The standing of the missionaries in the country was illustrated by an incident recorded by Dr Pierre Babel.

"On our return (from a holiday by Lake Kivu in 1960), after passing through the forest we began to pass columns of African fighters armed with spears. At one point we met a group of them who asked us to stop the car and, having recognised me as the doctor at Kigeme, told me that a Belgian helicopter had crashed near by and I should go and give them medical attention. They promised to guard our children while Andrée and I were away. We walked for about ten minutes to what remained of the crashed helicopter on the side of a hill and found four Belgian soldiers, wounded but not seriously. We gave them first aid and tried to make them comfortable, then left, assuring them that we would alert the authorities so that they would come for them . . .

"That evening, about 10 pm, a military camionette arrived with soldiers bringing food for the wounded but, in the blackness of the moonless night, they did not know where to find them and needed a guide. I went with them. On the main road with headlamps, there was no problem but we had to leave the road and continue in wooded bushland. For me to remember the route on such a dark night was a miracle. God was with us and guided us. Suddenly, in the dense blackness of the night there were loud war-cries all around us. The soldiers seized their arms ready to repel an attack. The first of the fighters arrived and pointed their spears in our direction. Then they recognised me and the tone of their cries changed, *'N'umuganga! N'umuganga w'i*

Kigeme!' (It's the doctor, the Kigeme doctor!) they shouted. From then onwards we were completely safe. They went ahead of us and showed us the way to the wounded soldiers."

It was nearly two years before the violence reached the Gahini area. Joe Church told the story: "A few weeks ago we at Gahini had our biggest testing. Tribal warfare, that up to now had not entered this part of Eastern Rwanda, flared up in three villages across the lake; and we watched the marauding bands through our binoculars and heard the shouts. Refugees arrived and we had to prepare emergency accommodation for them and plans to protect them in hospital. But there weren't many of them, nothing like those at Kigeme and Shyira in the past. We have often been threatened and many times I have walked round the station in the moonlight, and have given fear into the hands of the One Who alone casts out fear." Later that year many more refugees fled as bloodshed and violence spread to every part of Rwanda.

Godfrey Hindley, as Field Representative, was situated at Buye from where he was able to visit other stations. "On all our mission centres," he reported, "we are trying to offer some help to those in need but there are many problems to be overcome. There are also wonderful opportunities for preaching the Gospel. I have frequently visited all our centres during the last month and wherever there are refugees one of the things that has been most noticeable is the peace amongst them, whereas elsewhere in the country there is fear and panic. At Gahini . . . nothing could have been quieter or more orderly, and each morning practically the whole community met to hear the Gospel, and many were blessed."

Between Butare (then Astrida) and Shyogwe is the

town of Nyanza, near which is the church centre, Hanika. Because of its proximity to the King's court, this was a strongly royalist area largely untouched by the strife which divided the country elsewhere. In August, 1961, a combination of invasion from marauding bands and subversion from within resulted in fierce attacks on the local royalist majority. Soon streams of refugees poured into Hanika and were received by the Pastor and his wife, Misaki and Dorothy Vuningoma, and the headmaster of the school, Gershom Gakwaya. "We cannot thank God enough for these three and their testimony of quiet peace and patience and love," reported Peter Guillebaud. "They were a team prepared by God for what was to come. We never saw them angry or seriously disturbed, and God used the spirit of calmness and confidence He had put in them to pervade the whole place."

The situation became increasingly tense as huge numbers fled from burnt houses, devastated fields and bloodshed. "Again and again Pastor Misaki was accused of harbouring undesirables and of protecting those responsible for acts of violence," continued Peter Guillebaud, "until he found himself in serious danger of imprisonment on a false charge – or worse . . . his life was threatened more than once." For several weeks a number of missionaries including Peter and Elisabeth Guillebaud, Alan Lindsay, Doreen Peck and Bert Osborn, took turns to camp there. During this time the number of refugees rose from 2,000 to between 5,000 and 6,000 before they were dispersed elsewhere.

A Republican Government was declared in October 1961, and the authorities began to exert increasing pressure on refugees to return to their homes. They were embarrassed by the massive exodus of refugees to neighbouring countries. Slowly refugees dispersed from the Mission centres and either returned apprehensively to their homes or fled to refugee rehabilitation areas such as the Bugesera in the east of Rwanda, or they fled to join the thousands already in adjacent countries.

In the Orukinga Valley in Uganda, in the Murwanza area of Tanganyika and at Buye and Kirundo in Burundi, there were still many refugees for whom the missionaries were either directly or indirectly concerned. At Buye, Godfrey and Phyllis Hindley were responsible for several thousand refugees. "Here at Buye," wrote Phyllis Hindley, "we feed 12,000 people and we also have to send to four other camps of 8,000 in all. This is a big responsibility and without God we would be unable to undertake it, but we claim his promise: 'My God shall supply all your need'. So we trust and go forward."

The violent upheaval affected not only the politically orientated rebels, expressing itself in the driving out of *Tutsi* elements, the burning of their houses and crops, and the killing of many of them; it also affected the running of church, school and hospital. Joan Nicholson highlighted the educational dilemma at Shyogwe:

"In recent months Satan has been fighting hard. The Church has been sharply divided over the appointment of a school head – a question of race and political affiliations . . . We need prayer for wisdom in extremely tricky situations. When is it right to give way to pressure for certain lines of action, and when is some Christian principle involved? If certain members of staff are not acceptable to the local population do we agree to transfer them elsewhere or not? If refugee boys want to come back to the school, do we accept them, even if there are complications? If a boy has to be severely punished can we be sure that the opinions given by the African members of staff are unbiased by the political repercussions of any decision taken? If a brother seems to be wandering away from the Lord because of politics how do we challenge him without seeming ourselves to be 'leaning to one side' politically? These are the sort of questions we are facing day by day and for which we need much prayer."

A United Nations Commission of Inquiry was sent to
Ruanda-Urundi in April 1960 and meetings were organised between the political parties in order to arrange for
elections. In October 1960, a provisional National
Assembly was constituted with a *Hutu* Prime-Minister,
Gregoire Kayibanda. On the 28th January 1961, a mass
meeting, organised by the political party of the *Hutu*,
PARMEHUTU, was held at Gitarama, some 6 kms
from Shyogwe. Rwanda was declared a Republic and a
new provisional National Assembly and President were
elected. A United Nations mission proposed elections to
the National Assembly, combined with a referendum on
the status of the Rwandan King. The elections were held
in September 1961. They were followed by claims and
counter-claims of unfairness and "rigging". They also
sparked off a new wave of violence and thousands more
Tutsi fled the country.

At the final meeting of the United Nations Commission, with the leaders of the parties in both Rwanda
and Burundi, it was decided that the two countries
would become separate independent states while retaining a number of common institutions. On the 1st July
1962, Rwanda and Burundi were separately granted full
independence by the Belgian Government.

In 1964, a fresh outburst of violence swept Rwanda.
The Kigeme area again suffered severely. Doreen Peck
reported from there, "Several school, hospital and
church workers, as well as many other Christians were
killed; others fled thus leaving sad gaps in every
department and empty houses all around."

At Nyamata, the refugee centre in the Bugesera, the
situation became particularly tense towards the end of
1963. The camp was in the east of the country and it was
from this general direction that, from time to time,
exiled *Tutsi* raided Rwanda. Such attacks fanned the
hatred already there among the *Hutu* against the *Tutsi*

and spread desperate fear in any *Tutsi* who still remained in the country.

Yona Kanamuzeyi was Pastor of the church at Maranyundo. Yona had been one of the schoolboys at Gahini in 1936, when Blasio Kigozi was headmaster. There, he had come to experience that inner revival which is not dependent on dramatic outbursts of God's convicting power in other people. He shared that close walk with God which he had learned then, with Mary, his wife.

In a renewed outbreak of violence, soldiers eliminated anyone whom the authorities considered was either aiding the *Tutsi* insurgents or appeared to show sympathy to them.

Sympathy! Compassion! Do those words mean something different depending on the object of them? "There was no colour-bar with Yona," wrote Joe Church; "he was completely free of politics. No one quite knew (or cared) whether he was a *Tutsi* or a *Hutu*." Yet it was the fact that he treated anyone, whether *Tutsi* or *Hutu*, in a loving, caring way, which incurred the anger of the anti-*Tutsi* soldiers.

An entry in the church register of services at Nyamata shows that on Sunday, 19th January, Yona took as his text Romans 6:4, "We were therefore buried with Him through baptism into death in order that, just as Christ was raised from the dead through the glory of the Father, we too may live a new life." Those who knew Yona would not find it difficult to imagine what he said. He could speak from personal experience of "new life" in Christ.

On the following Thursday morning, 23rd January, Ian Leakey visited the Kanamuzeyi family.

"At the luncheon table alone with Yona and his wife," recorded Ian, "I was able to review the whole situation more freely. Clearly Yona realised now that he was in more danger than he and others had previously thought. Information had leaked out about a list of victims who were due to be called out of their houses and dispatched during the hours of darkness. It was the normal thing to hear gun-shots at night . . . So we prayed, and in his prayer Yona pleaded for God's people, that they might bear a true witness. He remembered the authorities who had charge of the country's affairs and the leaders of the Roman Catholic Church. He rejoiced that his true home was in heaven, that his life was in God's hands whose way was perfect, whether it involved going to be with Him or staying in His harvest field."

At the bridge which marked the boundary of the Bugesera, Ian and Yona parted – Ian back to Shyogwe, Yona to Maranyundo.

As darkness fell, six soldiers came to Yona's home and took him away. It was only for questioning, so they assured the family. They drove him to the bridge from where he had a few hours previously smiled good-bye to Ian Leakey.

There the soldiers shot Pastor Yona and threw his body into the river Nyabarongo.

Just before Yona was killed, Andrew, a schoolmaster, sat with another prisoner expecting the same fate. He watched the soldiers march off with Yona. "They (the soldiers) were all amazed." he lived to record. "They had never seen anyone go singing to his death or walking as he did, like a man just taking a stroll." Yona died singing, praying for those who were going to kill him.

For some inexplicable reason they told Andrew to go home. And remarkably, he found someone who was able to lead him through the bush to safety in Burundi.

The news of the death of Pastor Yona reached East Africa and Europe. Joe Church wrote a moving biography of him with a title of which he would have approved: *Forgive Them*.

A letter from Dean E. R. Matthews of London announced that "The Dean and Chapter have decided to add the name of Yona Kanamuzeyi to the list of Modern Martyrs in the Memorial Chapel in St Paul's Cathedral."

The revolution in Rwanda proved to be a severe testing of the young church. Revival had left a strong heritage of fellowship between individual Christians and a powerful determination not to succumb to ethnic jealousies and persecution at the individual level. The uncompromising stand of Pastor Yona was repeated in many other less publicised circumstances and many suffered greatly for it.

There was not, however, a comparable public condemnation of ethnic discrimination and violence by Rwandan church leaders. Was this a failure of the church? Part of the explanation may be that the leadership of the church was still in missionary hands. The condemnation and protest which *was* made, was in the name of the Mission and directed towards the Belgian authorities, who appeared to allow, if not actually support, the uprising. There were not, therefore, any Protestant Christian Africans in sufficiently senior positions to be able to speak in the name of the church to the African authorities. Whatever may have been the reasons for this silence, many considered the Rwandan Church to be the weaker because of it.

Chapter 15

Youth catches
the fire
1963–1985

The fires of revival, as witnessed in the extraordinary
events of the 1930's and 1940's, died down in the
early 1950's. Occasionally, usually in some outlying
church or school, or at a local convention arranged by a
group of churches, God broke through the increasingly
formal ways of worship and teaching of the truths of the
Bible. On such occasions, following some public confession of sin or reconciliation between estranged co-
workers; between husbands and wives; or teachers and
their pupils; a deep conviction of sin would be experienced followed by the exuberant joy of the assurance of
sins forgiven. Such events, however, became less frequent and were largely confined to the older generation
and among those who remembered the days of revival.

Many new missionaries, hearing some details of the
momentous events of past years but seeing little around
them that was unusual, asked what revival was all about!
Unfortunately, stories of those years concentrated on
the startling and dramatic. Less appears to have been
passed on of the spiritual battles which had been fought

and of the deep fellowship experienced. Some missionaries entered immediately into the heritage of fellowship which existed in many places; others felt disillusioned, believing that they had been misled.

During the 1950's and 1960's there was a great deal of activity in every area of missionary work in all the three territories. Medical work was straining missionary resources in personnel and finances, educational work required all the energies of the increasing number of teachers in church schools and administration, and the few ordained missionaries engaged in training a church leadership felt understaffed for their task. The spiritual needs of both missionaries and Africans were greater than ever, but there seemed to be less time to seek the God who had worked so greatly in the past.

In the mid to late 1960's, God began to work again in two unexpected ways – firstly in some missionaries and then among the youth.

John and Doreen Sharp led the medical team at Kisiizi Hospital in Uganda. In May 1965, he wrote from Kisiizi Hospital,

"We want you to know that for the past few months things here have been difficult spiritually. Many of the Christian staff who are normally happy and ready to speak about the Lord Jesus and what He is doing for them, have been silent or apparently half-hearted. Then, with the help of others, we had to discipline some Christians and non-Christians for immorality . . . We are hoping to have a Mission at Whitsun but do not yet know if this will prove possible."

Later that year, he wrote, "We are praising God for His blessing on us and for your answered prayers . . . There was no Mission at Whitsun but many attended the Kabale Convention. This was a good time but we wished for more power in the meetings. How easy to become so familiar with Christian truths and yet they can lack vitality if God's power is not there. We praise for news of God's gracious working in many parts of the world in many different denominations, through a fresh understanding of the Person and work of the Holy Spirit. We are especially thankful to our Lord for giving Doreen and myself a share in this experience – new and yet as old as the Acts of the Apostles. We were much helped during our holidays through contacts with those whom the Lord Jesus has baptized with His Spirit in Kenya, and also through reading the New Testament again in an attitude of prayer and expectancy. Now the Lord has begun to work in Kisiizi and in other places – some have been filled with His Spirit and others have an awakening awareness of what the Lord can do for them."

John and Doreen gave testimony to fellow missionaries to the way God had blessed them. It was at this time that the first signs of John's illness appeared. In February 1966, John and Doreen returned to the UK. John was diagnosed as suffering from a serious brain tumour. They did not return to the field.

Before leaving the work, a number of missionaries, having heard of John's and Doreen's experience, contacted them and indicated that God had met them too, in similar ways. A number were experiencing the gift of tongues, were given discernment of evil spirits and were praying for miraculous healing of the sick.

"Wherever I went," commented Bill Butler, on one of his visits as General Secretary of the Mission, "missionaries were playing Fountain Trust cassettes." Many missionaries testified to a new blessing in their lives but this was almost always as individuals and not so much in fellowship with others, as had been the case in times of revival.

Far from receiving encouragement there appeared to be considerable opposition to this apparent challenge to the new expressions of revival, coming mainly from older missionaries and senior Africans. Nevertheless, more missionaries now spoke of what God was doing in them through what was understood to be Renewal, than those who spoke with experience of Revival days!

The second strand in the new way God was working began at Shyogwe, in Rwanda. In 1969, Festo Kivengere visited all the Mission centres in Rwanda and Burundi and met little response except at Shyogwe. While there he spoke to the students of the secondary school. They were predominantly boys but three girls came under conviction of sin. They stood up before the rest of the school and testified that God had spoken to them. Little further happened immediately, but those three girls were to be used greatly in the days to come.

The scene of action then moved to Kigeme. In 1965, Doreen Peck had started a school there for girl auxiliary teachers (*Ecole de Monitrices Auxiliaires*). Doreen was succeeded by Mabel Jones the following year.

In September 1967, the first class of a higher level school for girls began on a very modest scale. The girls, who would otherwise have little hope of studies beyond the primary level, were thrilled to be on the ladder leading to higher education and competition for entry was great.

Some parents of disappointed girls went to sorcerers in an effort to put curses on the successful ones. One girl failed to turn up in January 1968. Mabel Jones takes up the story:

"We asked permission to visit her and pray for her. As we approached the house, the noise of the girl's shouting could be heard. We prayed for her deliverance. It was a beginning, but we didn't realise what a battle it would be before she was set free. On her return she stayed in my house for five days. The next day the parents visited her and while I was fetching coffee for them, a conversation began between the demons in the girl in her room and the demons in the mother in the sitting room. I read Deuteronomy 18:9–12 and tried to tell the mother who was a powerful sorceress what the Lord thought of such practices. The following days were pretty traumatic. There was great pressure from the uncle, a witchdoctor, and the mother, and there were great battles. The demons were many and very wily. Two brothers came and took her home. I felt very sad. After some weeks the father brought her back and she was supposed to be 'cured', but most evenings a group of girls would call us to the dormitory. What a joy it was that most of the girls were able to see for themselves the power of the sword of the Spirit. The demons hated hymns of praise. The girls learnt how to pray and use the Bible.''

In order to relieve the pressure on the girls, another house was made available and six of the girl's friends volunteered to sleep in the same house. All went well for a time but political agitators took advantage of the house's isolation. They stirred up hatred among the girls and this spread to the rest of the school, coming to a crisis in July 1969. The term ended with the girls being sent home a day early.

The following term a change was discerned. Many of the girls came to the voluntary prayer meetings and were keen to read their Bibles. Attendance at the weekly fellowship meetings grew steadily.

As in 1936, so in 1970, God began to move in a remarkable way in a girls' school in which spiritual war was being waged against satanic forces. The power of sorcery and witchcraft, now reinforced by political and racial hatred, was focused on a few girls at Kigeme Girls' School, some of whom were the victims of demonic powers while others were seeking the victory which they knew came through Christ alone.

On 13th January 1970, the girls met for their weekly meeting. About 80 girls tried to squeeze into the little *kazu* (prayer hut). It was typical of many such buildings. Circular in shape, built of mud-bricks and thatched with grass, with a seat all the way round on the inside except for the doorway. Above the seats rectangular openings served as windows to let in air and light – and through which people could look in!

"I remember distinctly," continued Mabel, "we sang a hymn, which was really a prayer, that the Holy Spirit would come down and fill our hearts with a flame of love and burn up all the hatred and jealousy. This really happened. The girls (deeply divided on tribal lines), began to repent and get reconciled to each other. They repented of having sticks hidden in their mattresses which they were going to use to beat each other up at the end of term!"

Then followed jubilant expressions of liberty and joy. From outside the hut they "queued up at the windows to testify," remembered Mabel. "Later we went up the hill together in the dark singing."

Later still, Mabel supervised the girls doing their homework. "I had started to mark exercise books but one girl was already on her feet testifying. I was handed a hymnbook and a Bible and we continued until 'lights out'."

From then onwards the students had to abandon the prayer-hut for fellowship meetings and use the new, more spacious dining-hall. The hospital staff began to join them, and also teachers, carpenters and other workers. "At first some came out of curiosity or 'for fun'," observed Mabel, "then the lads and lasses from the local market began coming. One lad, a real tough, asked for prayer for his older brother who was even tougher. Now too he is saved. The rest of the family are coming to see 'what happens up there'!"

And the battle against satanic powers continued. Frequently, in the days that followed, groups of girls would stay up late into the night, praying for and seeking to help, those of their number whom they recognised as being "demonised". In a way that was well-known to

Africans, demons spoke through girls so possessed while in a trance, using strange voices, blaspheming and acting in a violent manner. A number of girls were delivered from satanic possession but only after much prayer and prolonged "spiritual warfare". Then, as in the past, signs of God working in power were accompanied by signs of spiritual battle against evil forces.

Soon after this all the secondary schools in the country sent delegations to a special public event at Gitarama, the nearest township to Shyogwe. The girls from the Kigeme school made a banner with the words, in Kinyarwanda, TRUTH AND LOVE and depicting a flaming torch and a dove. This they held joyfully aloft in the procession through Gitarama!

While lodging at Shyogwe, the girls asked if they could give their testimonies to the students at the boys' secondary school. It was agreed that one girl only should give her testimony at morning prayers. She did not speak for long but told with great boldness and authority how God had worked in her. The boys were amazed that a girl would dare to stand up and give her testimony in front of all of them. It acted like a spark igniting dry grass. After the prayers were ended the girls were questioned by the boys. Some of the young men there were 'saved' then and a number played a leading role in the years that followed as young people caught the fire.

At the ETFP (*Ecole Technique Féminine Presbytérienne*), the girls' school at Remera, the headmistress, Mlle Geertje DeCombe, Mlle Jacqueline Lugtenborg (both missionaries of the SBMP), and Concessa, the Rwandan school secretary, had been praying that revival would reach their school.

"In May 1970," wrote Jacqueline, "the MEPRA (*Mouvement des Etudiants Protestants au Rwanda*) invited two of our students for a meeting in Shyogwe. One of them was Thamar Hitimana (daughter of the African

Presbyterian Pastor). They met some girls from Kigeme and students from Shyogwe who told them about the wonderful things that had happened at Kigeme. Thamar and Ruth came back completely changed. The Lord had done a new thing for them. That was the beginning of the revival in our school."

Seven of the girls, with Jacqueline Lugtenborg, attended a Scripture Union camp at Shyogwe. On returning to Remera, the joy they expressed was evidence of the way God had changed them. "A wave of curiosity and expectancy swept through the school," remembers Jacqueline. "At the next weekly Bible Study and Prayer Meeting almost the whole school attended. It was then that the Holy Spirit came. In an atmosphere of quiet and deep reverence clear testimonies were given and many girls expressed their desire to accept Jesus as Lord."

During the renewed outburst of God's working at Kigeme, Maureen New was posted as nurse to the hospital there. "The hardened hearts of the nurses began to melt as they witnessed the changed lives of the school girls and heard their testimonies," she wrote. "One of the hardest nurses had a vision of Jesus on the cross when she went to bed and she sobbed as she saw large nails in His hands and feet and the blood running down His brow. She came to hospital the next morning, "a new creature in Christ". Others quickly followed her. Their repentance of sin was real and costly – they returned to me drugs and dressings they had stolen from the hospital . . . the most wonderful sight was to see their loving care of the patients without us having to check whether it was being done."

Also at Kigeme, the nurse, Elspeth Cole, knew of the demonic power of sorcery which had been experienced in the girls' school. She wrote home at that time about a child in the hospital who had been unconscious for nearly twelve weeks. The Doctor could find no medical cause for his unconscious state. During this time his father became a Christian and he was completely changed from being an aggressive, difficult person to one who spent his time in helping others. "We often saw him reading his Bible with other patients whose children were ill, comforting them and speaking of Jesus. Maureen New and I often spoke together and prayed about this child's strange illness."

During the next few days, Elspeth continued to pray for guidance until one morning,

"I turned to my Bible reading for that day: 2 Chronicles 28, which tells of spiritual corruption and idol-worship. In it God confirmed His words to my heart. I shared this with the other missionaries and God showed us that we must tell the father that God had shown us that witchcraft was behind his son's illness. I asked him if any among his family or friends were involved in witchcraft. 'Yes', he said, 'I was. But I have given it all up now.'

"So we saw the opening that Satan had used. We went back to the ward and, with the African nurse working there, we prayed with him for his child. We prayed that all the satanic work be undone in the Name of Jesus, then again in Jesus' Name that this child be healed completely and saved to bring glory to Him alone. A short, simple prayer, that was all. Next morning as I helped the nurses to wash the patients we heard a loud cry. We rushed over to the boy's bed. 'What do you want?' we asked, calling him by name. He saw us. He tried to sit up and answer us. After three months of unconsciousness he was conscious! A few hours later he began to swallow milk from a spoon. Four days later he was enjoying sweet potatoes and attempting to walk a few steps with our help. The next day I left Kigeme to work at Gahini but I know that in answer to many prayers the boy has recovered, a living proof of the power of the Lord Jesus Whose we are and Whom we serve."

That God was working among the young people at Kigeme and elsewhere was evident, but there was no recognised leadership to guide them as had been the case in the early days of revival. What the old conventions were to revival, Scripture Union camps became to the new movement of God's Spirit.

Camps for youth were not new. The first SU camp under canvas had been attended by 45 girls and four officers at Gisenyi, on the shores of lake Kivu in 1958. Phil Hindley, who organised the camp, wrote of the event:

"For the past three years we have had camps during the Easter holidays, but this year it was different. Tents have been known by the girls for a long time as the 'houses' that the missionaries take with them when they go on 'safari', but this year the girls themselves were to sleep in tents . . . We were able to pitch our tents on a wonderful grassy site, reserved for us by the Belgian Administrator. From under the shade of big trees there was an unobstructed view of the Lake which was only about 100 yards away . . . Each day we started with a meeting, sitting by the edge of the lake, when we read together the SU portion and remembered other times when Jesus called, 'Come and follow Me'. The afternoon meetings were held under the shade of the trees when with flannelgraph illustrations we saw the two hearts, one ruled by Satan and one ruled by Christ, and Jesus again called, 'Give Me your heart'."

Also in 1958, Nina Putman recorded, "In December we were very pleased to welcome about 150 children from outschools for a special Children's Weekend. Dr and Mrs Adeney were in charge of the meetings and many children had a real hunger to hear more of the Lord Jesus, and were all especially thrilled to see slides of *Pilgrim's Progress*. The outschool children slept on dried grass in the classrooms, packed close together to keep each other warm. We did a 10:00 pm round and found them all with beaming faces, obviously enjoying every moment. It was quite evident, too, that they were full of beans (and sweet potato)!"

A camp for boys from schools at Butare and Shyogwe in Rwanda, and from Kibimba and Bujumbura in Burundi, was held at Bufundi, a peninsula on Lake Bunyonyi in Uganda, in July 1960. The 76 campers were led by missionaries and Africans. Pat Brooks reported: "You will remember that July was a time of tension, following on the Independence of Congo, and refugees were streaming through Uganda. However, we felt that God was telling us to go straight ahead and, as we did so, the way opened up wonderfully . . . At the time, there did not seem to be very many visible results but I have heard since that a number of boys made definite decisions there. It was surely a significant time in the lives of many."

In 1961 a girls' camp on the shores of Lake Bunyonyi included a visit to Bwama, the leprosy settlement. "That evening," wrote Phyllis Hindley, "round the camp fire, one after another testified to re-consecration and others to a vision of what the Lord Jesus wanted of them. Many realised afresh what they owed to Jesus because they had so much, while many of the patients they had seen were maimed, some blind and quite a number without hands or toes or feet and yet full of the joy of the Lord and praising Him."

There was, after this, a gap of some ten years during which camps were impracticable because of political tension and violence. When Peter and Elisabeth returned to Africa from leave in 1969 it was as SU workers.

"When the blessing began to come and people were saved at Kigeme," said Peter, "we just had to organise camps. From the first camp at Shyogwe in 1971, things 'took off' and the camps ran themselves! Campers came from all over Rwanda, from different churches, including the Pentecostal churches. The fellowship meetings in those days would go on all night. People would be saved and there was great joy in receiving those coming to the cross with their sins."

On one occasion, a boy who had just been saved was tossed into the air by the others as they welcomed him in their delight. A missionary from the Presbyterian Church was heard to ask, "Is this a new form of confirmation?" A Pastor of the Presbyterian Church, Naasoni Hitimana, was greatly used in those camps. They were characterised by remarkable times of prayer as the young people came to know the reality of a living and present Christ among them.

A year prior to the "rekindling of the fire" in the girls' school at Kigeme, a new missionary couple were posted to Shyogwe for youth work with the special task of developing the Boys' and Girls' Brigades. The Rev. Eric and Ruth Townson found themselves immediately involved in this upsurge of spiritual life among young people. "I saw myself as a youth evangelist," Eric affirmed. "I had offered as a missionary and had just been converted at Liskeard Lodge (CMS missionary training centre). I was born again and filled with the Spirit. I talked with various people in the college; some did not understand at all and thought that I had had a nervous breakdown; others said 'Praise the Lord' this is revival, this is what happened in East Africa."

Eric found himself in a dilemma. He welcomed all the evidences of revival which were still being manifested, but he also recognised the reality of experiences which could all too easily be considered as "pentecostal" in character. He met strong resistance from church leaders against what they considered to be "non-Anglican" activities.

From his own experience, Eric recognised that it was

useless to train youth leaders in techniques and skills and
give them material help, if they were not "saved". The
spiritual side of the work had to come first. If the leaders
were not motivated for spiritual reasons they would give
up as soon as the missionary with his money and expertise moved on. This attitude was highly unpopular with
some church leaders.

"I had no Boys' Brigade experience," Eric explained,
"but I saw that this was a tool that could be used to get
alongside young people and as a Mission we were
already involved in it. When we got out there, I discovered that, as far as the church was concerned, what I
had gone out for was to put the Boys' and Girls' Brigades
on the map – to give them status. I could see danger
there and that proved to be true when, later, the political
coup occurred. The Boys' Brigade folded up then because it was based on marching and uniforms which we
were not allowed to do any more. That did not break my
heart. We kept on the Bible Studies, the leadership
training and the games." Eric's quiet and discerning
counsel was sought by many of the young people among
whom God was working so powerfully.

Eric and Ruth visited every church centre where there
was a Boys' or Girls' Brigade Company, or the possibility of starting one, to run courses for leaders. He
wrote of one such visit: "The course in Kigeme resulted
in at least twelve new Boys' Brigades and we are not sure
how many Girls' Brigades. We praise the Lord because
on our visits to parishes at least four youth leaders have
been saved . . . In the parishes we have witnessed
miracles – we have been given real freedom by the Lord
to speak in Kinyarwanda where necessary and to discern
what is happening though hearing very little. What a joy
to see the team absolutely on fire for the Lord, pouring
their hearts out to vast congregations. We could weep
with joy and often do."

On one occasion he visited Kigeme and on seeing what God was doing among the girls there, he invited one of them to Gahini. There she spoke in church to a congregation which included the staff of the Bible School and the teachers and boys of the secondary school. "She had tremendous authority," wrote Eric. "Although there were some who, in their ignorance, mocked; the ground had been well prepared beforehand by the Holy Spirit and many of those boys accepted Christ into their lives. In the afternoon 45 of the boys came to seek for Jesus. Three weeks later nearly every boy in the school testified to new birth in Christ."

At this time, one feature of life among the youth of the country concerned Peter and Elisabeth greatly. They could recall the 1940's and 1950's when one result of God's work among young people in Uganda was that saved young men began to look for marriage partners who were also committed Christians. The *Abalokole* saw the importance of "marriage in the Lord". This had never been accepted in the same way in Rwanda and Burundi. Exceptions were Eustace and Marion Kajuga, and Yona and Mary Kanamuzeyi in Rwanda; and Paulo and Dorotiya Rutwe in Burundi. All three men were ordained and, with their wives, were greatly used by God.

"When the blessing came at Kigeme in the early 70's," commented Peter Guillebaud, "Elisabeth and I had a great burden for this. What distressed us was that saved boys were not asking for saved girls in marriage! They would look rather for someone who was good at cultivating or of whom the family approved or whom they felt would give them a good home. The Christian girl seeing this, thought that she would never get a Christian boy so she had better take the first boy who came along."

The Scripture Union camps proved ideal occasions to

pursue this theme. The camp programmes always included a session on Christian engagement and marriage. Peter and Elisabeth noted that, "on those occasions they listened politely but were not at all amenable to what they took to be our western ideas". Then, in January 1975, Paulo and Dorotiya Rutwe were invited to a camp at Shyogwe. Paulo handled this subject with a very light touch. He said that he was so determined to find a saved wife that he crossed the Akanyaru (the river separating Burundi from Rwanda) to find one – incredible! The story was told of one *Mulokole* in Uganda who was being pressed to get engaged before he went to study in Europe because by the time he returned all the nice *balokole* girls would have been snapped up. "Oh No!" he replied, "God has a cupboard full of nice *balokole* girls and when I come home He will open the door and mine will come out!"

Turning to his wife Dorotiya, Paulo said that he prayed, "Thank you God for keeping this girl in your cupboard for me!" The campers got the message! From that time the saved boys began asking for Christian girls. Christian girls saw that they were being asked for and they waited. Elisabeth remembered that "within two or three years there were about 40 couples that we were praying for who were starting up Christian homes."

In Burundi, as in Rwanda, the new life shown by young people was not always appreciated by the African church leadership. Paul and Lucie Bell wrote of "minirevivals" a few weeks before the 1972 troubles and again in 1980. "Teams began to go out as far afield as Nyabigina," wrote Paul. "Hymns were composed in *Kirundi* and things began to move ahead among the young people. Indeed, I felt the church at that time was rather like a cheese we bought once from a local farm. It had been stored too near the oven. Lucie brought it to me one morning looking like a Michelin tyre and emitting a menacing hissing noise. The young people were like the active middle and the church hierarchy like the restraining rind!"

A new feature of God's working occurred in the Roman Catholic Church. "While in 1970, the Spirit worked first in Anglican schools, then among the Presbyterians and other churches," wrote Peter Guillebaud, "since 1973 we have seen something quite new: the mushroom growth of 'Catholic charismatic prayer groups' (a term which out here often means no more than a free prayer meeting based on Scripture, something that is quite new to Catholics). It is true to say that in many places it is the Catholics who have taken the initiative in starting prayer cells, and the blessing that is resulting is two-way, to them and to us."

That God was at work in the youth of Rwanda and Burundi was undoubted. Many were brought to Christ and God raised up leaders from among them. God does not necessarily work in exactly the same way in each generation. Youth had "caught the fire" in the 1970's it is true, but it was also among young people that the "fire burst into flame" in the 1930's. Yesterday's boys and girls become today's old men and women! Africans, especially at Gahini, who had known God working in revival in the old days, began to feel spiritual oneness with younger men and women who were, in their turn, seeking to know the power of God in their lives. From the 1970's onwards, there was a greater recognition of gifts of the Holy Spirit but whenever there was a deep work of God, there was always repentance, confession, restitution, joy in sins forgiven, great praise, lively prayer and powerful witness to the reality of the living Christ.

Chapter 16

The partnership years 1966–1973

"*Parentalism* is 'out', but *partnership* is very much in," pronounced Lawrence Barham as the retiring Bishop of Ruanda-Urundi. The churches which the Ruanda Mission had founded had "come of age". "In March 1966, the final stage of this important development took place when the former diocese of Ruanda-Urundi disappeared and its missionary bishop also, and the two bishops were installed as diocesans over the two new dioceses, one of Rwanda, the other of Burundi." Partnership in an advisory capacity was exercised, in Rwanda by Canon Albert Brown, and in Burundi by Canon Ian Leakey.

In an unexpected move, Dick Lyth was consecrated Bishop of Kigezi in January 1967. This was at the express request of the African leadership despite protests that an African bishop would be more appropriate at that stage in the country's development. In the context of existing tribal divisions, an expatriate would be able to exercise an impartial influence, it was affirmed, until a suitable national was found.

At the first Diocesan Council at which he presided as bishop, in January 1967, Dick asked the members what they considered they should concentrate on in the new diocese. Stewardship, finance, administration were proposed but, after considerable discussion, it was decided to ask God for a mission to the diocese.

"In July of that year," reported Dick, "200 missioners came invited from different parts of Uganda and Rwanda. Four by four they visited every part of the district, into schools, hospitals and dispensaries, churches, police stations and prisons; markets, bus stations and drinking places – wherever there were people, the Gospel of the redeeming love of God was preached and testimonies were given during the whole of those two weeks. Everywhere there was an immediate and overwhelming response, and literally thousands of men and women and boys and girls gave their lives to Christ. Many wonderful reconciliations followed, often with restitutions and restorations. Many a headmaster's table and police station desk were piled high with things that had been stolen. Of course, sadly many of those who gave their lives to God at that time took them back again, but the church was never the same again. And naturally the giving was doubled in the first year, doubled again the next year, and has continued at a very high level ever since."

Itself the product of missionary activity, the diocese determined to promote a missionary outreach. The giving at Pentecost each year was to be devoted to this end. This determination was focused in a visit from the Rev. Janani Luwum, later to become Archbishop of Uganda and die a martyr's death. He gave his testimony as one who had spent nearly all his ordained life serving God away from his own homeland. He ended by appealing for men and women to do the same and to go as missionaries outside Kigezi. Six men responded to this call and, supported by the mission fund of the diocese, went off to serve God in distant places: two to the wild people of Karamoja, another to the west of Uganda, two to join the army as chaplains and one to England for six months to preach the gospel and to share his testimony and the testimony of the church.

At the end of 1966, the first Missionaries' Conference after Independence, took place at Kabale. Writing about this later, Ian Leakey commented that it was, "held against the background of some speculation as to whether it was tactful these days for a large number of missionaries to come together for meetings." The main theme of the conference was the new relationship of missionaries to the church leadership. Among the questions discussed was who should be pastorally responsible for the spiritual welfare of missionaries working under African bishops. Bishops traditionally fulfilled this role in Anglican thinking and it was decided to follow this path in the new church situation.

Whatever may have been the historical reasons, the leadership of the churches in Rwanda and Burundi lagged behind that of Uganda. At the conference Ian Leakey pointed to the "considerable contribution in manpower" which the missionaries still constituted and also to the delicate situations in which they would have to work under the authority of an African leadership that was not yet fully effective.

The office of Field Secretary was replaced by that of a Mission Representative in each territory. Efforts would be made to combine an effective caring for missionaries from the UK with a rightful subjection to church leadership authority. This required much behind-the-scenes discussion, thought and prayer as well as more frequent visits from the UK to Africa of the General and Home Secretaries.

In the Kigezi Church, apart from Bishop Dick Lyth, the only missionary involvement was in the Canon Barham Divinity School where, in 1963, the Rev. Andrew Bowman was appointed Principal. The training of ordinands began in that year. Andrew returned to the UK for leave at the end of 1965.

An unusual event occurred at Kabale on the first day of 1968. The District Council of Kigezi organised a celebration in honour of the foundation of the Republic of Uganda. Six "foreigners to Kigezi", three from elsewhere in Uganda, a Roman Catholic priest and two Protestant missionaries, Constance Hornby and Algie Stanley Smith, received symbolic "blood-brotherhood". In a simple "old-time ritual ceremony", each of the six was honoured for their services to Kigezi. Algie Stanley Smith described the proceedings:

"The Secretary-General of Kigezi, as titular head of the District and clothed in every-day dress with an open shirt, stood before the people, wearing a short brown cloth robe lined with flesh-coloured cloth to represent the traditonal goatskin worn in the old days by the men of Kigezi. He held a spear and a bill-hook, (the emblem of Kigezi), and recited the deeds and services rendered by each one in his turn. In my case he mentioned specially medical services, and the translation of the Bible into the language of the District."

After a similar recitation of Miss Hornby's services to Kigezi, the Speaker of the district Council, acting as the Master of Ceremonies, called out in a loud voice to the people, referring to each candidate in turn, "Is there any reason why this man (or woman) should not be admitted to our blood-brotherhood?"

And each time all the people answered, "No!"

"The Secretary General mounted the table," continued Algie Stanley Smith, "and sat down on a stool, and I followed on the other opposite him. The Master of Ceremonies first turned to the Secretary General of Kigezi and said for all to hear, "You, Secretary-General of Kigezi, you have in the name of the people of Kigezi, made blood-brotherhood with Dr Simiisi. If ever Kigezi

lets him down, may this oath turn back on it!" Then
turning to me he said, "Simiisi, we have allowed you this
day to make blood-brotherhood with the people of
Kigezi. If you ever let men down or betray them, may
this oath turn back on you! . . . From now onwards we
give you a new name, *Rugangura* (Overcomer), because
of your victorious struggle against sickness and Satan,
which when you came here you found robbing us of
peace. Hail *Rugangura!*"

Constance Hornby was named *Kaa-ka* (Grandma),
"for she has been a true 'Mother' to the women and girls
of Kigezi."

In his speech of thanks, Algie Stanley Smith replied,
"What a remarkable thing it is that this custom of
Omukago was so very widely practised among the
nations; a sign that the 'partaking of the blood ends the
enmity between man and man, and between clan and
clan; and this is surely a God-given parable of the
'precious blood of Christ', the only means by which
we can be reconciled to God, and thereby admitted
into that blood brotherhood in our Lord which is
now uniting people of every tribe and culture in the
world."

In the years 1962 to 1965, just prior to the churches
becoming independent, events took place in a most
unexpected quarter, which were to influence greatly the
atmosphere of Protestant church work in all the three
territories in which the Mission was working, but especially in Rwanda and Burundi. It was at this time that
the Roman Catholic Church held its Second Vatican
Council. Whatever may or may not have been changed
in that Church's structures and doctrines, the transformation in the attitudes of many Roman Catholic priests
and laity to Protestants was dramatic indeed in Africa, if
not equally so in Europe. The phrase, "Since Vatican
Two . . .", became a kind of passport to relationships

between Roman Catholic and Protestant missionaries which often became as friendly and helpful as they had been hostile and antagonistic in the past. Some mistrust continued, however, between African leaders of both churches.

Equally dramatic was the changed Roman Catholic attitude to the reading of the Bible. Considered dangerous in the past, reading it was now being openly advocated. Where there were Protestant vernacular translations of the Scriptures, as in Kigezi-Ankole, Rwanda and Burundi, Roman Catholics were recommended to read these until such time as officially accepted versions were available. At one time, the sale of Bibles to Roman Catholics exceeded that to Protestants! The effects of this revolution were incalculable.

On the 14th March 1965, tragedy struck in the sad death of the Rev. John A. Clayton. John had come on to the staff at the Theological College at Buye in order to help implement the higher level theological ordination training. On that Sunday morning he had been writing a circular letter when three Africans broke into the house with the intention of robbing the safe which contained College money. They were drunk and shouted in a garbled mixture of French, Kinyarwanda and Kiswahili. One of the men opened fire with an automatic gun. He had never handled such a weapon before. Bullets rained everywhere indiscriminately and two hit John. He died an hour later. He was sorely missed. Barbara, his wife, a nurse, returned to the UK later that year with her baby daughter.

The team at the Buye Theological College was now reduced to two missionary couples – Ian and Joyce Leakey, posted to Buye on the death of John Clayton – and Keith and Ruth Anderson; and a French-speaking ordained African, Samwuel Ndayisenga, who became the Principal of Buye Bible School. The higher level ordinands' course in French was stopped and the students were found places at other theological colleges in East Africa.

In Burundi the position of Bishop Yohana Nkunzum- wami was particularly difficult. Three factors played important roles – race, churchmanship and social in- tegration. Burundi society was dominated by the min- ority *Tutsi*, the reverse of the situation in Rwanda. The Bishop was a *Hutu*. This made it almost impossible for him to be an effective leader, particularly when dealing with officials of the Government. It is difficult for those not deeply immersed in the culture to under- stand the fear that inter-ethnic pressures produce. This was coupled with the traditional 'big-chief' view of leadership which militated against a sharing of responsibilities.

The ordinary clergy also seemed to be frustrated by their lack of preparation for leadership. This was illus- trated by their reactions to a visit to Buye, in 1969, of Terry Waite, who led a Provincial Training Team from Kampala to the Diocese of Burundi.

"The aim was to help the church leaders to see what resources they had within themselves for solving their own problems," recorded Keith Anderson. "Terry Waite led the sessions very well indeed. Two thirds of the way through the second day there was an explosion of anger from the Burun- di pastors who objected to the methodology being used by Terry to get the pastors together in small groups with tasks to identify and suggest solutions to their felt needs. Their objection was that the expert from Kampala was the person who had all the answers because he was their 'teacher', so why did he keep asking them to discuss questions in groups to which he already knew the answers? . . . So the group discussion method was dropped and Terry had to 'lecture' to the group which was what they had expected and wanted.

They felt more secure having others come and tell them the answers."

The first years of Church independence in Burundi were made more difficult by the influence of two men, Wilson Makokwe and Eustace Kinama. Wilson completed his training as a teacher at the Alliance teacher training institution at Kibimba in 1960, the same year that Eustace Kinama was ordained by Bishop Jim Brazier after completing the ordination course at Buye. In their different ways, both men were visionaries in that they held high hopes for the future of their Church in an independent Burundi. They were both very critical of the inadequacies of missionary development of Africans. Pat Brooks recalls a remark of Wilson Makokwe which typified the attitude of both men. Referring to a senior African leader of the Burundi Church, Wilson said, "He is typical of what you Europeans have done. You've got people to a certain stage and no further. He is like the man Jesus touched who saw men as trees walking but needed a second touch. You have left us after the first touch!" The second touch to which he referred had a very strong ethnic-political emphasis. Wilson was eventually ordained by Bishop Yohana Nkunzumwami.

Wilson was posted to Bujumbura to fill three different posts in the Protestant Alliance and Burundi Episcopal Church. He was eventually found guilty of financial malpractice and defrocked but not before his influence had caused a great deal of damage to the church. Eustace Kinama was posted to Matana where, as a strong *Hutu* nationalist, he influenced the local Church against the Bishop. He too was defrocked. For several years the influence of these two men brought division to the church as feelings were roused against both whites and their own leaders.

A major concern of Keith Anderson was to explain and gain the acceptance of the aims and methods of Theological Education by Extension (TEE). It was rejected on two principal grounds. The first was that TEE had been introduced some eight or nine years before then in Guatamala by the Presbyterian Church. "The idea was thought to be un-Anglican," commented Keith, "and my attempts to persuade the church to take it up were viewed as attempts to subvert the Church from its Anglican roots and turn it into a Presbyterian one!" The second objection arose from the aim of TEE to extend theological training away from the Bible School to the parish where the pastor could apply his study to his own situation. This was construed as depriving clergy of formal instruction in a residential institution culminating in a diploma.

The threat, as it appeared, of "Presbyterianising" the Church reflected the "churchmanship" tensions. The missionaries' aim of the establishment of a united, truly African, evangelically based Church was met by two even greater pressures from the newly independent Church. The first was the very strong criticism on the part of the group led by Wilson Makokwe, that the Anglican Church was foreign to Burundi and to Africans in general. The group broke away from the main body of the Church but, after a few years, disintegrated because of the corruption of its leadership.

The second pressure was in the opposite direction, that of integrating the Church more completely with the world-wide Anglican fellowship. Keith Anderson illustrated this by two incidents. "I well remember the day at the Bible School at Buye when I walked into the Chapel to take an afternoon lesson only to discover that the Principal had installed a communion rail thus marking a division of rank between clergy and laity. It was clear to me that traditional views of Burundi social structures were being read into the Bible and used to establish a "pyramid" model of leadership in the Church – the model is almost endemic in Anglicanism anyway. I remember sitting later at my teaching desk in front of the class for about five minutes or more with my head in my hands almost in tears as I thought of the theological implications for the future development of the church that this symbolic act of installing the rail would mean."

At about that time the Principal of the Bible School persuaded the Bishop to introduce the wearing of stoles because this was the way the majority of clergy dressed for worship in England and in the rest of Anglicanism. It was clear that strong elements of the Church leadership believed that the Evangelical stance of the missionary clergy was a form of colonialism by which they were trying to prevent the Burundi Church from entering into the fullness of the world-wide Anglican Church. "The demand for (foreign) catholicity in vestment," commented Keith Anderson, "became, rather strangely, a rallying point for African nationalistic identity! Had the move been towards more authentically African styles of worship and dress I think we would have had less misgiving. . . . We knew that we were powerless in the independent nature of the church to do anything about these trends."

The political violence of 1972 made any further attempts to further the TEE ideal impossible and the following year Keith and Ruth Anderson moved to Nakuru in Kenya where the project was much more openly received and achieved a great measure of acceptance and success. In 1972, Ian and Joyce Leakey returned to the UK. There was no further missionary involvement in the staffing of Buye Bible School.

When Rwanda became an independent diocese, Albert and Joan Brown moved to Gahini to establish the

Church training centre for the diocese. In November 1965, the first twelve deacons to be trained in Rwanda were ordained at Gahini.

"Since we started the theological college here two years ago," wrote Albert Brown, "we have had no name. We've simply been 'The College' at Gahini. However, last August, at the Diocesan Synod the naming of the college was carefully debated by the church leaders. It was interesting to hear them discussing past and present missionaries and other Christians whose name might be given to it. The final decision was that we should be called the Stanley-Smith College. We must be one of the few theological colleges in the world to be named after a medical doctor!"

"There are few professions that involve a man's wife as much as the ordained ministry of the Church," wrote Joan Brown. "For this reason when our new college was opened here for Rwanda we followed the tradition, started by Julia Barham and maintained by Catherine Lindsay at Ibuye, of running a course for the wives of the men in training. This course covers practical subjects such as cooking, sewing, hygiene, housewifery, writing as well as Scripture, preparation for talks and the running of women's meetings. As the Mothers' Union is being introduced throughout our diocese we are giving special emphasis to this and the twelve wives will shortly be enrolled as members. We join daily with the men for the time of worship in the chapel. We hope that they will go out from here with not only the desire to be co-workers with their husbands in the Lord's work, but also to pass on to other women what they have learned . . . What we desire most of all for them is that their two years here will draw them into a closer walk with the Lord Jesus and give them a vision for work amongst other women."

Douglas Paterson joined the staff of the Stanley Smith Theological College in 1967. A year later Albert Brown was called to work with the Bishop in Kigali and Canon Eriya Kanyamubari was appointed Principal of the College. The need for missionary staff became so acute, however, that, in 1970, Bishop Sebununguri invited Malcolm and Jeanette Bole to return to Rwanda. Malcolm had already served a tour as a teacher. After leave and training at Oak Hill College, he had been ordained in 1967 and served a curacy in Yorkshire. From there he, with Jeanette, returned, in 1970, to the Stanley Smith Bible School at Gahini.

In addition to the ordinands drawn from the older, experienced church teachers, another class was started in that year. This was a smaller group, composed of younger men, all in their twenties, relatively well-educated, French-speaking but with little or no experience of church work.

With the background of his previous experience in education and now observing the church scene, Malcolm wrote,

"I felt strongly that far more attention should have been given to the catechists (church teachers). The worship and teaching of the indigenous church was largely in their hands and yet they were quietly despised, virtually unrewarded and offered little teaching. Among them were some fine and godly men. By contrast, huge resources were poured into the extravagant training of a few wealthy theological students, none of whom had any testimony to a living faith and some of whom had their eyes set on promotion and prestige rather than on serving the Lord among His people. Their names had normally been put forward by their local *bourgmasters* (local African government officials) for political reasons and the church seemed powerless to resist this. I began to feel that if the Holy Spirit was to bring blessing to the country it would have to come about apart from the church and that would be regrettable."

In 1972, the Stanley Smith Bible College at Gahini suffered a financial crisis and it was decided to close the school. Four from the 'advanced ordination course' were ordained and the remaining four students sent to the interdenominational *Ecole de Théologie* at Butare. Malcolm joined the staff, whose principal was a missionary of the Danish Baptist Mission.

Butare is the university town of Rwanda and the proximity of the theological school to the influences of the university soon became evident in unrest among the students. A number of strands could be observed. Some of the unrest in the School probably stemmed from what Malcolm Bole described as, "current differences of opinion about what is needed to train a pastor. The church attaches great importance to the teaching of what we call the 'prestige subjects': Greek, English, philosophy, typewriting, etc. The missionaries still emphasise the teaching of Bible subjects, doctrine and pastoralia. This leads to tension unless we agree to bolster the image of the pastor as a high-powered intellectual rather than the shepherd of his flock. We long to send men out to preach a clear Gospel to the ordinary folk in the country."

On a personal level Malcolm became the centre of some controversy. "Since September," he wrote, "I have been the object of continuous criticism by the students, and a regular flow of accusations has been sent by letter, without prior discussion, to the highest authority in the three churches. It has been tremendously hard to go on teaching in such an atmosphere. It is clear that such behaviour is common throughout the country these days and we are experiencing a reflection of the general unrest. What is disappointing is that it should come from future pastors. It makes us more than ever concerned that there should be more careful selection of candidates, so that those who come for training are able to testify both to their conversion and to their call to the ministry." The situation became intolerable and Malcolm and Jeanette Bole returned to the UK in 1973.

In 1972, Dick Lyth was succeeded by Festo Kivengere as Bishop of Kigezi, and Dick and Nora returned to the UK. Ian Leakey and Keith Anderson left Burundi, and Albert Brown, Malcolm Bole, Eric Townson and Douglas Paterson left Rwanda in 1972–3, making a total of seven ordained men and their families leaving the field in those two years. Only in Kigezi was there an ordained man remaining, Andrew Bowman, and he was involved in theological training.

An urgent need for the new dioceses in Rwanda and Burundi was for buildings in which to establish diocesan offices in the capitals of the countries. In response to requests, two substantial gifts to the Churches in Rwanda and Burundi were made from the Church in Canada in 1967. In Bujumbura, an existing building near the centre of the capital was acquired and this was used as the diocesan centre.

In Rwanda, three houses were built in Kigali, the first for the Bishop and the other two for Church officers. In 1968, Albert and Joan Brown were posted there with Albert as Chaplain to Bishop Adoniya Sebunguri.

As the churches in Rwanda and Burundi became more centred on towns and the church leadership concentrated in them, so grew the pressures of compromising with the world and the seeking of prestige and power. The Gospel was still being preached but the fire had gone. It was in the rural areas that God was still working in power; not everywhere, but enough to indicate that the flame was still alight. Eric Townson described a visit to a rural outschool.

"We have just spent the most fantastic weekend of our lives. I don't think we will ever forget it. After lunch on

Saturday we set off into the bush. As we got nearer to
Rukira, the country got wilder and wilder . . . When we
arrived the car was surrounded by the happiest people I
have ever seen. They were singing 'Tukutendereza', which
means Praise the Lamb . . . We woke to the sound of many
African voices . . . During the morning we felt something
happen to the crowd of nearly 2,000 people. We could feel
Jesus working . . . But straight after dinner Satan began to
attack, it was really uncanny . . . To cap it all a woman at the
convention started to have a baby. Everyone began to pray
for her but the baby was stuck and wouldn't be born. There
was no one else to take her to the hospital nearly 20 miles
away so I had to do so.

"When we got back we discovered that the talks had
finished and a time of open speaking had begun. The Pastor
gave the news that the baby had been born safely and the
crowd all praised God. Then suddenly I saw an opportunity
to talk about being born again. Then the Spirit really came
down. People confessed their sins and claimed the power of
Jesus. It was the most fantastic meeting I have ever seen.
People testified and sang praises. For minutes at a time they
sang 'Tukutendereza'. After the meetings had finished the
singing continued. People who had crossed each other were
making it up. Hands were waving in the air in sheer joy of
living. Every single face was spread out in a smile. As we
went to bed I felt a miracle had happened . . . I couldn't help
comparing this with Evensong in England. It seems so
wrong, humanly speaking, that such poor people, with
hardly enough to eat should have such joy when people in
England, with more than these people ever dreamed of,
should be so lacking in joy!"

Throughout the partnership years, medical work continued in the church hospitals of the three territories.
And, with church primary schools incorporated in the
government education system, missionary involvement
in education was concentrated at the secondary level.
Political upheavals in all three territories acted as a

restraint on all missionary activity at this time and made the holding of conventions virtually impossible.

Chapter 17

The church under fire 1972–1985

The revolution in Rwanda was a testing time for the church moving towards independence. Missionaries were in positions of leadership and it was easier for them than for nationals to remain impartial in ethnic-based, political differences, especially when these turned into violent conflict. By the early 1970's, peace had been restored and there appeared to be a genuine effort on the political front to integrate all sections of society into a unified nation. The choice of leaders was, at times, delicate. For the Church, this dilemma was more acute than for the government. It was not difficult for political leaders to be chosen on ethnic grounds. The majority ethnic group had triumphed in the revolution and political justifications were understandable. It was a more difficult problem in the church where spiritual qualifications were held to be more important than ethnic or political ones. In practice, leaders were chosen from the dominant ethnic grouping who were also considered to be spiritually fit for office. It was a time of great heart-searching for the African Christians involved and for the missionaries as they looked on. Fellowship was severely strained at times, but there was never any withdrawal of missionary support for the African leadership.

After political independence in all three countries, the violence seen in the Ruanda revolution was experienced in even more intense forms in Burundi and Uganda. The church was severely tested.

In Burundi, under the Belgian authorities, the king, Mwami Mwambutsa IV, continued to exercise his traditional authority until September 1961 when a provisional National Assembly was formed with the king's son, Prince Rwagasore, as leader of the dominant political party, which had a large majority. Trouble first occurred the next month, October, when Prince Rwagasore was assassinated by a Greek gunman in the pay of one of the leading families of the country. From that moment onwards any semblance of unity between representatives of the *Hutu* and the *Tutsi* elements began to disintegrate and power became concentrated more and more in *Tutsi* hands. Nevertheless, the hand-over from Belgian to independent government was achieved peacefully.

On the 18th October 1965, the king, Mwami Mwambutsa, was deposed. He fled to Europe and his son, Prince Charles Ndizeye, succeeded him as king. On the 28th November 1966, the Prince was deposed and Captain Micombero assumed power as Prime Minister of the *Conseil Supérieur du Pays*. Burundi was proclaimed a Republic.

Political control of the country deteriorated until, on 20th October 1971, Micombero set up an advisory body which he called the Supreme Revolutionary Council (*Conseil Suprème de la Révolution*) comprising 27 army officers. This appeared to release tremendous tensions in the country which Micombero could not contain and on 29th April 1972, he decided without any warning to dismiss all the members of his cabinet. Within a few hours the *Hutu* rose in rebellion.

The uprising was centred on Bujumbura and the southern provinces of Burundi. Within this area the rebels killed or wounded every *Tutsi* they could find – it is estimated that some 2,000 lost their lives.

The government forces then proceeded to prevent a recurrence of this uprising in the most systematic, efficient and ruthless way imaginable. Thousands of *Hutu*, especially the more educated and influential men from Government offices, business houses, banks, schools and churches, were rounded up, imprisoned and killed. Secondary schoolboys were herded into 'death lorries' and then disappeared. An estimate in *The Times* of London, gave the number of those who died in such ways at between 80,000 and 120,000.

The loss of *Hutu* workers to the country was enormous. Churches were denuded of their leaders. Buhiga hospital lost all its *Hutu* workers. Joan Nicholson described those days: "On the Friday after the first trouble, three men were arrested at Buhiga, two teachers and one hospital dresser. On the Sunday our Pastor and the head hospital dresser, two of our dearest brethren in the Lord, were taken. The following week we could hardly keep count – school teachers and supervisors, hospital workers, catechists, watchmen. We dreaded the sound of the lorries roaring round the hill knowing that soon the word would be secretly passed round: 'They've taken Mary's mother and Pastor X and Teacher Y'. Rumours were already rife, and later to be proved true, that those who were taken would never come back. Yet in the horror of it all, the strength and courage of some of our brethren awed and humbled us."

Everywhere the educated *Hutu*, even schoolboys, were arrested, executed by thousands, and buried in mass graves. Attempts were made, in vain, to stem the terrible genocide.

All the hospitals found themselves in difficult situations similar to those experienced in Rwanda a decade previously, seeking to serve all who needed medical attention, irrespective of their ethnic or political background. At Buye, the *Ecole d'Aides Accoucheuses* continued under difficulties. "We tried to carry on in the nurses' training school as normally as possible," recorded Ruth Anthony. "It was a time when the girls became much more open to the Gospel. Almost all of them were affected in one way or another – most of them losing a relative. They would come and share their problems and we would be able to pray together. Some certainly had their faith strengthened and learned to put their trust in Jesus. Even in those dark days there was some light."

The darkest days were not without humour. Joan Nicholson records an incident in those weeks of tension: "One day we had to take the whole (Buhiga girls') school to a public information meeting. They, along with the boys from the Trade School and a few other people, were given a talk about the situation and then the official addressing them said: 'In many schools there has been trouble and schoolboys and even schoolgirls have been arrested, but here in your schools there has been peace. Now who is to thank for that?' Our 160 lassies thought for a moment, then looked up and, almost to a girl, chorused quietly and confidently, 'God is!' A little ripple went round the other listeners. The official opened his mouth and closed it again and then even he relaxed and said, 'Well, all right, all right, God is. But who else?'"

On the 24th June 1972, Ian Leakey and a doctor of the Danish Baptist Missionary Society were arrested and they spent a night in a prison cell in Bujumbura. Ian recalled his experience: "The power of evil seemed heavy and cruel and at first waves of fear and self-pity swept over me. I could not believe it was really I who was there . . . I remembered the Swiss Roman Catholic

father who had recently been held in a cell at this very
place for three days without food and water . . . As I
poured out my heart to God in prayer the powers of
darkness seemed choking . . . Gradually increasing victory came and a deep assurance of the mighty power of
Jesus and those everlasting arms. I spent the night in
prayer in different postures with shoes and cardigan for
pillow, and bed-bugs and scores of mosquitoes for com-
panions. In the morning we were eventually released."
Ian Leakey was accused of expressing concern about the
ferocity of the reprisals following the abortive *coup* and
was given 48 hours to leave the country.

In November 1974, Pat and Pam Brooks were due for
furlough, flying from Bujumbura. As they were boarding the plane a man tapped Pat on the shoulder and
asked him to move away from the plane. The man
proved to be a Government agent who forbade Pat to
leave the country. He withdrew both Pat and Pam's
passports. The following day, permission was granted
and their passports were returned to them on the steps of
the plane as they boarded. Their permits to return to
Burundi after leave had been annulled.

It appears that this cancellation of permission to
return was done without official sanction. Investigations
showed that, officially, they had been commended for
their work in the country and had been given complete
clearance to return after leave. How the annulling of
their re-entry visas had been organised was never fully
discovered, but it became clear, later, that it was en-
gineered by some church leaders. They had been
angered by Pam Brooks who, in charge of the church
accounts, had refused to release money in a building
fund for purposes other than those for which they were
given.

The violence subsided but a series of changes in
government leadership made the situation of churches –

Roman Catholic and Protestant – even more precarious. Regulations were introduced which limited the number, location and occasions for all meetings of Christians. It became increasingly difficult for foreign missionaries to renew their residence visas annually until, in 1985, almost all expatriate missionaries were expelled. At very short notice, William and Melanie Challis and Stephen and Marian Coffin were forced to leave the Bible School at Matana in which they were teaching and return to the UK. Apart from associate-missionaries Graham and Sarah White, working at the University in Bujumbura, no missionaries of the Ruanda Mission remained in Burundi.

The Protestant churches of Burundi were to bear the scars of the massacres for a long time. About one-third of all Protestant Pastors had been killed as had also many school and church teachers. The churches suffered the cruel blow of losing what in many ways they most needed: leaders. They had not, however, lost their faith. Many were the testimonies to God's peace in situations of crippling losses, particularly among thousands of newly widowed mothers of large families.

In September, 1987, a *coup d'état* brought President Buyoya to power. He brought new freedom to the churches and an attempt to broaden the ethnic base of the government. The situation began to ease and greater liberty for worship and meeting in groups was granted. The struggle for a truly representative national leadership in all areas, including that of the Church, continued slowly.

In the same year that Rwanda and Burundi gained their independence, on the 9th October 1962, Uganda also became an independent state with Sir Walter Coutts as Governor General. It later became a Republic with the Kabaka, Sir Frederick Mutesa, as President and Milton Obote as leader of the Uganda People's

Congress and Prime Minister. Later still the Kabaka was forced to flee the country and Uganda was declared a republic with Milton Obote as President.

At first the country progressed in a climate of peace. Slowly Obote's government deteriorated and he lost his popular support leaving the way open for violent change.

The peace of the country was shattered by a *coup d'état* in 1971 in which Major General Idi Amin came to power, ousting Milton Obote who fled to Tanzania. The disorder became a "reign of terror" which touched every part of the country. A year later, in August 1972, the Asians, many of whom were traders, were evicted from the country and its commercial life came to a virtual stand-still.

Uganda, under Idi Amin, was notorious for its flagrant disregard of human rights. Men in positions of authority were given the right to kill all who opposed them and the torture chambers in Kampala evidenced the appalling lengths to which Amin was prepared to go to eliminate all who would speak out against his terrifying regime. Worldwide condemnation was evoked when he, either himself or by direct command, murdered Archbishop Janani Luwum on the 16th February 1977.

Following the death of the Archbishop, Bishop Festo Kivengere was advised to leave Uganda and in the same year he was awarded the International Freedom Prize in Oslo for his stand on freedom and human rights.

In these conditions the church in Uganda suffered greatly as its leaders protested at the corruption and violence of the regime. The centre and north of Uganda suffered most; the south-west districts, including Kigezi, far as they were from the centre of the country, suffered less severely. Kisiizi hospital was able, with difficulty, to continue working throughout this period.

The new regime was anti-Christian. Idi Amin was a

Muslim and did not hide his aim of converting Uganda to Islam. In 1974, John Whitlock, a missionary laboratory technician at Kisiizi, wrote, "The country chief arrived and announced that we should not conduct prayers any more on the wards or in the prayer room. We were told that if we wanted to hold prayers, we should do it out under the trees far away from the ears of the patients. The result was that the Christian staff were all the more determined to preach the Gospel, and are doing so. Five months have passed and no more has been said. Praise Jesus!"

After the chief had left, one woman who had worked at the hospital since it began remarked to nurse Margaret Walker, "Others have died for preaching the Gospel. Does he really think we are going to stop!"

In April 1979, Tanzanian soldiers with Ugandan exiles invaded the country from its southern border and Amin fled. Professor Yusufu Lule was made President. He was, however, ousted two months later and was succeeded by President Godfrey Binaisa. In April, 1980, Binaisa was himself ousted and Milton Obote returned to power, backed by the Uganda National Liberation Army (UNLA). In December of that year, elections were held for the first time since 1962 and Obote again became President of Uganda. The atrocities, far from decreasing, actually increased, and the country sank lower still into anarchy. Obote had had a bad human rights' record when he had been President in 1971; now things went from bad to worse. Public executions in Kabale and Kampala in 1972 had aroused great fear and left an indelible impression in many minds, including those of missionaries who were there at the time. Later, between the years 1983 and 1985, it was estimated that some 300,000 people were massacred.

In the face of the atrocities and bloodshed, church leaders, notably Bishop Festo Kivengere, protested strongly at the highest levels. The witness of the church was clear. Church leaders might well have suffered more had there not been world-wide revulsion at the murder of Archbishop Luwum.

In 1981, Yoweri Museveni formed the National Resistance Army and began a long fight, commanded from "the bush" to gain control of the country. His forces were young, very young, some mere boys of school age, but they were well disciplined and Museveni gained a reputation for ethnic impartiality and minimum violence to gain his ends.

In July, 1985, the Obote government was overthrown and the army came under the control of Tito Okello. Five months later a power-sharing agreement was signed between the Uganda forces under Okello and the National Resistance Movement under Museveni. This proved to be ineffective and, in February, 1986, the National Resistance Movement gained control of Kampala and Museveni was sworn in as President of the country.

For fifteen years Uganda was subjected to a vicious, oppressive, militarily enforced regime. The Christians suffered severely, including the leaders who dared to stand publicly against injustice and brutality. Many were the testimonies of those who found in Christ the strength to remain true to Him and to forgive those who so brutally ill-treated them and their relatives. The book, written by Bishop Festo Kivengere, entitled, *I love Idi Amin* expressed the triumph of God's love in Jesus Christ.

Chapter 18

Standards of living 1960–1973

The soil in the mid-African states of Uganda, Rwanda and Burundi is, in general, very good for cultivation. With an average altitude of 5,000–6,000 feet and a very undulating-to-mountainous terrain, most of the crops are grown on sloping hillsides or in valleys. The climate is good and normally the wet and dry seasons interchange with predictable regularity. The ordinarily plentiful rain, in the wet season, tends to pour off the hills and drain away quickly into the rivers, causing erosion if care is not taken to prevent it. Generally the supply of water is not a problem. Its purity is! Beans, sweet potatoes and *matoke* (green bananas), form the staple diets of ordinary people. It is from green bananas, too, that the local powerful alcoholic drink is made.

The very ease with which food can be grown tends to make the people improvident so that, when the exceptional drought occurs, disaster follows. The traditional diet, though plentiful, is unbalanced, and this, together with a low standard of hygiene, accounts for the prevalence of many tropical diseases and malnutrition from which they suffer.

Added problems have arisen from the rapid growth of

population in all three territories and the economic effects of limited, cultivatable land. The pioneers came to Ruanda-Urundi with a total population of around 5 million people. Rwanda and Burundi now have more than that number in each country and it is rising steadily. Profitable cash crops such as tea, coffee and rice are now grown on good land which is, therefore, no longer available for local cultivation. Forest areas have been destroyed in order to gain more cultivatable land in Rwanda and the collapse of the world coffee market has drastically affected the economies of both Rwanda and Burundi. Before the independence of these countries, the Belgian administration made notable contributions to the solving of these problems: by initiating terracing on the hillsides; in providing grain stores; and in promoting research into possible animal and agricultural development. But this rarely brought immediate great benefit to the ordinary peasant.

With the early proclamation of the Gospel came the ministry of healing on medical safaris and in rural hospitals. It was soon recognised that a large proportion of the sickness treated in the Mission hospitals could have been prevented by a more balanced diet, better hygiene and, above all, by using clean water for drinking and cooking.

The first moves towards helping Africans to raise their standards of living were concerned with cultivation of land, raising livestock and improving hygiene. Here the preventive medicine that was increasingly being taught in the hospitals and through women's work helped. But this was not enough. It was soon recognised that this was not an extra to the task of evangelism and church-planting. In its preventive aspect, those influenced were mainly mothers of children suffering from the many preventable diseases. The problems, however, had much deeper sociological implications and required the co-operation of the whole family to tackle them, with the greatest responsibility lying with the man. Both in local culture and from the Christian point of view, the man is the head of the family, a great responsibility to be taken very seriously.

The first move outside the hospitals arose, surprisingly perhaps, not from a direct desire to raise standards of living but rather from a concern for the many boys who did not pass the entry examinations to secondary education.

In 1960, while David Weston was the Head of the secondary school at Shyogwe, in Rwanda, he wrote, "I have to confess that my own thoughts are turning more and more to the need to provide technical education for the many boys who fail to get into the 'grammar school' stream of the secondary schools. We have long felt that we have a special responsibility towards them and that we should start with a more practical bias. This we hope to do this term at Shyogwe, and it is very much in faith that we launch out; it may even be true that the type of school that we envisage will become the pattern for others elsewhere in the country."

Details of the suggested, non-subsidised, agricultural farm school were sent to the Belgian Governor of Ruanda-Urundi. The proposal evoked an enthusiastic response which was accompanied by the unconditional gift of the equivalent of about £180 together with four cows and a subsidy to pay for a teacher for the first year.

The Farm School was begun and great interest was aroused. Two American foundations provided some financial help and the "Freedom From Hunger" Campaign provided a small diesel tractor. However, Shyogwe was geographically near the centre of the political troubles which spread throughout the country. Many local *Tutsi* were violently ejected from their homes and a number of students at the school were forced to take refuge in Uganda and Burundi. The Farm School was forced to close down.

A need had, however, been recognised and a Rural Service Project was started in its place. "The service is an outreach from the Shyogwe farm, an attempt to help local Christian people to improve their standards of living through agriculture," David continued. "We have arrived at the stage where we must call on an agriculturalist to give direction and drive to the project. We are praying for such a man."

James and Margaret Brown were the first missionaries to bring a farming background in the UK to the problems of this part of Africa. Located for a few months at Shyogwe, overseeing the Farm School, they then worked for eight years at Maranyundo, in the refugee area of the Bugesera to the east of Rwanda, and three years at Kigeme. Their main task was to look into the reasons for malnutrition and then advise sufferers, or their parents, on the crops needed to remedy the deficiencies.

"I was unable," James concluded eventually, "to find a single case of malnutrition which was caused by a lack of knowledge of how to grow suitable crops. I found that the main cause of malnutrition was that 75% of the food which could be used to remedy the condition was turned into alcohol. This conclusion was supported by a Government report in 1972. A secondary cause was that some Africans were under the power of the witch doctors to such an extent that they were not feeding their children properly. When children who were suffering from malnutrition were brought into health centres and fed with food which they produced themselves, they were restored to good health."

James' conclusion supported the view held by other missionaries who were in close contact with malnutrition, that the most effective remedy was for the parents, particularly the father, to be "saved"! As Christians, their change of heart would bring about a change of conduct and sense of responsibility to wives and children.

While looking for ways of improving agricultural methods, James could see no way of great improvement apart from radical changes which he honestly felt he could not initiate. These included the socially unacceptable merging of the usual small-holdings into larger farming units.

Meanwhile, in 1964, similar concerns prompted Dick Lyth to launch the Christian Rural Service at Kabale. "The Church was responsible for starting both medical and educational work in Uganda," he wrote, "but by 1964 these had to a large extent been taken over by the State. However, the Church continued to see the Gospel, in its broad sense, as being concerned with the whole of life, and accordingly felt that she should have a contribution to make in areas of health and hygiene, of agriculture and animal husbandry, of youth, literacy, home-improvement, the economy, and so on. A small pilot project was begun – just two young African men operating on bicycles – with funds supplied by an American organization, concerned with self-help schemes of this kind around the world, called World Neighbours."

Dick planned a scheme to train a carefully selected team of men and women who, after training, would live in villages under the same conditions as the local people they set out to serve. There they would seek to help to raise their standards of living and so demonstrate God's concern for the whole of people's lives.

"As over 60% of the men and 80% of the women of the district are unable to read and write," reported Dick Lyth, "one of the early tasks that the field workers threw themselves into was the formation of adult literacy classes and the training of volunteer teachers for these.

The publication of the whole Bible for the first time in the local language was an added incentive to these classes, and the field workers had many opportunities for teaching about the Lord."

Village industries were encouraged. Bee-keeping courses were arranged, an improved type of hive was demonstrated, and arrangements made for marketing honey and wax. A more direct contribution to the Church included a homecraft course for the wives of men in training for the ministry and, for the clergy themselves and other church leaders, a course dealing with health and first-aid, accounts and stewardship, agriculture, adult literacy and youth work.

"Of course there were a great number of failures and disappointments and frustrations," Dick reported, "and naturally some of the field workers were better than others. One or two found the work and dedication demanded too exacting and moved into other jobs; but most were caught up with the excitement and satisfaction of the work, which very often involved helping people at the deeper levels. One field worker was called in to advise about a disease affecting coffee plants. But afterwards over a cup of tea he discovered that there was a worse disease in the farmer's home – quarrelling and unhappiness – and that the marriage was just about breaking up. The field worker was one of those who was married, and his testimony of how God had helped him and his wife to ask each other's forgiveness affected the farming couple very deeply. Soon they began to turn to God themselves, and in time the whole home was transformed. In this kind of way the field workers constantly saw the practicalities of health or agriculture becoming keys to open doors to the Gospel. And nearly everywhere they were at work, too, the local pastors saw church attendance increasing and the level of giving going up."

Concern for the growing number of young men, educated to a post-primary level but unable to go further and so joining the ranks of the unemployed led to a new venture at Gahini. Funds were requested from the government to build, equip and staff a Trade School. Permission was given and grants made which enabled the construction of buildings and the provision of tools and other equipment. With high hopes the school opened in 1960. Ted Sisley was in charge and 53 boys from all the Mission areas in Ruanda-Urundi were enrolled. The first course ended in 1962 and the successful trainees found employment without great difficulty.

"We had some good lads from Burundi in training at Gahini," reported Ted Sisley, "but the Burundi Church wanted a Trade School in its own country. So during 1962 we started at Buhiga a school run by the Church. The boys were local so that there were no boarding expenses. Each boy paid 1,000 francs (£7) for the year, the church provided buildings and classroom equipment, and I collected tools for them." The Buhiga experiment proved to be a success.

A year later the government discontinued its grants and the school at Gahini was forced to close. This appeared to be the sad conclusion of a very promising venture. However, the Gahini Church leaders were not at all happy at this end of the only school where Protestant boys could gain practical training. They had heard of the successful Buhiga venture and they decided to try something similar in Rwanda. "So," reported Ted Sisley, "we started helping the local churches which requested trade schools, to organise them. God provided us with a car in which we were able to carry wood and equipment. So the process of building up began."

Seven rural trade schools were started. However, for three years the help given to them was limited due to the absence of Ted and Beryl Sisley on furlough in the UK and, on their return to Rwanda, the appointment of Ted as headmaster of the secondary school at Shyogwe.

Leave for Ted did not mean abandoning his efforts on behalf of the Rural Trade Schools. While in England, he often spoke of the problem of obtaining the much-needed but expensive tools. "After I had spoken at a meeting in Manchester, a man suggested that friends might find some spare tools in their sheds for me, and I left with a large box of them. Others are taking up the idea and in some places a crate is being placed at the back of the Church for tools of all kinds."

Armed with these tools and back in Rwanda, despite his duties as headmaster at Shyogwe, two further trade schools were opened in 1966. Two years later this number had risen to eleven.

Ted and Beryl Sisley were posted to Shyira in 1968 to take over the headship of a secondary school there. However, this did not prevent Ted being approached about beginning another Trade School in a way which illustrated the enthusiasm of some church leaders for these schools.

"It was at a parish called Rugendabari," recalled Ted Sisley, "in the north, not far from the Uganda border. The Pastor arrived at Shyira saying that his Christians wanted a Trade School for their boys. I told him that we already had eleven schools and there was no money left to buy tools, also I was running the new secondary school and I did not have time to help them. He would not take 'no' for an answer, so I agreed but insisted that they must first put up a mud and wattle workshop with grass roof, get boards to make benches, put up the money for the basic tools, about £250, and enrol at least twenty boys with their fees paid. I would then look for a teacher. I thought that this would put them off! Within ten days the Pastor was back, the £250 had been collected, they had almost finished the workshop building and would I come the next day to see the students and parents with the tools. How he imagined I could get the tools and be at his parish the next day I do not know, but that was the kind of enthusiasm we met with."

Pressure of work again made it impossible for Ted Sisley to continue supervising the Rural Trade Schools. Church leaders, however, considered their continuation sufficiently important to justify appointing a supervisor, Andrew Nyirimanzi, an ex-trade school student.

From time to time, a number of young men and women served with the Mission for one or two years in a variety of tasks arranged under the Voluntary Service Overseas (VSO) scheme. Some, later, returned as missionaries. One such VSO volunteer was Bob Venning. He was posted to Shyira in 1968 to assist Ted Sisley in organising the Rural Trade Schools. "At that time," Bob wrote, "I was privileged to witness the beginnings of the Holy Spirit's work at Kigeme school and to come personally into blessing particularly through the ministry and witness of Eric and Ruth Townson. It was wonderful to see the Lord doing a new thing in the lives of many African Christians, missionaries and volunteers."

In 1974, after further training for missionary service, Bob returned with Julie, his wife, to open CEFORMI (*Centre de Formation Micro-Industrielle*), a technical training centre in Kigali. "I saw my work," explained Bob, "as being part of the local African church's concern for the whole man, and in particular, in showing its love for young people who were unemployed. In the training of young men as skilled trades people, we had the opportunity of sharing the Gospel with them during the three or four years of their training. Our desire was to train Christian technicians who would go out into industry, co-operatives, trade schools or similar enterprises, and there share their new-found faith."

With grants from Christian Aid, Oxfam and Tear Fund, CEFORMI provided a much needed training ground in the manual skills of carpentry, vehicle repairs, servicing machinery including grinding mills etc. Over a period of ten years the centre grew from very small beginnings until, in 1984, it was handed over to African management. Since then the number of 53 students in training in six different trade skills has grown to a figure nearing 80.

In contrast to some of the early efforts to improve levels of agriculture and animal farming, CEFORMI enjoyed whole-hearted support from the African church leadership. In 1984 a government commission examined 21 centres in Kigali which were concerned with training for young people. CEFORMI was, "voted best centre in the capital for the training being given there," wrote Bob. "There was much good publicity on the national radio, so one can only praise God that the centre was recognised in this way. The certificates that our students receive when they leave now have a government rubber stamp on them too!"

In Burundi, Steve and Ann Stordy began in 1973, to form teams of Christian Rural Service workers on the lines of those in Kigezi. For three years, rural development work was carried on through trained workers in six church centres. In 1977, *TEAR* Fund provided two workers, Terry Withers and Dave Jones, to work on projects for improving water supplies, planting trees and developing the experimental and demonstration farm at Buye.

"Are African farmers ready to learn?" asked Steve Stordy. He answered his own question: "The farmer is not the problem. There is often a very good reason for what he does. Projects are introduced, but if they fail, it is due not so much to the farmer's ignorance or unwillingness to change, but to planners like myself who do not take the time to relate to the farmer's needs."

When Steve and Ann left for the UK in 1980, a great deal of good work had been done, but the upheaval of the political situation, a reluctance on the part of the

Burundi Church to understand and support the aims of Christian Rural Service and no one to carry on the work, resulted in much of the ground gained being rapidly lost.

In the late 1970's and early 1980's, Richard Rowland was the doctor in charge of Gahini hospital in Rwanda. He, with Prilla his wife, were very concerned for the preventive side of their medical work. "What shocked us, as we understood better the Rwandan people and their way of life," he wrote, "was the tiny effect the Hospital had had on the overall health of most people in fifty years . . . Ordinary farmers have the ability to improve their own health and that of their families, and they do not know it! Too often, it has been doctors and nurses who have been at fault. We have thought that medical knowledge was something to be jealously guarded, rather than to be widely shared."

A trained agriculturalist, Geoff Price, with his wife Hope, were posted to Gahini in 1976.

Working together, Geoff and Richard set about establishing facts about the health of the local people, the way their children were growing and what they felt were their most urgent needs. "In 1977 the Gahini Family Centre and School for Parents was opened," Richard wrote. "We hoped that parents would learn in a kind of school how their children could enjoy better health and growth. It was not only the parents who learned. We did, too! We made mistakes, perhaps chiefly through being paternalistic."

Realising that there would never be enough health-professionals to go round in a developing country, Richard applied to the government and was granted the possibility of training a primary health-worker or Health Scout. "The people from one far-off area elected a local farmer, named Reho, to come to Gahini to train as a part-time health worker . . . Reho came to Gahini for three weeks' simple training and returned to his home.

After that, once a week, he would come back to Gahini for further training and report on his work. We would visit him once a month . . . After a year's effective work, the government stopped him giving out medicines, but let him carry on teaching about health." Other Health Scouts followed.

Learning from a successful method used in Nigeria, health information was incorporated into song and drama. "Our latest Health-Scouts," added Richard, "are natural story-tellers. They are adept at composing songs about health, with all the rhythm that antiphonal African singing lends."

At Gahini, the Christian Rural Service was linked to the Family Health Centre of the Hospital. Around the Centre, Geoff and his colleague, the Rev. Emmanuel Ndababonye, supervised gardens where nutritious crops were cultivated and rabbits reared. TEAR Fund promoted a successful tree-planting project. "We had a good relationship with the local Church," commented Geoff. "At the diocesan level, we got on fine with people personally, including the Bishop and Church hierarchy, but we were under pressure because they required us to bring in more funds and promote prestige status projects."

The success of the Christian Rural Service in Uganda in raising standards of living among rural Christians was not repeated to the same extent by any organisation in Rwanda or Burundi. Such activity requires the active approval and support of church leaders. This, the Church in Kigezi was prepared to give to a much greater extent than in Rwanda and Burundi. Nevertheless, foundations had been laid on which others were to build.

Chapter 19

The trumpet of Jubilee 1973–1980

"The trumpet of Jubilee" was sounded by the Mission in 1971, in gratitude for fifty years of ministry in Kigezi, Rwanda and Burundi. The retired Bishop Lawrence Barham reminded Mission supporters that Jubilee meant a *setting free of slaves*, interpreted as "slaves of sin". "We thank God that from a very small beginning with two missionary couples at Kabale in 1921 there are today thousands of Africans in these territories who are able to give that witness. . . . Yet there are still millions in Africa, Europe and elsewhere who have no idea that there is deliverance. We have a great responsibility to let it be known."

The phrase "set free" had other applications. There were those in African church leadership who wanted to be "set free" from overseas domination. There were missionaries who began to feel that the original mission of the pioneers had been accomplished and it was now time to be "set free" to obey other calls from God.

A simple understanding of the call to the pioneer

doctors to "take the Gospel of Jesus Christ to the peoples of south-west Uganda, Rwanda and Burundi" would suggest that that "mission" had been fulfilled. "Taking the Gospel" has, however, implications, declared by Jesus Christ Himself, of "making disciples of all nations" and "building His church".

From 1921 to 1966, a period of 45 years, missionaries had taken the lead in the evangelisation of Rwanda and Burundi. In March 1966, that leadership had been handed over to African bishops. During the "partnership" years, 1966 to 1973, Albert Brown and Ian Leakey worked closely with the bishops of these new dioceses as they grappled with their new responsibilities. Bishop Adoniya Sebununguri was particularly warm in his appreciation of the contribution to the setting up of the Kigali diocese that Albert Brown was able to make. With the departure of Bishop Dick Lyth from Kigezi as well as that of Albert Brown from Rwanda and Ian Leakey from Burundi in 1972–3, there was no further direct influence on church leadership in these countries.

The Mission was guided by a few clear principles, summarised by Bishop Dick Lyth: "To be clear in our own thinking about what the church really is: a fellowship of blood-bought brothers and sisters in Christ, of all races, working together for His glory; to continue, as expatriates, to be a contribution to the overseas church where, and for as long as is needed, always giving priority to the training of nationals to do our jobs; to help the national churches to have vision for the preaching of the Gospel, both to their own people and to people of other countries, so that we and they may share with the churches in all other countries in God's plan of international mission and fellowship."

The working out of these principles was, in practice, a day-to-day meeting of the demands of the existing work and responding to the requests of the African leaders, using the resources, in finance and personnel, that God provided.

Andrew Bowman returned from the UK to join the staff of Bukuuku College in the Ruwenzori Diocese, in West Uganda, in September 1970. He had, in fact, been prepared to leave for Africa after leave in 1966 when he was diagnosed as suffering from a brain tumour and an operation was necessary. He married Susan a year later but it required a further three years of recuperation before they were to resume missionary service in Uganda.

In 1972, the College was renamed the Bishop Balya College, after the famous Bishop, then aged 92, who was remembered as "the Bishop who never wore shoes!" Its Principal, the Rev. Yona Kule, was transferred to Mukono Theological College and Andrew succeeded him. Andrew and Susan left finally for the UK in 1977.

In Burundi, the Bible Schools continued, under African leadership, to train church teachers. Bishop Yohana Nkunzumwami was concerned to see trained women working in his diocese and requested a missionary teacher, Etta Johnson, to undertake this work. After a year at Trinity College, Bristol, the Bishop ordained her as a deaconess in November 1977. A year later the first course for women church workers started at Buhiga. On Etta's retirement in 1980, Rosemary Preston succeeded her, assisted by Euphrasie Niragira, a trained primary school teacher and daughter of the Bishop. Six years later, Rosemary was able to hand over the school to her.

Girls were selected who had completed six years of primary school and were at least 16 years of age. The aim of the course was to prepare them to teach others a variety of subjects and to assist in pastoral work, particularly where this related to women. Funded by Christian Aid, TEAR Fund, the Mothers' Union and the SPCK for books, the course included study of the Bible, practical home skills, hygiene and some arithmetic for accounts.

Despite many difficulties, not least in finding places for the trained girls in parishes which were unaccustomed to women workers, courses have continued to the present. Eventually Euphrasie Niragira was ordained deaconess by the Bishop. Some of the ex-students have married. Most of them work in parishes where they make a very worth-while contribution. "As in England," commented Rosemary Preston, "it varies with the Pastor as to what responsibilities they are given, but some lead services and preach and most are engaged in women's and children's work." It was a bold initiative by Bishop Nkunzumwami. Later, the presence of a few women students in other Bible Schools showed that note was being taken of the need for the contribution to the churches of trained young women.

After a period of four years during which there was no ordained missionary in Rwanda or Burundi, Roger and Miranda Bowen were posted to Bujumbura. It was a strategic posting but with no clear objectives. Roger was curate to the Vicar of the Cathedral Church, Canon Yeremiya Kabuye, but his ministry was extended to school and university Christian groups and to developing a youth and community centre.

"The initial vision and impetus had come from missionaries rather than Africans," reported Roger, "and it was not clear to me that the African Church had any idea of what they were expecting . . . In fact, that vision was unrealistic from the start because the site of the community centre next door to the President's offices made any such activities unacceptable. That sort of activity should have been sited in the shanty town . . . As a recreation centre it never fully got off the ground because there was no African colleague who had any vision or experience for 'open' youth work as opposed to Christian activities, equipment was difficult to obtain and maintain, and Christian young people were not interested in leisure activities, in some cases viewing them as irrelevant at best and at worst worldly. All their spare time was spent in fellowship meetings for prayer and testimony."

In his second tour, Roger Bowen was involved in overseeing the refurbishment and adaptation of a partially derelict primary school at Matana so that it could be developed as a Bible School and Seminary. The Matana Bible School, which served the Diocese of Bujumbura, opened in September 1981 with a one year ordination course in Kirundi for eight senior men. A year later, in addition to the training of senior church teachers and clergy in the vernacular, Roger began a 3-year French-speaking higher-level course.

During the years that Roger worked in Burundi he had ample opportunity to study the after-effects on the church of the political risings in Rwanda and Burundi.

"The thing that struck me during my years in Burundi," he commented, "was the need for a fuller interpretation and application of the Gospel. The church was strong on the vital aspect of personal salvation but needed to emphasise Christ's lordship over all of life, the doctrine of God as Creator and Judge, the role of the servant of the Lord who, 'will bring justice to the nations' (Isaiah 42 1:4).

"The churches we have established in Rwanda and Burundi are stamped with the strengths and weaknesses of the pietist tradition. The strengths lie in the strong emphasis on the necessity for personal conversion and holiness of life. The weaknesses of that tradition lie in a withdrawal from the public life of the nation. Thus there is little concern for God's 'will to be done on earth as it is in heaven' except in the area of winning people to Christ. There is little concept of training in Christian discipleship for life in the world as light and salt. The church leadership has little concept of being the conscience of the nation, pleading for justice and human rights in the face of the most appalling abuses. This is often not their fault because they have not been given a theological framework in which to think through these issues, e.g. because man is made in God's image anything that abuses man is a blasphemy against God and is therefore the church's concern. The use of torture, imprisonment without trial and racial discrimination are God's concern and the church cannot dodge them by saying, 'Oh! that's politics and we don't get involved'. . . . The role of the foreign missionary may be politely, respectfully, graciously but firmly to keep asking awkward questions at the same time as showing their solidarity with and commitment to the national church."

The heritage of revival includes the ability, illustrated by many, to make an unflinching personal stand in the face of political injustice, racial discrimination and violence. Pastor Yona Kanamuzeyi in Rwanda was a notable example. The apparent weakness of the African leadership to protest publicly in the same way may be attributed in part to the strong missionary concern for spiritual holiness of life leaving insufficient room, particularly in the training of church leaders, for applying it to social situations.

A further milestone in the development of the churches structure was reached in 1980 with the formation of the Anglican Province of Burundi, Rwanda and Zaire led by Archbishop Bezalel Ndahura. Kigezi Diocese remained in the Anglican Province of Uganda led by Archbishop Silvano Wani.

The leadership of the churches was now wholly in African hands and the influence of missionaries was negligible in terms of their status in the church structure. The value of missionaries in the work of the churches depended, rightly, on their personal contribution as members of those churches. To their individual tasks they could bring, but not impose, aspects of their technical and Christian cultural heritage.

Chapter 20

Servants of Christ and of the Church 1973–1980

From 1973 onwards the Ruanda Mission became a servant to the churches it had, under God, brought into being. Each missionary ultimately worked under African authority even if he or she was the head of a hospital, school or other institution or organisation. The Mission continued its support of the churches by maintaining grants for special activities such as theological training, the salaries of a few key workers and the support of key church projects.

Missionaries were still relatively free to initiate new activities where these were seen to fit in with their evangelising and church-building aims. In the 1970's two such developments in the hospitals of Rwanda and Burundi gave them new perspectives and areas of outreach – nutrition and preventive medicine, and physiotherapy.

Over Christmas 1970, TEAR Fund raised money for a Health Education and Malnutrition Project at Kigeme, in Rwanda. As a result new buildings were added to the

Hospital. Jeff and Pat Newth were in the forefront of this new venture in preventive medicine.

Besides the usual illnesses treated in every hospital, typhus, typhoid, leprosy, tuberculosis, malaria and worms, the Kigeme area included many patients suffering from gross malnutrition. To the outpatients' department, with its dispensary busy six days a week, were added the special consultations undertaken by the nurse and doctor in the Nutritional Centre and the large daily nutritional and ante-natal clinics.

Dr John Henderson was in charge of Kigeme hospital during a number of structural changes. In 1974, he wrote, "The hospital was built in 1933–34 and the original buildings for the men's and the women's wards and the outpatients are still in use. The two wards are desperately shabby with the foundations eroded and are now fit for nothing but demolition. New fabric has been going up: a maternity building with an operating theatre in 1963, a house for a second doctor in 1970, a laundry in 1971, and the Nutritional Centre with the kwashiorkor ward was opened in 1972. An infectious diseases unit should be operational soon. Today we had a shock. We thought we had 150 to 160 patients in our 110 beds, but when we came to count, there were 223! Such a total means that 113 sleep on the cement floor with only a grass mat under them and a thin blanket, if that, over them at night when the temperature drops to 12° C or lower."

A serious situation arose at Gahini in early 1973. "At the end of February," wrote Joyce Windebank, the nurse in the hospital, "the local Secondary School boys started to terrorise the *Tutsi* on the hill, both in the school itself and in the hospital. This resulted in eleven of our nurses and technicians having to leave work, leaving a great gap as we now have only eleven left . . . we have closed the Children's Ward and combined it with the Women's ward. All operating, except for the emergency cases, has stopped. General Outpatients is on three days a week only."

It was only slowly that the situation returned to normal in both hospital and school. As in all such events, the scars in relationships took longer to heal.

In 1975, a crisis developed in all the Church hospitals of Rwanda. The Government unexpectedly doubled the salary scales officially prescribed for accredited medical personnel. The hospitals were responsible for finding a considerable part of the salaries of African qualified staff from the fees paid by patients. This dramatic rise, without notice, presented an almost insuperable obstacle to maintaining the three hospitals in Rwanda – Gahini, Shyira and Kigeme.

Faced with this situation, the Ruanda Mission Council was forced to reduce its responsibilities to the hospitals. Of the possibilities suggested, one – that the Mission would assume responsibility for staffing adequately one hospital while leaving the Church and the Government to work out between them ways and means of keeping the other two hospitals going – was accepted by the Church. The staffing by missionary doctors and nurses of Gahini hospital was designated to be the Mission's responsibility. It was a unanimous decision over a potentially divisive issue.

In 1976, the new physiotherapy unit, built with funds provided by TEAR Fund, came into use at Gahini. This was a great step forward for Liz Hardinge, who had pioneered the unit. The work grew and gained recognition at Gahini and elsewhere in Rwanda. "There are lots of exciting possibilities," Liz wrote, "but I feel very strongly that whatever we do, we must start teaching others to take over. It seems to me that there are two ways of doing this, one being to start some kind of training here which would have government support;

the other would be to spend more time visiting other hospitals to teach nurses and generally to help and advise . . . My regular visits to Kigeme are proving very worthwhile. I've recently been asked to go to Burundi and to a hospital in Tanzania, in both cases to teach nurses some simple techniques, and I'm sure there are other hospitals in this country which would welcome this kind of visit." Both possibilities became realities in the years that followed but the most significant, as well as taxing in energies, was that of visiting hospitals – Protestant and Roman Catholic – throughout Rwanda.

As in Rwanda, so in Burundi, in the early 1970's all the church hospitals suffered from shortages of money and personnel, especially doctors and nurses. It became clear that all these hospitals could not for much longer be staffed with missionary personnel unless God sent many new missionary recruits. These were not forthcoming and the Mission was forced to face withdrawing its responsibilities. There were other considerations.

For the missionaries, hospitals were primarily a means of evangelism and, in their earlier days, the training of leaders. "The Ruanda Mission started as a medical mission and in the grace and love of God much of the blessing which spread out in Revival started among medical workers," commented Harold Adeney. "Later the 'nuts and bolts' of medical work tended to take so much time that many of us lost the spiritual vision of medical missionary work. And the church's attitude to the hospitals was more and more at variance with that of the missionaries. In common with medical missionaries in other societies, we became more and more confused as to what our aims really were and how to achieve them."

It was often difficult to reconcile the "Protestant prestige" value of hospitals which church leaders appeared to consider very important with the evangelistic outreach and caring for the poor and needy which the missionaries and some African Christians saw as more important.

The situation became critical in Burundi in 1975. At Buhiga, Mary Hammond and Gwen Whitaker ran the hospital, as there was no resident doctor since Harold and Isobel Adeney had moved to Matana. The following year, 1976, a unique arrangement was agreed with the Burundi authorities. The hospital would be "lent" to the Government until such time as missionary medical personnel were available. It was agreed that the Government would be responsible for providing a doctor but, in the event, only a Medical Assistant was appointed. Later that year the two nurses were posted to Buye because of the greater need of the Midwifery and Nursing school there and Buhiga hospital was reduced to the status of a dispensary.

Harold and Isobel Adeney returned to Buhiga late in 1976 in a pastoral capacity – Harold had been ordained – but from then onwards there was no missionary involvement in the hospital.

At Matana, discussions with the Government were requested with a view to the possible handing over to it of the hospital. In August 1977, the Government requested an inventory prior to take-over. A month later a Murundi doctor was appointed. By the end of the year the Government had taken over full possession and control and did so, towards the end, in a rather aggressive way. It had, at first, been agreed to reimburse the Church for hospital and surgical equipment. In the event no payment was made and, contrary to an initial agreement, the Health Centre was also taken over. Dr Marion Wright was forbidden to work there or in the mobile clinics unless she agreed to become a Government doctor.

At Buye, Dr Marguerite von Bergen was joined, in 1975, by Dr Luc and Jacqueline Lisimaque, from France, and a German nurse, Karen Heidrich. They were followed by Dr Joel and Bernadette Ceccaldi also from France. In 1978, the French doctors returned to France and Karin Heidrich left for leave in Germany. During the next two years the hospital was run by Dr and Mrs Forkel of Germany, helped by Mrs Irmgard Klinger. Towards the end of 1979, the hospital was handed over to the Burundi Government.

Brian and (Dr) Marion Wright worked on at Matana until 1980. Marion was involved in the teaching of health and hygiene to Church workers with only a tenuous link with the hospital.

Gwen Whitaker and Jill Singyard, the two nurses at Matana returned to the UK for leave. Jill returned to Burundi in 1981 and worked at a Brethren Mission dispensary, at Vugizo, near Bujumbura. When she left in 1984 there was no further Ruanda Mission medical involvement in Burundi.

For the Mission this constituted a "closed door" to evangelism. For African Christians "it made us feel like orphans", to quote a leading church Pastor at Matana. "We lost our parents and the care we had always been able to count on." For the church leadership, hospitals were an important prestige activity. In this service the Protestants had been strong whereas they appeared to be so poor and behind the times in almost every other activity compared with the Roman Catholic Church. The loss of the hospitals was felt to be a severe blow to the Church's standing in the country.

In Kigezi, the hospital at Kisiizi flourished under the happy leadership of Dr John Davies and Bishop Festo Kivengere. An incident in the hospital while John was in charge revealed how spiritual life "burst out" from time to time, as in the past.

John wrote of a special mission to the hospital in May
1972.

"On Sunday we had an open air service to which many
people came including the whole parish! At the close of the
service several people gave testimonies but suddenly the
whole crowd was electrified into full attention when our
VSO (Voluntary Service Overseas) volunteer Sister also
walked to the microphone to make a public stand for Christ.
She had accepted Him as Saviour during the weekend but
this was the first any of us knew of it. As the mission closed
we started packing things away feeling that the whole
weekend had been well worth the effort and we were really
praising the Lord for all that He had done for us at Kisiizi.
We were, therefore, taken completely by surprise when on
the following Tuesday we discovered that although we
thought that we had finished, the Holy Spirit had in fact only
just begun!

"At Kisiizi there has always been a real hardness to the
Gospel among the female nurses and as a result there are
practically no female nurses who follow the Lord Jesus. It
was a shock to us all when on that Tuesday one of the most
senior and most difficult nurses stood up to say that she had
decided to follow Jesus. It then seemed as if the dam which
Satan had built up to stop a spiritual flow into the Nurses'
Home suddenly burst and that evening two more girls came
to Christ. Two days later another two were converted and as
they stood up to give their testimonies at morning prayer,
the Spirit brought two more senior girls under conviction
and finally to faith in Christ . . . The work continued among
the staff and at 3:00 am on the Sunday morning one male
dresser, who had the distinction of being quite easily our
most difficult member of staff but to whom the Lord had
been speaking during the week, realised his desperate need
of a Saviour and turned to Christ. He was so full of praise
that he woke up the nurses on night duty and they had a
praise meeting in the ward at 4:00 am to thank the Lord for
His grace and love."

John moved to Mengo Hospital in Kampala in 1974 and Kevin and Sheila Vaughan succeeded him at Kisiizi. Both served and suffered in the trauma of Uganda at that time. From the coming to power of Milton Obote, then of General Idi Amin, there were great tensions for the hospital due to the political corruption, persecution and violence described elsewhere. Throughout all those years the leadership of the hospital and local church combined to witness to the power of Jesus Christ to break down barriers and bring reconciliation. Throughout this period, Pat Gilmer continued her itinerant care of leprosy patients in south-west Uganda.

In education, there were missionaries on the staffs of several secondary schools. All but one were women. "These few lines," wrote Ted Sisley in the 1972–3 Review Number of Ruanda Notes, "are being written by a practically extinct specimen – the male missionary educationist in Rwanda. I am the last survivor and extinction of the species will be complete by September of this year!" Ted was referring to his expulsion, together with *Tutsi* members of staff from the *Groupe Scolaire*, Shyogwe. "We have always sought to preach the Word of God to the young people, many have responded over the years, and in the last two or three years, during my tenure as headmaster at Shyogwe, the Lord in His love and grace has allowed us to see revival amongst the secondary school students. Now . . . there are no longer religious education lessons, there is no chaplain, no morning prayers, about 80 out of 250 students meet down at the church on Sunday morning. Yet through the difficulties the Christian Union has continued to meet each evening, with 30 to 40 attending. The students themselves are telling the Good News and this pattern is being repeated in most of the secondary schools in Rwanda."

At Kigeme, Lilette Honoré was headmistress of the

Girls' School. Considered to be one of the best girls' schools in the country, it had benefited greatly from western aid agencies which had made grants for buildings and equipment. Many primary school teachers owed their Christian testimony and professional training to the staff led by Lilette.

The outburst of spiritual life at this School in 1971 continued to bring a dynamic vitality to the witness of several girls. A number of them later married young men who were equally active and to the fore in Christian witness and service. That generation of young people formed the basis of a lively, educated and able witness to the power of Christ expressed in a truly African leadership.

In Burundi, Joan Nicholson was headmistress of the Girls' Secondary School at Buhiga until September 1972, when the Government handed over the headship to an African headmaster. Joan remained on the staff. The school suffered from the aftermath of the 1972 holocaust. "On the whole the girls are peaceful and cheerful and school life goes on normally," she wrote, "but one is aware that not far underneath the surface is sorrow and perplexity and uncertainty. There is one lass who when she went home in July found that her father was still alive but all five brothers were gone, and there are many others who have lost relatives. There is the knowledge that two of their fellow schoolgirls were killed in the holidays and three others are missing as well as a number of ex-students . . . As the Christian girls meet to pray and share their testimonies and prayer-requests, one is very conscious of the spiritual battles being waged. The bursts of joyous praise that were so frequent earlier last year are not heard very often."

In south-west Uganda, Joan Hall completed ten years as headmistress of Bweranyangi Girls' School in 1973. She was succeeded by an African. She served a further year as headmistress of Kyebambi Secondary School at Fort Portal, Uganda, before returning to the UK. Liz Traill was on the staff of Kigezi High School.

These Ugandan girls' secondary schools were government institutions. Although meeting a very important need in the community, they were not sufficient for the needs of the Church as seen by its leaders. In 1974, at the request of Bishop Festo Kivengere, Liz Traill began a Church secondary school for girls at Muyebe, some six miles from Kabale. Beginning with one classroom, it received no grants from the Government and, over the succeeding years it grew in size as the local Church and sympathetic aid agencies contributed to building expenses and the Ruanda Mission posted a few missionary teachers there.

By 1971, Kabale Preparatory School was recognised as a full primary boarding school totally integrated into the country's educational system. It remained a church school run by a Committee of Management which was responsible to the Government.

The year 1971 was a dramatic one indeed for KPS. The coming to power in Uganda of Idi Amin and the régime he inaugurated brought a number of unhappy consequences to the school. The expulsion of Asians from Uganda robbed the school of an important section of its pupils. The closing of the borders to Rwanda led to several missionary families south of the border teaching their children at home. Some African parents from a distance feared to expose their children to the indisciplined or drunken soldiers who often manned the frequent road blocks. Idi Amin sent a number of his own children to the school and this, although accepted as a God-given opportunity to show them the love of Christ, added to the tensions of daily life. The way that food and transport was provided during those fifteen years of political chaos and violence is a story in itself. The local people helped the staff to learn where and when supplies of food were available and their one vehicle was kept on the road with just enough petrol to enable it to fulfil its essential runs.

By 1978, the number of pupils had risen to 120, nearly half of whom were boarders. Within three years all the pupils were Ugandan.

It was in these years that three of the pioneers were called to their heavenly reward. Esther Sharp had died in 1962, but it was not until the 2nd March 1976 that Len Sharp died peacefully in retirement at Mombasa. Two years separated the deaths of Algie Stanley Smith on the 28th July 1978 and of Zoe on the 26th April 1980. Their lives, linked together since college days at Cambridge in 1908, now continue with thousands of those brought to Christ, directly and indirectly, through their ministry, in heaven where the master they served on earth is Lord of all.

Four senior missionaries, Peter and Elisabeth Guillebaud and Harold and Isobel Adeney were still in service in this period. They had witnessed and participated in God's early working in revival and later in the renewed outburst of spiritual life mainly among the youth. Their wise counsel was always given a hearing by the African church leaders; sometimes it was received in deep fellowship, at others it was ignored or even resented. Being a servant of Christ and of the Church was not easy either for these experienced missionaries or for the later ones. But there was also a great deal to encourage and give great joy in service.

Chapter 21

Building for the
future
1980–1991

In the 1980's, the part played by missionaries lay in fulfilling specific tasks at the request and under the direction of the African bishops, with the aim of building up the churches and assisting in their evangelistic outreach. The number of missionaries in active service dropped steadily from 82 in 1973 to 30 in 1990. The reason for this lay less in reduced opportunities for service than in fewer candidates offering as recruits.

Increasingly the African churches pursued their tasks without any reference to outside agencies, missionary or otherwise. It is true that grants were forthcoming for specific projects but the churches were, in their normal running, entirely self-supporting and self-governing. There were, however, problems that arose in financing activities which transcended parishes and the chief of these was the training of church teachers and clergy. The Ruanda Mission made grants for running costs but these were insufficient for capital outlay in buildings and equipment.

In three areas, missionaries worked directly with the

African church leadership: secretarial, the training of clergy and the pastoral visits of Canon Ken Barham.

From 1979 and throughout the 1980's, Felicity Angus served as secretary to Bishop Adoniya Sebununguri. Located at Kigali, the diocesan centre, she was able to work with the African church, liaise with the Mission and welcome the many missionaries and others who visited the capital. It was a task which God enabled her to fulfil with great tact, grace and patience.

Attempts to set up a Theological College for the Province of Burundi, Rwanda and Zaire failed and an insufficient number of ordained missionaries offering for service made it impossible for the Mission adequately to meet the requests for missionary staff to assist in the provision of theological and pastoral training of clergy in each diocese.

In the early 1980's, Roger Bowen was the only missionary of the Ruanda Mission engaged in the training of clergy. Located at the Matana Bible School in Burundi, he and Miranda were joined, in 1982, by William and Melanie Challis and Ephraim Radner. Ephraim was an ordained American invited directly by the Bishop from the Episcopalian Church in the United States. Ephraim succeeded Roger as Principal in July 1984. He was expelled from Burundi by the politically sensitive Government in January 1985. William Challis succeeded him as Principal. Steve Coffin and his family moved to Matana from Gitega to fill the gap in March 1985. Both William and Steve were clergymen.

"We never questioned," commented William Challis, "that the Church in Burundi was the Church of the *Barundi*, although there were occasional tensions over whether we were under the Bishop or the Ruanda Mission. Actually, we sometimes thought that the *Barundi* were more Anglican than we were and often had a stronger sense of being part of a worldwide

Anglican communion than we, from the Church of England, had. . . . We also didn't see our role as establishing the Church at the time we were working there, but rather strengthening it, and offering, as 'foreigners', a skill which the Church in Burundi did not possess."

The rapid series of changes of staff at Matana came to a sudden and dramatic end when William and Melanie Challis and Steve and Marian Coffin were, with many other Protestant and Roman Catholic missionaries, forced to leave the country in the political unrest which reached a climax in the upheaval of August 1985.

The eight members of the French-speaking course were ordained deacons at the Burundi Church's Silver Jubilee celebrations at Matana in August 1988. Those ordained on that day included the first woman *Murundi* deacon, Godelive Ndikumana.

None of the three missionaries later involved in church leadership training in Rwanda was ordained. Andrew and Kate Ross spent five years, 1984–1989, at the Stanley Smith Bible School at Gahini. Andrew's triple concern: to give a good biblical grounding; to establish rural clergy and church teachers in their agricultural and animal farming setting; and to promote a stronger literature backup to their teaching ministry, led both him and Kate to develop new methods in all these fields. It was an unusual approach which was welcomed by some and opposed by others who held a more traditional African concept of church leadership.

A further input to the training of church leadership was given by Mike Greig, but more about that later. In 1989, David and Odile Stringer were posted to Gisenyi to build up a Bible School for the relatively new diocese of Shyira.

From 1979, the Rev. Ken Barham, son of Bishop Lawrence Barham, visited the three territories while he was a travelling Secretary of the Mission. From 1983 onwards, while vicar of a parish in England and with financial assistance from the Mission, he made periodic visits to some of the African churches, to assist clergy who could benefit from his pastoral experience. His help was particularly valued in the formation of the new diocese of Muhabura, Kigezi, in 1990, when he was appointed its first Canon.

From 1980, Ken Barham was able to make further visits to Africa, particularly Rwanda, to assist rural clergy improve their pastoral role; his upbringing in Africa and knowledge of the language qualified him well for this task.

Among the other tasks undertaken by missionaries that of Rose Everett was new. She was the first mission- ary given the special task of developing materials and workers for Sunday Schools. Her base was at Shyogwe where she was able to produce and display suitable materials for the courses she ran for Sunday School teachers. Selecting Pastors and teachers with a concern for children to attend the course was difficult, but once found, many of them were able to start or improve Sunday Schools in their parishes. When she returned to the UK in 1983, she handed over the training facilities at Shyogwe to an enthusiastic African pastor, the Rev. Faustin Kanyandekwe. Sad to report, he was killed in a car accident not long after her departure.

The team at the Gahini Family Centre and School for Parents was joined in 1981 by Susan Oakley and, in 1983, when Richard and Prilla Rowland returned to the UK, by Paul and Jean Daltry. Paul was a trained Environmental Health Officer. Under the title of *Santé du Milieu* (Environmental Health), they were able to take further the work of Richard Rowland. A programme for training Parish Community Health Workers was developed in which trainees were instructed in providing advice and help over a wide range of community health needs. "It is the belief of those who are involved in the project that through the various technical training schemes, people may begin to understand the Lordship of Christ over every area of their lives and so create a movement of change within the church, which can touch areas outside those covered by the project."

When Paul and Jean returned to the UK in 1989, they were able to hand over the responsibility of the Development Training Centre to an African, Louis Muvunyi.

Mike and Zena Greig arrived in Rwanda a few months before Geoff and Hope Price returned to the UK. They were posted to Shyogwe, the scene of the first venture into Christian Rural Service nearly twenty years previously. Learning from his predecessors, Mike, an agriculturalist, worked cautiously. Also at Shyogwe was the Bible School which trained Church teachers for the Butare Diocese. Mike was invited to work with the students. He soon discerned a vital principle: If raising the standard of living by agricultural methods was really to succeed, the zeal and expertise of one African Pastor or Church Teacher who had "caught on to the idea" was of more value than the verbal teaching and demonstration plots of many "foreign" experts!

Mike concentrated more and more on the students training in the Bible School and on the Pastors whom he visited regularly in the hill parishes. "It is apparent," he wrote home, "that a key factor in the process of changing the way people live and farm is by the example set by a respected person in their neighbourhood. The church has a network of Parishes and within each Parish a network of hill-churches. These are small, local congregations that are led by a Church Teacher who is usually a local farmer, well known to everyone. He works under the authority of the Parish Pastor and is, therefore, very important for the growth of the church and for the church's contribution to the development of the country."

The success of Christian Rural Development is now measured more in terms of leaders who have caught the vision of raising standards of living rather than in the demonstration fields and resource centres, as at Shyogwe, important as they are. And furthermore, this raising of standards of living is seen as linked with raising levels of spiritual life, which is a prime objective of proclaiming the Gospel of Jesus Christ. Mike and Zena Greig were later posted by the Bishop to Butare where Mike was able to pursue this aim within the Butare Bible School, thus giving both a Biblical and practical relevance to the training of church teachers and clergy in the diocese of Butare.

During the 1980's, doctors and nurses of the Mission worked at Kisiizi and Gahini hospitals. Elspeth Cole, in the premature baby and nutritional centre at Kigeme hospital, was the sole missionary representative there. Shyira Hospital, still a Church responsibility, was staffed by Swiss and German doctors through "technical assistance" agencies quite apart from the Mission.

Each of these missionaries had stories to tell of God's reaching out to those in need through the ministry of healing. One such was told by Elspeth Cole at Kigeme.

"I was called up to the Hospital to see a very ill premature baby. She had been brought to us at four days of age, thin, cold, dehydrated and very underweight. She had seemed to be doing well but that evening she had suddenly developed great difficulty with her breathing and had turned a dusky blue colour. She was unconscious. All we could do seemed to be of no avail – obviously she had a severe lung infection.

"As the hours wore on, it was obvious to us all that she was getting worse, not better. I looked at the mother's sad, resigned face – she had watched all her previous six children die – who could understand her feelings and help her now? – I certainly could not!

"I asked her if she would take the baby in her arms while we all prayed together and, weeping now, she gladly agreed. The nurse and I knelt down on either side of her and we committed the child to God's loving care and wisdom. He knows all things – He must know what is best for the baby. We prayed for the mother and her husband too, that they would experience God's peace and healing love whatever the outcome of their baby's illness.

"At about 4:00 am I said to the nurse-aid, 'I must go home now, I have a busy day ahead, there is nothing more we can do for the baby – just leave it to die'.

"When I returned to the ward at 7:30 am, imagine my surprise to see the baby a lovely rosy pink colour! She was breathing normally and sleeping quite peacefully – I couldn't believe that it was the same child. The little nurse, Judith, was very troubled: 'Sister', she said unhappily, 'we said last night that there was nothing more we could do for the baby. We said that we would just leave her to die. We should have said that we would leave her in God's arms. We must both ask God to forgive us for thinking and speaking like that'.

"So, then and there, we prayed together for His cleansing and forgiveness. His joy flowed into our hearts – Wonderful Jesus! The parents on the ward were filled with that 'awe and fear' that St Luke writes about in the Acts of the Apostles; we all gave "Glory to God!"

An isolated incident? A thousand times No! Can a single story like this, which demonstrates so clearly God's working in the Ruanda Mission, give even a brief glimpse of the many thousands of occasions when God has broken into the lives of Africans and missionaries alike? He has worked miracles, many of them un-recognised as such, of spiritual and physical healing, given joyful assurance of sins forgiven, *triumphed* over the destructive powers of darkness and *revealed* depths of sacrificial self-giving in Christ's name.

In Uganda Kevin Vaughan was succeeded by Dr Amos Twinamasiko in 1986 to become the first Ugandan Doctor in charge of the church hospital. The clear Christian witness of the hospital continued and in the years that followed a number of missionary doctors worked with Amos Twinamasiko in a way which allowed him the freedom to train as an eye-specialist.

In February 1977, Dr Felton Ross of the American Leprosy Mission, Inc. visited Kigezi and was able to see the extent of the work supervised by Pat Gilmer.

"Pat is running a remarkably effective and economical programme," he wrote in his report, "caring for nearly 1,800 patients and undertaking leprosy control in a population of 2.7 million. The programme demonstrates a remarkable degree of integration and co-operation with the government health facilities where the leprosy patient care and leprosy control activities are carried out, and with the government-employed staff who work in them. The nature of the programme is such that Pat is continuously training government staff to the point where they can accept full responsibility for leprosy patient care and leprosy control. Her role is a vital one but becomes progressively less needed as the work goes on; soon no leprosy control officer will be needed in the Kigezi District."

The extent of the medical achievement of the work of Pat Gilmer as the Leprosy Control Officer in South-West Uganda, of the Mobile Unit and its staff, and of the training that Pat was able to give to government health workers may be gleaned from the remark of Jill Rendle, a New Zealander who helped Pat for a time in her secretarial and statistics gathering responsibilities. "We are working," she wrote in 1979, "towards a gradual disappearance of the disease." Unrecognised in the medical statistics are the mental and spiritual achievements. Leprosy is not simply a physical condition. It was in the relief of the mental suffering and in pointing those bound by evil spiritual forces to the One who can truly set them free that Pat and her Christian African colleagues fulfilled this great ministry of which the effects are still seen in Uganda and will be there in heaven! Pat Gilmer continued the strenuous itinerant care of leprosy patients in south-west Uganda until 1988 when she returned to the UK.

In the sixty years from the establishment of its first treatment centre at Bwama in 1930 to 1990 when leprosy was successfully being controlled and treated like any other disease, the Ruanda Mission was privileged to play an important part. In medical terms this was a remarkable achievement. And there are two other great, though less obvious, reasons for the Mission to be grateful to God.

The first is the thousands of leprosy sufferers who discovered that, despite the disease which made society despise them, they mattered to God, that Jesus Christ had included them in His saving death on the Cross and that, one day, in heaven, they were assured of "new bodies" in which they would be truly whole.

The second is the band of missionaries who have found that, in devoting themselves in God's name to serve the outcasts of society, often grotesque and repulsive in appearance, and by patiently ministering to them, they themselves gained an inexpressibly rich experience of God and a deep fellowship with those with whom they worked.

In 1977, at a meeting of the Literature Committee of the Protestant Alliance, Rosemary Guillebaud had been asked to write a devotional commentary on one of the books of the New Testament. Two years remained before she was due for retirement and the choice of book was left to her. "I thought and prayed about this and chose Hebrews, as being a book which has been a great blessing to me and yet without help is very difficult to understand. It took longer than I had expected, as I needed to read a lot and think of Kirundi ways of saying things. It was really exciting to write rather than translate, enabling me to make use of their wide variety of proverbs in explaining a point."

Rosemary was, in fact, unable to complete the work before her retirement in May, 1979. In 1981, she was able to return for six months to complete it. *Yesu n'Agaheta* (Jesus is Supreme) was printed in 1982, and the first, and to date, the only commentary on the Scriptures available in *Kirundi* or in *Kinyarwanda*.

A new service, SECLAR (*Service Chrétien pour la Litérature au Rwanda*), with the aim of providing Christian literature in the vernacular for Rwanda, was pioneered by Margaret Court in 1978. Considerable funding was received from a German aid agency and through SPCK. Initially some of the early books, such as *Umuhuz'umwe* (One Mediator), were revised and reprinted. Then additional titles, translated from English into Kinyarwanda, were produced, mainly relating faith and life style – Christian marriage, Christian attitudes towards work, stewardship, etc.

It was planned to distribute literature through a network of parish bookshops, but this did not prove successful and the scheme was discontinued. SECLAR staff spent most weekends visiting parishes, so providing opportunities to share in the preaching ministry and to sell books. This proved to be the most effective way of making literature available to the people.

Margaret was joined by two Rwandan colleagues: Rev. Alphonse Karuhije from 1979 and, later, Jean-Nathan Sezibera. Their linguistic gifts proved invaluable in translation and editorial work; also in their fellowship and unity of purpose in a work which was not widely understood or valued. Alphonse Karuhije left in 1983 to pursue further studies, and in 1984, Margaret Court returned to England to join the Mission's home staff. For three years Jean-Nathan "held the fort" alone. In 1987, he too left to begin a four-year course in Christian communication in order to equip him better to lead and develop SECLAR. In the intervening years, the work of SECLAR has declined awaiting fresh impetus from Jean-Nathan.

In 1979, Peter and Elisabeth Guillebaud were due to retire but, in fact, were asked to return the following year to Rwanda for Peter to work as co-ordinator of a team of translators drawn from the Presbyterian, Seventh Day Adventists, and, most remarkably, the Roman Catholics. Under the aegis of the Bible Society they started work on a new translation of the Bible into *Kinyarwanda* that was to be both modern and colloquial in style and acceptable in vocabulary to all the participating churches.

It was a formidable task to undertake, particularly working with the Roman Catholic linguists. At the time Peter Guillebaud wrote, "The Roman Catholics – 80% or more of our population – are now beginning to thirst for the Word of God. But they find our version particularly hard to understand, because traditionally many important doctrinal terms have been differently translated by Protestants and Catholics (Cf. in English 'repentance' and 'penitence'!). The Roman Catholics are so keen to have the Bible that if we refuse to work with them on a joint version (the only kind the Bible Society will now sponsor), they will eventually go it alone and do their own translation, which would, I am convinced, be a pity."

The Rev. Giles and Christine Williams joined Peter and Elisabeth Guillebaud in Kigali, Rwanda, in 1986. When, at the end of that year, Peter left, Giles succeeded Peter as co-ordinator of the team. The New

Testament, accepted by all the participating churches, was published in 1990.

Seventy years of missionary work had resulted in the whole Bible being available in the languages of Kigezi-Ankole, Rwanda, Burundi and Bubembe (a region of Zaire). A heritage indeed for the peoples of these countries.

In education, two girls' schools only remained in which missionaries of the Ruanda Mission were on the staff – the Bishops' Girls' School at Muyebe in Kigezi, Uganda and the Girls' Secondary and Teacher Training School at Kigeme, in Rwanda. Liz Traill was headmistress of the first and Lilette Honoré of the second. From time to time, in both schools, God worked in remarkable saving power.

While Oliver and Elisabeth Ross were on the staff of the school at Muyebe, they wrote of just such an event

"There was an extraordinary time . . . when there was a powerful surge of the Holy Spirit and quite a number of the school made confession of faith in front of the school. We had been leading a group of S4 (4th. year secondary) girls in a discipleship course and they had definitely 'gone deeper' during that time. But this event happened during the course of prayers held every evening by the girls themselves – where as they confessed and witnessed to each other – it seemed they felt and experienced the effect of their sin – turning pale and being quite overcome. Oliver called another meeting soon afterwards and deliberately tried to remain unemotional and calm but the Spirit was at work and the girls' changed lives were a testimony to that."

When Liz Traill returned to the UK in 1986, the headship passed to an African, Jason Turimumahoro. In 1990, Mick and Pat Moorse were the latest missionaries to join the staff.

In 1981 Jean Sumner became headmistress of Kabale

Preparatory School. There were two other missionary
staff but the majority were Ugandan led by Naris Tiben-
derana, the deputy headmaster. In 1989, Jean Sumner
returned to the UK and missionary involvement in the
school ceased.

Today, the Scripture Union in Rwanda and Burundi is
the principal organiser of camps for young people.
These continue to be very popular as well as being
effective means of communicating the Gospel by
teaching, example and testimony. The Scripture Union
is also the most important source of instruction for
young people on Christian marriage, family life, relationships, and behaviour in contemporary society. The
SU also organises teams of young people to go out with
the Gospel. Many are gifted singers and their music is an
important method of communicating the Gospel.

During this decade Graham and Sarah White, associate-missionaries working at Bujumbura University,
were able to combine a support for the Christian students at the university with a greatly valued link with the
church leaders when missionaries were excluded from
the country.

In 1986, due largely to the initiative of David Vail the
General Secretary, a departure from previous practice
was introduced. Hitherto all financial support had been
directed primarily to maintaining the missionaries in
their tasks and to supporting work that depended on
them. The need was becoming urgent for help in areas of
work not directly associated with missionaries. Of immediate concern was the need for new buildings and
equipment for African staffed Bible Schools, for bursaries for the further training of staff for Bible Schools,
for help in replacing low-standard church buildings in
Burundi where existing buildings were threatened with
demolition by government order, and for literature and
cassette ministry equipment.

"I came back from my trip to Africa," reported David Vail, "burdened as never before by the sheer extent and urgency of the work to which our African brethren in Uganda, Rwanda and Burundi are committed. True, the Church is devastated in some respects by political pressure . . . but there is a great work going on underneath. Young people are coming to Christ, schools and colleges are open to evangelism, the dioceses are moving forward and churches are expanding in numbers . . . But building for the future is costly. Bricks have to be bought, training bursaries have to be paid for, pay packets have to be filled." The "Building for the Future" project was initiated with the aim of meeting some of these specific needs.

Solving the many problems facing the African churches is not going to be an easy task. Increasing populations, political instability and lack of economic resources will continue to aggravate them.

The extent of church development can be gauged by the increase in dioceses that has been achieved. In the territories in which the Ruanda Mission worked there are, to date, three dioceses in the Anglican Province of Uganda, and seven in the Province of Burundi, Rwanda and Zaire. There is a strong prospect of Zaire becoming an independent Province soon. Rwanda and Burundi would then jointly form one Province, but in the not-so-distant future they will probably separate to form two separate Provinces. Many of these dioceses have forged links with overseas churches in Europe, the United States and Canada.

There is no claim here that these African churches are a perfect expression of the aims and prayers of the Mission from which they came. African leaders are now facing on their own the moral problems of ethnic tensions and cultural adaptation without having solutions imposed on them by missionaries. They are under strong pressure by the temptation to compromise with the world, by status-seeking for the church and its leaders, by the misuse of power to promote family interests (nepotism) and by concentration on prestige-orientated projects. Inevitably the Mission is sad to note these trends, yet when, by the power of God, the leaders overcome them, their testimony to God's grace will be the greater. Even now there is much to encourage among grass-roots church members, in the evangelistic zeal of many village congregations and among young people.

In 1988, the Bishops of the dioceses of Rwanda and Burundi wrote to the Ruanda Mission requesting that urgent consideration be given to changing its name in view of the embarrassing interpretation that the name "Ruanda", however it was spelt, caused in their countries, Burundi in particular. The Mission was also urged to state clearly and publicly that it no longer held a monopoly of serving the churches there. Freedom was desired to seek links with any other organisations anywhere, without having to pass through the Ruanda Mission.

The Mission Council recognised the strength of the argument for the first request but was surprised at the second. There had been no attempt to insist that aid requested by the African churches which it founded, from whatever source, be channelled through the Mission, nor be subject to its scrutiny. An exception was the normal procedure by which all requests for assistance from these churches, made to the CMS, the parent society, were referred to the Ruanda Mission. Nevertheless, a public statement along the lines requested was made and the process of seeking a new name was launched.

After two years of prayer, heart-searching and consultation with present and former missionaries, home church leaders and CMS (the parent society), a new vision for the Mission was discerned, a revised relationship with CMS was agreed and . . . a new name: Mid-Africa Ministry (CMS).

"God has no grand-children," is a truism. Each child of God has to appropriate for him or herself the gift of salvation in Christ and work it out in personal experience. Similarly, each Church must learn for itself the truths of God's Word and apply them to its own situation. This the Churches founded by the Ruanda Mission, have begun to do. The Mid-Africa Ministry assures them of its continuing fellowship and prayer as well as support in material ways and seeking personnel of God's calling, to share with them in their ministry to their own people.

Furthermore, it is confident that, as the churches preach the full counsel of God as it is written in His Word, expose and condemn sin in all its forms, and offer salvation on the basis of Christ's death on the cross, and as they continue to depend on God alone in prayer, the breath of God will once again give them life; the fire of God will again purge them and set them ablaze for Him as He did so powerfully in their missionary brothers and sisters in the past.

Chapter 22

The heritage

In the Preface to *Road to Revival*, published in 1946, Dr Stanley Smith wrote: "We believe that behind each story of missionary enterprise there is discernible some expression of the thought of God. It has always been God's way that when He wants to speak to the world, He seeks out a man or a body of men through whom He can express Himself. We seek to know the thought of God in calling this Mission into being."

Algie Stanley Smith is no longer with us to discern that *Thought of God* which he strove to discover. Now, 45 years later, a similar question is asked with equal urgency: what may God have been seeking to teach His people, missionaries and Africans alike, during the 70 years of the Mission's history?

When a person acts genuinely, that action is an expression of that person's will and character. Thousands of men and women, illiterate and educated, black and white, experienced or witnessed God acting in power in Rwanda, Uganda and Burundi. Within that activity can be discerned an expression of God's character and will.

The first decade of missionary work was marked by much zealous activity, with some success, measured in terms of numbers of converts to Christianity. There were, in some places, encouraging signs of spiritual life as witnessed by the missionary zeal of some African Christians. Some missionaries, however, felt a deep sense of impotence in the face of powerful spiritual enemies. As they came to the end of their own resources, they were driven to plead with God to vindicate His Word and bring honour to His name. It was a devastating experience, but, having gone through it, they could never boast that their particular zeal or faith or methods of working somehow enabled God to act in a special way.

The "bursting into flame" of spiritual life, and that is an apt description of what happened, was God's work, not man's. The missionaries insisted that they stood by watching what God was doing. He acted when and how He chose. It was for the missionaries and Africans to proclaim the truths He so dramatically energised and not to stifle what He was doing, either by contrived support or by indisciplined laxity.

The new thing that God was doing was never seen to be in contradiction to what the missionaries had been proclaiming as God's truth for the world, nor did it add any new truth. The opposite was true! However, God not only made real the truths taught from His Word but He brought some of them into sharp relief and defined others more clearly. It has become part of the Ruanda Mission heritage to testify to these insights. This is not to imply a unique claim to them. Far from it! But, because God so clearly endorsed them in the life and work of the Mission, they have become, in a special way, part of its special heritage.

The first clear element in this heritage was the way in which God vindicated the simple, unequivocal proclamation of the way of salvation through Jesus Christ that was based on an acceptance of the Bible as God's final, authoritative Word. Missionaries went directly to the Bible to declare God's message to the people to whom He had sent them. They were careful not to present a "gospel" that was merely the "message of Western Christianity", nor that of the "Church of England", nor the wisdom of theologians who had studied the Bible. "God so loved the world that He gave His one and only Son, that whoever believes in Him shall not perish but have eternal life," (John 3:16), meant, for them, exactly what it said. There were no reservations about the nature of the deity of Christ, about His substitutionary death on the Cross where He suffered in the place of sinners, or the reality of heaven and hell. Sin was proclaimed as rebellion against God, without cultural or situational modifications. It was simply: *The Bible says . . . therefore God says . . .*

The second truth clearly highlighted throughout the Mission's history is that of the centrality of the cross of Christ in every human experience. At the heart of all the teaching and preaching was everyone's need for a transforming personal encounter with the living Christ, described by the Bible as being 'saved'. This is made possible only through the death of Jesus Christ, God the Son, in the sinner's place. "If we confess our sins," wrote the Apostle John, "He is faithful and just and will forgive us our sins and purify us from all unrighteousness" because "the blood of Jesus, His Son, purifies us from all sin" (1 John 1:9, 7). That means exactly what it says, if we repent of our sin, God so deals with that sin by the death and resurrection of Jesus Christ that God no longer remembers it and it no longer exists as a barrier to oneness with Him.

When those in whom God worked so powerfully testified to what they had experienced, invariably what Jesus Christ accomplished on the cross for them was foremost. The power of the 'blood of Christ' to make clean from the defilement of sin, to reconcile the sinner to a holy God and to liberate him from the power of evil, became a reality which transformed thousands of lives. And all this was entirely of God's grace, unmerited by the sinner in any way. It is a precious element in the Mission's heritage.

The Ruanda Mission shared these two elements of its heritage with the Keswick Convention as was affirmed in its Constitution: 1. The Ruanda Council and the missionaries of the Ruanda General and Medical Mission stand for the complete inspiration of the whole Bible as being, and not merely containing, the Word of God. 2. Their determination is to proclaim full and free salvation through simple faith in Christ's atoning death upon the Cross. 3. They are satisfied that they have received from CMS full guarantees to safeguard the future of the RGMM on Bible, Protestant and Keswick lines.

The roots of the third element in this heritage go back to the number of occasions when missionaries on the field pleaded with home supporters to join them in prayer that God would intervene in His work and, 'breathe life into the dry bones' of their ministry. Behind this repeated call to prayer was the recognition of failure. In addition to the often very low spiritual level of many converts all was not well in relationships between missionaries. When God worked in power, it was in answer to much earnest prayer.

Even before God began to work in a general, more widespread way, says Bill Butler, in Uganda the prayer most often sung in meetings of hungry searchers for God was the chorus, *Spirit of the Living God fall afresh on me. Break me, melt me, mould me, fill me.* As God worked in saving power in many lives the power of evil to thwart His work became so evident that prayer became even more urgent.

Before, during and after God worked in such power, the need was felt for earnest and continual prayer. And

God answered that prayer. That is a precious part of the heritage.

The fourth element emerged unexpectedly. Again and again when the Spirit of God was working there was public confession of sin. Men and women would stand up and say, "I want to repent . . ." They would then give details of the sins of lying, theft, deceit, hatred, slander, or whatever, of which God had convicted them. They would describe the awful sense of condemnation by God and separation from Him which they felt and their sorrow for what they had done as they turned to Him in repentance to ask His forgiveness. Then would follow a clear testimony to an inner assurance that their sin was forgiven indeed. Often the reactions in others were dramatic. God used such public declarations to bring about a deep conviction of wrongdoing and almost to overwhelm people with a sense of the awfulness of sin in the sight of a holy God and of the hell that would follow if there was no repentance. This happened so frequently without any missionaries present that they could never be accused of stimulating people to hysteria.

Because those under deep conviction of sin almost invariably said, "I want to repent . . .", the missionaries naturally concluded that God worked in power when people truly repented of their sin. This was a correct conclusion, but it was not the full picture. It became clear later that the significant element in what happened was not so much that people *truly repented of their sin*, important as that was, but that, in addition, they *confessed openly before others that they had sinned, that they had repented of their sin, put right the wrongs committed, and God had forgiven them*.

The distinction is an important one. Many of the sins confessed were unsuspected even by close friends; some were grievous wrongs done to others; many were sexual sins; while others were seemingly trivial acts of thieving, lying, deception and unkindness. The Spirit of God so convicted people that the sins could not be tolerated until there was deep repentance expressed in a full confession to God and a full confession before others of the sin, repentance and forgiveness received.

Many leaders, missionary and African, were unhappy that all the detailed exposure of sinful acts should be made in public. Others, however, felt strongly that to limit such open confession was to quench the Holy Spirit and that He would heal any damage that might be caused.

The truth so clearly highlighted was, nevertheless, a very profound one. What mattered was not so much the public detailed admission of sins, rather it was the willingness to admit in public, that a person was a sinner, owning openly that he or she was a sinner before God in need of forgiveness and that forgiveness had been received from Him.

The public admission of having sinned in particular ways is a humbling experience, particularly for a leader. To do so became known as being *broken* – humbled before God and humbled before others. Before God, *brokenness* expressed an attitude of heart and mind which said "Yes! you are right about my sin and I am wrong", especially where this related to the seemingly less serious or less obvious sins such as pilfering, jealousy, deceit, lying, impurity of thought and unkindness. A *broken* person prays, "Lord bend this proud and stiff-necked 'I', help me to bend the neck and die" – the words of a chorus written at the time. Before others, *brokenness* meant being humble about one's status and position and being willing to follow the way of the cross as a servant of Jesus Christ. "Revival," said Festo Kivengere, "means to be exposed for what we really are. The presence of the Lord is very revealing." (Bishop

Festo Kivengere *Love Unlimited* G/L Regal Books
p 35.)

Joe Church illustrated *brokenness* in a picture in
which an *unbroken* man is standing stiffly upright, then
as he is *broken*, he kneels humbly, meekly before the
cross. "Not I but Christ" is written underneath the
picture showing the bent shape of the C in Christ contrasted with the proud, unbending "I". The powerful
way God used *broken* people, missionary and African,
make *brokenness* an important element indeed in the
Mission's heritage.

Fifthly, as missionaries and Africans were humbled or
broken enough to expose to each other what they were
really like in their thoughts and motivation and were
able to testify to God's forgiveness and love, so there
developed a great *oneness* between them which, for
many, was the lasting memory of revival days. *Oneness*
with others meant living in the *light* and *love* of God.
Light – no lying, no deception, no wearing a mask to
cover a defeated life, and *love* – "Calvary love" for one
another, sacrificial love that enables people to feel
"safe" with one another, love that always seeks the
highest interests of others. The link between *brokenness*
and *fellowship* was illustrated by Joe Church in a picture
of two brothers who have been reconciled at the cross
and clasp their hands to form a V for victory.

In the reality of this fellowship, the words of 1 John
1:7, became a watchword: "But if we walk in the light, as
He is in the light, we have fellowship with one another
and the blood of Jesus, His Son, purifies us from all sin."

God bound *broken* missionaries and Africans in a
loving, trusting fellowship, and used them as channels of
his love, compassion and reconciling power. This is a
precious element in the Mission's heritage!

A sixth element in the heritage concerned the work
of the Holy Spirit in convicting of sin and filling to

overflowing the cleansed heart. Before revival came to Gahini and Kabale, some had, in a quiet way, entered into a new personal experience of the fullness of the Holy Spirit.

In a "charismatic" understanding of the work of the Holy Spirit, the emphasis seems to be mainly on God bestowing particular spiritual gifts such as "speaking in tongues", "prophecy", "healing", etc. In the experience of those who were first touched by revival in Rwanda and south-west Uganda, these evidences were largely either missing or considered of secondary importance. Their experience of the Holy Spirit led rather to an overwhelming sense of the holiness of God, of the sinfulness of sin, of the effectiveness of the blood of Christ shed on the cross to cleanse from sin, of the assurance of sins forgiven, of the reality of the presence of Christ and of the enabling power of the Holy Spirit to overcome sin.

Joe Church often spoke of the victorious life, but it was a "sinners' victory" as, day by day, they allowed the Holy Spirit to convict of all that fell short of His Highest will in their lives and to lead them to Calvary. He often spoke of the High Priest, "on the last and greatest day of the Feast" (John 7:37), standing with his golden water-pot of water. Before Him people stood in line holding out empty cups into which He poured out His precious Holy Spirit. But how could Jesus, the Great High Priest, fill dirty cups with His precious water of life? Hearts needed cleansing for the Holy Spirit to fill them. "Some are not open to the Spirit", Joe would add, "they hold their cups upside down. Sadly the High Priest passes them by".

Joe Church, Yosiya Kinuka, William Nagenda and others often spoke of the Holy Spirit and of His work in them but did not link it with any particular, personal "second blessing" experience. Joe would refer to the

Day of Pentecost and point out very significantly that
when those men and women were baptised by the Holy
Spirit in the Upper Room in Jerusalem, "they went out
and preached, not the Holy Spirit, nor 'speaking in
tongues', nor the 'Baptism of the Holy Spirit', but . . .
JESUS!"

Whether or not any of those in whom God worked so
powerfully could testify to some crisis experience of
receiving the Holy Spirit, there was no mistaking the
power of God in lives which He was constantly making
clean from repented sin. Such lives bore the marks of the
fullness of the Holy Spirit. From them there flowed a
power in service, authority in proclaiming the truths of
the Gospel, discernment of evil powers and victory over
Satan's designs: a precious element of the heritage.

A seventh element for which the Mission is grateful to
God is that, by His grace, he has enabled different
strands in the life of mission and church to hold together,
resisting strong, internal pressures that could have
driven them apart. The *Abaka* in Rwanda and Burundi
and the *Abalokole* in Uganda stood out against all whom
they saw as compromising with sin and worldliness in the
church. The missionaries in their turn, tended to polar-
ise along the same lines. Some of them now regret the
harsh attitudes adopted in those early, fiery days. Nevertheless, the uncompromising, even hard stand of the
Abaka never took them to the point of splitting off and
forming another church. They valued their Anglican
traditions and background and were content to go on
working together in churches, schools and hospitals,
with those with whom they did not feel at one spiritually.
And missionaries, divided as they were by the uncompromising stand of some of them, nevertheless
continued to work together in the "fellowship of the
gospel".

After the expulsion from Mukono in 1941, the *Abalo-*

kole in Uganda and elsewhere in East Africa, were tempted to leave the Anglican Church, spiritually dead as it appeared to them. The temptation was, however, strongly resisted by those who were leaders in revival, even though it might mean putting up with harsh discriminatory treatment from some Church leaders on account of their uncompromising testimony. They argued that the Anglican Church was their church, the one in which they had been saved. If they left, who would witness to those remaining? To respond to opposition by splitting off and starting a new church would have appeared to them as evidence of *unbrokenness* and refusal of the way of the Cross. Similarly, the Mission itself, with its very strong evangelical heritage has resisted the temptation to "split off" from the Church of England or from its own parent society, the CMS.

In the 1960's and 1970's, as in the 1930's and 1940's, God touched many lives in reviving and renewing power. There were differences of emphasis. In the early days, it was the devastating conviction of sin and the power of the cross of Christ to make clean and enable a holy life and bold witness through the "fullness of the Holy Spirit" which was so distinctive. In the later outburst of God's working, it seemed that the Holy Spirit emphasised ministries of deliverance from evil powers by taking authority in the name of Jesus; and of healing – spiritual and physical – in co-operation with medical colleagues.

Far from these later expressions of God's working being an alternative or superseding the earlier manifestations, they were seen to be complementary. It became clear that expressions of what some people called "renewal" were incomplete, inadequate and even dangerous, when an up-to-date experience of repentance and of the "power of the blood of Jesus' to cleanse

from sin were lacking. The spiritual heritage, for which
the Ruanda Mission is grateful to God includes the
freedom to move wherever the "wind of the Spirit"
leads, benefiting from any expressions of ministry and
worship where these are based on faithfulness to the
Scriptures and that holy relationship with God and with
others which revival highlighted so clearly.

God has honoured this refusal to divide or separate
over different expressions of His working in diverse
people and situations to such an extent that it has
become part of the Mission's heritage.

The God-given commission of the Ruanda Mission is
not yet wholly accomplished. In His wisdom, God was
pleased to use its missionaries to found churches in
south-west Uganda, Rwanda and Burundi. These
churches are now, rightly, independent – independent in
their organisation and leadership, but not cut off from
the hearts and affections of those whom God used to
serve them.

In his letter to the Corinthian church Paul wrote,
"Even though you have ten thousand guardians in
Christ, you do not have many fathers, for in Christ Jesus
I became your father through the gospel" (1 Corinthians 4:7). In the sense that Paul referred to the Corinthian church, so the Ruanda Mission, as Mid-Africa
Ministry, relates to those who are now their brothers and
sisters in Christ in these countries. More than that, it
shares with them the call to join hands in proclaiming the
gospel of Jesus Christ to those whom those churches
would reach for Him among their own peoples.